Frank Middle

MENINGA

MY LIFE IN FOOTBALL

MENINGA

MY LIFE IN FOOTBALL

MAL MENINGA

WITH ALAN CLARKSON

HarperSports
An imprint of HarperCollins*Publishers*

DEDICATION

to Debbie, Tamika and Joshua

Harper*Sports*
An imprint of HarperCollinsPublishers, Australia

First published in Australia in 1995
Copyright © Team Meninga Pty Ltd and Alan Clarkson 1995

This book is copyright.
Apart from any fair dealing for the purposes of
private study, research, criticism or review,
as permitted under the Copyright Act, no part
may be reproduced by any process without written permission.
Inquiries should be addressed to the publishers.

HarperCollins*Publishers*
25 Ryde Road, Pymble, Sydney NSW 2073, Australia
31 View Road, Glenfield, Auckland 10, New Zealand
77–85 Fulham Palace Road, London W6 8JB, United Kingdom
Hazelton Lanes, 55 Avenue Road, Suite 2900, Toronto, Ontario M5R 3L2
and 1995 Markham Road, Scarborough, Ontario M1B 5M8, Canada
10 East 53rd Street, New York NY 10032, USA

National Library of Australia Cataloguing-in-Publication data:
   Meninga, Mal, 1960–
   ISBN 0 7322 5189 3.
     1.Meninga, Mal, 1960– . 2.Rugby league football players — Australia — Biography.
     3.Rugby league football players — Australian Capital Territory — Biography.
     I.Title.
796.3338

Printed by Griffin Press

9 8 7 6 5 4 3 2 1
99 98 97 96

FOREWORD
BY WAYNE GOSS

I remember that Sunday afternoon in 1979, sitting in the outer at Lang Park with my mate Harro, watching our team Souths when the ball came out to the right wing. We couldn't help but be impressed by the speed and strength of this new kid as he bumped a couple of players out of the way to score in the corner.

Mal Meninga has since become one of the all-time greats of Australian sport. In his home state of Queensland, Big Mal holds a special place in the hearts and minds not only of keen sports followers but of people right across the community who recognise in the big man those extraordinary qualities that have put him head and shoulders above his peers.

Born in Bundaberg and taught to play and love the game of rugby league by his father, Mal Meninga grew to represent all that is best about the sport.

It is a remarkable achievement that, by the end of his playing career, Mal Meninga was the most capped Test player in the game's history and the most capped State of Origin player. Not only that, but his country has honoured him with the Order of Australia.

An outstanding player from his first appearance in senior grade football, Mal represented Queensland from 1979 to 1994, including the historic first State of Origin match in 1980, and Australia from 1982 to 1994.

Two of my greatest moments in watching rugby league were the Souths' premiership wins against Redcliffe in 1981 and Wynnum–Manly in 1985. The win in 1985, against Wally Lewis and all their big names, was particularly sweet for we Souths supporters after our crushing loss to Wynnum the year before, and, as so often, Mal played a key role.

His move to Canberra, where he remained until the close of his playing career in 1994, was a loss for Queensland but a huge gain for Australian sport as he loomed ever larger as one of the brightest stars of the game.

It was a great pleasure for me to be at each of Canberra's grand final wins in Sydney, but it was the 1994 grand final win that gave all those fans who had followed Mal over the years so much pride as we cheered him across the line for that last winning try.

It was fitting that right up to his last year in the game, this great player was captain of Australia, captain of Queensland and captain of Canberra and that he finished off his career with the Canberra Raiders riding high on the crest of a third premiership win. It was also fitting that in the same year Mal completed a record fourth tour with the Kangaroos.

The powerful form of Mal Meninga at full stretch lunging for the try-line has become and will remain one of the legendary images of the game of rugby league.

Mal Meninga has got a lot out of rugby league, and rugby league has got a lot out of Mal.

As he wrote in his final year, "I'll have some fabulous memories to reflect on." So will we all, Mal, so will we all.

Wayne Goss
Premier of Queensland
June 1995

CONTENTS

INTRODUCTION 9

1: THE LONG FAREWELL 29

2: MY FATHER'S SON 51

3: SOUTHS AND SAINTS 63

4: MATE AGAINST MATE 85

5: TRAVELLING SOUTH 103

6: GREEN AND GOLD 121

7: CHAMPIONS! 133

8: THE WINNING EDGE 147

9: ONE TOWN, ONE TEAM 159

10: AUSTRALIAN CAPTAIN 183

11: SUPER LEAGUE 203

EPILOGUE 207

CAREER RECORD 229

INDEX 238

INTRODUCTION
BY ALAN CLARKSON

In my decades as a rugby league writer for the *Sydney Morning Herald* and the *Sun-Herald* I have been fortunate to see many magnificent first-grade games, grand finals, inter-state clashes and Test matches. One moment is etched in my memory — the epic try by Mal Meninga that won the second Test of the 1990 Ashes series at Old Trafford.

Great Britain had won the first Test of that series, but the Kangaroos appeared in control of the second until well into the second half, when Ricky Stuart fired out a long pass which was intercepted by Paul Loughlin, the replacement British centre. Loughlin ran 60 metres to score near the posts.

Stuart was devastated. A simple conversion and Great Britain were in front. The little Australian halfback believed he had let his team-mates down. The fact that his pass could have ended with an Australian try — had it landed where it was intended — was no consolation. It seemed his one miscalculation had cost Australia the Ashes.

Luckily, the conversion swung wide. The score stayed at 10–all. The series was still alive.

Captain Meninga, despite the intense pressure, kept his players primed for a grandstand finish. The experience of the previous year's grand final against Balmain, when his Canberra Raiders had fought back from a 10-point deficit to triumph, was a factor in his on-field leadership. There was no panic in the Australian team, even when a couple of British field goal attempts slid just wide of the posts.

With only seconds remaining, the Australian team had possession but were trapped near their own line. A draw seemed inevitable. However, Stuart, to his everlasting credit, more than made up for that intercepted pass. He saw his chance, dummied, escaped a desperate attempt by the British hooker Lee Jackson and raced downfield. The predominantly English crowd shouted out a collective cry of anguish, while the Australians among them roared in anticipation. Stuart sprinted clear. Ten metres ... 20 metres ... 50 metres ... then 60 metres he raced, deep into British territory.

Then he heard the yell, "Inside, Ricky! ... Inside!"

Opposite: *Australian captain Mal Meninga during the second Ashes Test of 1990 at Old Trafford. This was one of the greatest days in Australian rugby league history, and culminated in a sensational last-minute try, set up by halfback Ricky Stuart and scored by Meninga; it gave the Kangaroos a 14–10 victory.*

Meninga

Above: Meninga in England in 1982; this was his first overseas tour with the Australian team.

Opposite: A clash of two Raiders. Meninga, the Queensland captain, is grabbed by his NSW counterpart, Laurie Daley, during the State of Origin series in 1994.

There, in support, was Mal Meninga.

Meninga shouldered aside an opponent — a tactic he had learned from his father, Norman, in his early footballing years — keeping his eyes on the ball. Stuart's pass was perfect. Meninga grabbed it and no human being alive could have stopped him as he pounded those final few metres to the line.

When he planted the ball down, the Australian skipper did not feel any special jubilation. Just relief. Defeat had been *that* close. Two weeks later, the Kangaroos wrapped up the series with a 14–0 shut-out of Great Britain in the final Test. Meninga scored another try, to finish with a try in each of the three Tests of the series. His place among the game's greatest was assured.

Yet there were many more famous days to come. By the time Mal Meninga's playing career concluded, he was universally acknowledged as one of the game's supreme achievers, a footballer whose remarkable feats may never be equalled and certainly will never be bettered. Meninga, who retired when the final whistle sounded to end Australia's 74–0 humiliation of France in the Test match at Béziers on December 4, 1994, has created a legacy of record-making performances which ranks him among the all-time greats of the game.

Introduction

Meninga in 1982, wearing the black and white colours of Southern Suburbs, his Brisbane club from 1979 until 1985. This was his first game back after dislocating his left elbow during his Test debut, against New Zealand at the SCG.

In a spectacular career in the top-grade, which covered 15 seasons, Meninga compiled a record that includes the following landmarks:

◆ an unprecedented four Kangaroo tours — 1982, 1986, 1990 and 1994 — including the final two as captain;
◆ an Australian record 45 Test-match appearances;
◆ a world record 270 points scored in Test rugby league;
◆ twenty-three Tests as Australian captain;
◆ a total of 86 appearances in an Australian jumper in Tests, World Cup and touring matches;
◆ a record 38 appearances for Queensland;
◆ a record 32 appearances in State of Origin football;
◆ a record 161 points scored in State of Origin football;
◆ a total of 306 grade games for his three clubs — Southern Suburbs of Brisbane, St Helens of England, and the Canberra Raiders;
◆ three grand final wins with the Raiders (1989, 1990 and 1994), all as captain;
◆ two grand final wins with Southern Suburbs;

Introduction

- eleven grand final appearances (five with Canberra, six with Southern Suburbs);
- an incredible total of 465 first-class matches in all.

◆◆◆

It is difficult today to comprehend how, less than a decade before Meninga's retirement from football, the prophets of doom were convinced he would not handle the pressure of the Sydney premiership. This was in 1986, following the announcement he had signed with the Canberra Raiders.

The theory was that as he played only a couple of tough matches each season for his Southern Suburbs club in the Brisbane premiership, the virtual Test-match standard of each weekend in the Sydney premiership would find him out. And in truth it did — it found him to be one of the finest footballers in the game, a player capable of turning in outstanding performances week after week.

But for every detractor, there were dozens who never doubted Meninga would silence those critics who had failed to recognise his enormous talent. The man who wanted Meninga in the Sydney premiership more than most was Don Furner (the Canberra Raiders then coach), who worked overtime to convince the giant centre that Canberra was the place to further his football career.

Before committing himself, Meninga spoke to his close friend and adviser, his former physical instructor at the Police Academy and then coach at Southern Suburbs, Wayne Bennett.

Bennett had recognised Meninga's potential seasons earlier and knew before most the impact Mal would have in rugby league. He also had great confidence in Furner, both personally and as a coach. Bennett advised Meninga to accept the Canberra offer.

Don Furner never had the slightest doubt about Meninga's talent. Back in the early '70s, Furner had successfully attracted players to Eastern Suburbs by signing the great Arthur Beetson from Balmain. Now he wanted Mal at the Raiders to act as a similar magnet to other quality players.

As it had done with Beetson, Furner's ploy worked again. Following Meninga to Canberra soon afterwards was a stylish young fullback named Gary Belcher and a tough, raw hooker, Steve Walters. Later, a clever centre, Peter Jackson, and Steve Walters' younger brother Kevin, a utility-back, signed as well. All went on to play for Canberra in the 1987 grand final — and for Australia.

Furner liked everything about Meninga's play but particularly his ability to take the right option nearly every time. Today, he speaks glowingly about Meninga's pride, and his will to win. He regards Meninga as "a complete footballer".

Over page: The Canberra Raiders, celebrating their grand final success of 1994. Standing (left to right): Mal Meninga, Steve Walters, Ruben Wiki, John Lomax, Luke Davico, David Westley (obscured), Quentin Pongia (in front of Westley), David Furner (at back), Albert Fulivai, Noa Nadruku, Jason Death, Ken Nagas, David Boyle, Brett Mullins, Jason Croker, Steve Stone. Kneeling: Brett Hetherington, Laurie Daley, Ricky Stuart, Paul Osborne. In front: Bradley Clyde, the J.J. Giltinan Shield and the Winfield Cup.

Meninga

Introduction

Opposite: A tearful but jubilant Meninga with Ricky Stuart after the 1989 grand final, won in extra time by the Raiders over Balmain. Of all the famous triumphs enjoyed during his career, this is the one the Canberra captain treasures most.

"I consider the Raiders were fortunate to get someone like Mal Meninga to come there. But now he has decided to retire, other players will take his place and the club can go on from there," Furner told me.

Mal knew success before moving to Canberra but, once there, he became an even more dominant player. Premiership victories, Test-match triumphs, Kangaroo tours and State of Origin glory combined to promote him to his inevitable destiny ... the Australian captaincy. His crowning achievement came when he was named captain of the 1994 Kangaroo touring team, as he had been in 1990. No man had ever captained the Australian team on two tours of Great Britain and France before Mal Meninga.

In Meninga's final year as a player, he had one of his most memorable seasons — leading the Raiders to the premiership and the Kangaroos to Ashes glory. But was it his greatest? How do you compare one great season with another?

Was the glory of 1994 better than the grand final triumph of 1989? Was it better than leading Australia to that magnificent second Test victory on the 1990 Kangaroo tour? Or was his proudest achievement being selected for his first Test against New Zealand way back in 1982?

Personally, I'd take 1994. If a script writer had been commissioned to come up with a fitting finale to Mal Meninga's league career he or she could hardly have done a better job than what really did happen in that amazing farewell season. But for Meninga, and undoubtedly most of his Canberra team-mates, pride of place in the achievement list is 1989, and especially that famous grand final victory over the Balmain Tigers.

This, I admit, does not surprise me. Many internationals have told me that playing in a grand final is a more emotional, gut-wrenching experience than playing in a Test match. And hence, more satisfying to win.

I have never seen a better grand final than 1989. There have been harder, more brutal premiership deciders, but nothing could equal the action-packed excitement of the courageous Canberra victory.

In fact, the Raiders' surge actually started five matches from the end of the premiership round, when the team appeared to be down and almost certainly out of the semi-final race, after a loss to South Sydney put them back in seventh spot on the table. But then came the guts and glory finish of this superb team, magnificently led by Meninga. They won nine matches in succession, to finally rip the Winfield Cup trophy out of the hands of Balmain's great captain, Wayne Pearce.

There were so many memorable moments in that match. One of the most decisive was a desperate dive by Meninga to ankle tap Balmain five-eighth Mick Neil about 15 metres from the Canberra line. But for that move, Neil would certainly have scored and the premiership would have been Balmain's.

INTRODUCTION

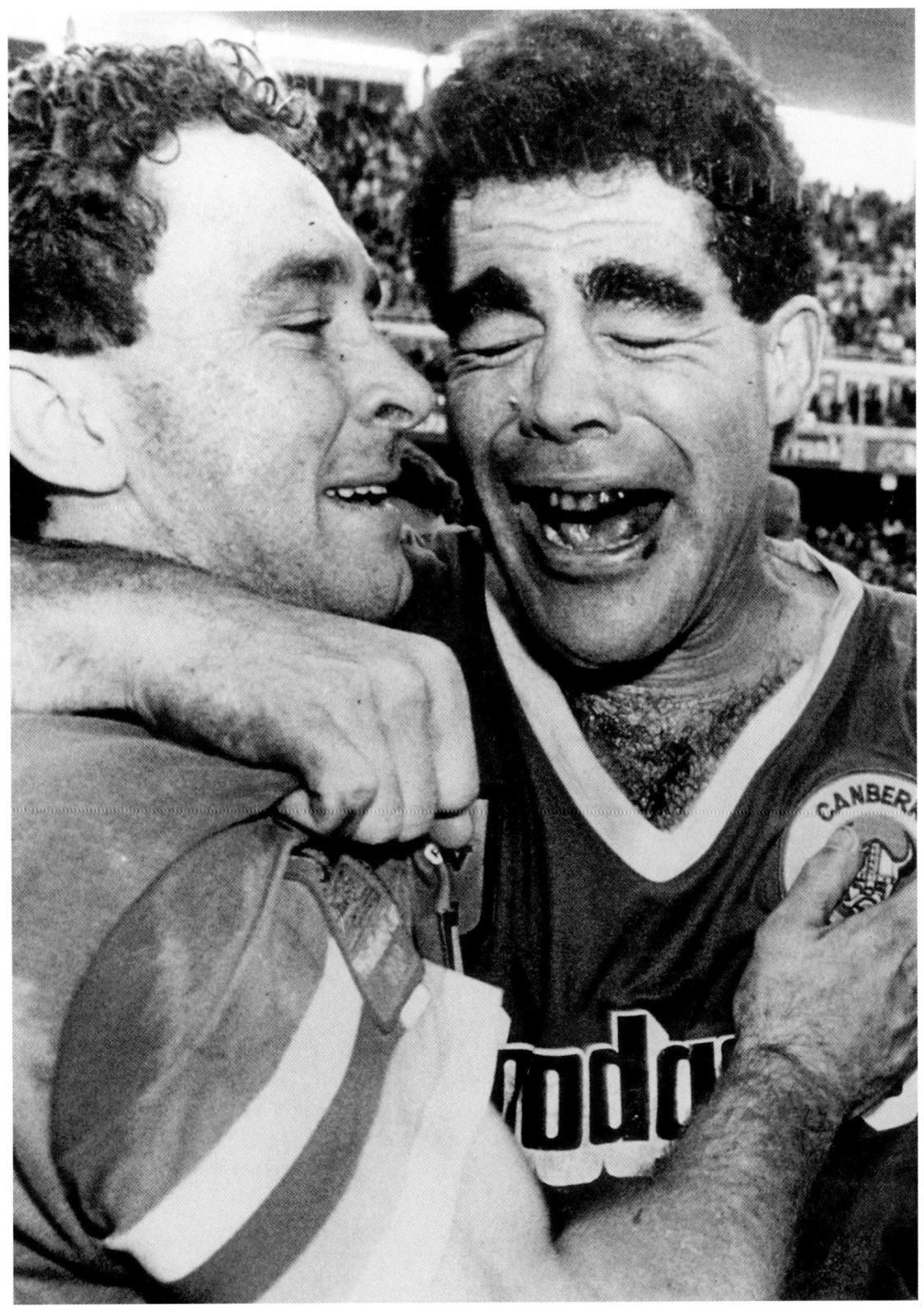

Meninga leaves the field after shattering his arm in the 42nd minute of the Raiders' 1987 match against Manly at Seiffert Sports Ground. This was the first of four matches (between May 1987 and July 1988) in which the arm was broken.

An incredible try by John Ferguson 90 seconds from the finish and a cool conversion by Meninga locked up the scores 14–all and forced the match into extra time and rugby league history. With Meninga leading by example, Canberra faced the next 20 minutes with supreme confidence. They knew they had the power to win. And so it proved. Not long into the first period of extra time, the Tigers fumbled, and Canberra had a loose head and feed close to their opponent's line. Meninga wanted to run the ball, but five-eighth Chris O'Sullivan wanted to kick a field goal.

"Okay, Sully ... go for it!" said Meninga and he watched in relief as O'Sullivan's field goal attempt went through.

Then, close to the finish, replacement prop Steve Jackson crashed his way over for the best and most important try of his career. The Green Machine were champions, the first team from outside the Sydney metropolitan area to win the premiership and the first team to come from the minor preliminary semi-final to win a first-grade grand final.

INTRODUCTION

Mal feels that this 1989 grand final victory ranks as his greatest moment in rugby league, a triumph for his team-mates, his coach Tim Sheens and himself. Who could argue?

●●●

Mal Meninga places a lot of emphasis on the importance of the friendships that develop in football, particularly those in a close-knit team like the Canberra Raiders. Yet, since his retirement from football, he has rarely made an appearance in the Raiders' dressing-room after a match. Although he knows he would be welcomed, he stays well in the background, not wanting to give the impression that he is hanging on to the past, reliving the Meninga glory days. This is not something that has evolved since the conclusion of his playing career: Meninga has always believed that the present belongs solely to the players involved on the day, those who sweated and bled to secure the win. As he says, "They are the ones who won the battle. I didn't do anything to contribute to the victory."

This is not being aloof, or false modesty, as some have suggested. Even in his playing days, when he was injured, Meninga found it difficult to go back into the dressing-room after a match. In such circumstances, he believed he had not contributed to the victory. If his team had lost, he felt he should have been out there trying to help them win.

●●●

Mal Meninga's unprecedented record of achievement tells one part of his rugby league story. But the statistics do not convey the drama, the pain and the frustration that have also been part of his private and public life.

Four times he broke his left arm.

The start of this drama was at Seiffert Sports Ground, in a match against Manly on May 2, 1987. The big man crashed into the bottom of a goal post and left the field, his arm cradled in his football jumper. I spoke to Meninga a couple of hours later when he came back to the Queanbeyan Leagues Club from the hospital. The left arm, he confirmed, was broken. There was no whinge from him, however. He accepted this terrible setback as one of the risks associated with the sport. His intention was to get back on the field as quickly as possible.

He came back a little too soon, though, and suffered a similar fracture in the match against Penrith 10 weeks later. Before that second break, everything had appeared to be going smoothly. Meninga did not spare himself, and was as dominant as ever, scoring a try and kicking four goals. But two minutes from the end, he was involved in a tackle and emerged clutching his arm.

Opposite: Meninga with the World Cup trophy after Australia's stirring 10–6 victory over Great Britain in the 1992 final at London's Wembley Stadium.

It looked as though he would be missing at least until the beginning of the 1988 season.

In the meantime, he lived the good life. He entertained and was entertained well and, inevitably, his weight exploded. But he was brought back to earth with a sickening thud when he was told, after Canberra had won their way into the '87 preliminary final against Eastern Suburbs, that the arm had healed to the point where he might be able to play.

Sure enough, a team of doctors gave him the all clear. With his left arm encased in a massive sponge cylinder, he lasted 64 minutes, and played a decisive role as the Raiders outplayed the Roosters to reach their first top-grade grand final.

This was an incredible performance when you consider he was well above his best playing weight and had been out of football for weeks.

As far as his injuries were concerned, Meninga believed the worst was over. But in the 1988 pre-season he smashed the bone again and, a month after his return, he suffered the same injury in a clash with a Papua New Guinean player in the match between Australia and the Rest of the World.

The two breaks in 1988 limited Meninga's contribution to just five matches for the Raiders that season, and this time there was no magic comeback to help lift his team past Balmain in the knock-out minor semi-final.

Broken arms have not been the only setbacks Meninga has needed to overcome. As a youngster growing up in Bundaberg, Maryborough, Wondai, Monto and Thangool there were difficulties created by the colour of his skin.

Meninga's father, Norman, was an Islander, born in Australia, whose great-great-grandfather had been captured and brought to Australia as a slave to work on the sugar plantations in Queensland. Norman Meninga's wife, Lee, was an Australian, of Scottish parents. Their marriage caused something of a storm, the consequence of racial prejudice among both white and black populations.

Lee, a wise and gracious lady, always told her son that name-calling was not worth worrying about. She explained that the problems caused by racism did not create any worries or difficulties for her, a philosophy Meninga has tried to adopt as his own, even though he recalls the battle his father had to gain recognition for his achievements in athletics and for his outstanding work in fostering junior football.

Mal speaks with pride about his father. He has great respect for the love Norman had for rugby league, the way he played the game and his marvellous coaching feats in the Queensland country districts. And he appreciates how much his father taught him about this great game. But, more importantly, Meninga treasures the fact his father also taught him

INTRODUCTION

In 1984–85, Meninga played a full season with the English club, St Helens. It was a stay that proved rewarding for both club (St Helens won the Lancashire Cup and the Premiership Trophy) and player. Meninga's last game before flying to the north of England had been the Brisbane grand final, in which his side, Souths, had been thrashed by Wynnum–Manly 42–8. After that debacle, the big centre admitted he had lost his enthusiasm for rugby league. But the warmth and friendship of the people of St Helens, coupled with the open style of football played at that time in England, rekindled his passion for the game.

the important things in life — how to be a good person, how to make friends and always to be honest.

Mal Meninga learned those lessons well.

Lee Meninga told me that young Mal faced hurdles from the very start of his football career. Because of his size, Mal was obliged to play in a higher weight division than other children of his age.

"But he handled it," she explained. "For some matches which had weight restrictions, Mal would have to run around the ground a couple of times and go to the toilet to try to get his weight down."

Introduction

On the question of the racial problems her son has faced, Lee Meninga's remarks were straight to the point.

"Mal has more brains than all those people criticising him," she said and then added, "I'm not saying this because he's my son, but I believe Mal was a great footballer ... And really, he's just a big teddy bear ..."

There are probably several hundred players spread throughout England, France, Papua New Guinea, New Zealand and Australia who would tend to disagree with Lee Meninga's assessment of her famous son. He may have been many things on the football field ... but a teddy bear was not one of them!

Some of the prejudice and the jealousy that impinged on Meninga's early life led to problems in the schoolyard. He estimates he averaged a fight a week, with a number of these squabbles triggered by youngsters who resented his remarkable ability in all sports. But some were more hurtful, the result of snide remarks about his colour.

Early in his football career, even after he had become a Test regular, the taunts continued. Usually, Lee Meninga's calming philosophy guided him through, but occasionally enough was enough.

The worst instance occurred in 1983, during a club match in Brisbane. Meninga was playing for Southern Suburbs in a match against Wynnum–Manly when he was verbally abused as he left the field. These were not the usual taunts players become accustomed to. These were racist. And Meninga, it should be remembered, had just returned from his first Kangaroo tour, the celebrated "Invincibles" tour in which the Australians, for the first time, remained undefeated throughout their stay in Britain and France.

Mal found it possible to ignore the remarks from spectators when he was involved in the game, but when he was walking off the field and the insults continued, it was too much. He asked a man to repeat what he had said, and when he did (not a smart thing to do in the situation!), Meninga belted him.

The support for Meninga following this incident was unanimous. Southern Suburbs coach Bob McCarthy gave voice to the public disgust at the treatment which had provoked his star centre to act as he had when he said, "It seems the worst thing he has done in his life is to become a sporting hero in Queensland."

Even in the latter years of Meninga's career, a period strewn with triumph and glory, all was not smooth sailing. There was the drama at Canberra in 1991 when there were fears the Raiders would fold because of a debt incurred by the licensed Mawson Club, and accusations of malpractice from other clubs after it was discovered that the football club had breached their salary cap restrictions.

Opposite: The Australian captain on the Kangaroo tour in 1990, against Wigan at Central Park. The Australians won 34–6.

For many weeks, Meninga and his team-mates did not know where their careers were heading. They were not even sure they would be paid. Amid the growing storm, players were insulted by sections of the public, and there were suggestions made that the Raiders should be thrown out of the league or stripped of their two premiership victories. Meninga recalls all too clearly situations where people would walk up to the Canberra players in public to call them cheats.

In the nick of time, it seemed, Mal received a massive offer of a four-year contract with his former English club, St Helens, where he had created such a huge impact in 1984–85. It was a deal most players dream about ... £100,000 a year for four years, a position as captain–coach after a couple of seasons (if he wanted it), a coaching job when he had finished playing, free accommodation, unlimited use of a car and all expenses met by the club.

Meninga admits he was tempted but, after meetings with his team-mates, and later with Raiders coach Tim Sheens (who had already re-signed with the club) and Kevin Grace, chief executive of the Queanbeyan Leagues Club, he decided to stay.

The main reason was his strong loyalty to the Canberra public which had rallied behind the battling Raiders and contributed $250,000 to a fund to pay the players.

This is a link that remains ironclad to this day, for Meninga feels a great affinity with the rugby league followers of the nation's capital, and the entire city regards their former captain as a living legend.

A drama of a different kind dominated Meninga's life in the lead-up to the final Ashes Test on the 1994 Kangaroo tour. The series was tied at one–all, but the tabloids' headlines were screaming the story of the Australian captain's young daughter, born in England after his first Kangaroo tour in 1982. Meninga was unmarried at that time.

Meninga had known when he went to England for the World Cup in 1992 that a paternity suit against him had been instituted by the mother of the girl. At no stage did he say the child, Nicola, was not his but, naturally, he wanted proof. Tests were done but, as far as Meninga was concerned, they were not conclusive. However, though he was not completely satisfied with the results of the tests, he believed his eyes.

"She's a Meninga, there's no doubt about that," Mal frankly admits. And he accepted the responsibility of assisting with the support of Nicola, who was 11 when he met her for the first time on that '94 tour.

For the English tabloids, it was an early Christmas present. And, apart from journalists trying to get some new angle on what they labelled "The Love Child" story, it seemed there was a swarm of solicitors knocking on Meninga's door. This was the price Meninga had to pay for his astoundingly high profile.

Introduction

Meninga on the training paddock in Sydney with Australian team-mates Allan Langer (left) and Steve Walters, two days before the second Test of the 1991 series against New Zealand. Australia, who had lost the opening match of the series in Melbourne, would win this game 44–0, and then two weeks later seal the series with another emphatic victory, 40–12, at Brisbane's Lang Park.

The pressure on him at that time was incredible as he tried to deflect media attention from his personal situation and at the same time focus on the task of leading Australia in the Ashes-deciding Test. What concerned him more than anything, though, was the embarrassment for his wife, Debbie, her family and his own.

Another controversy erupted within months of the Australian captain's retirement from football when, following the French leg of the '94 Kangaroo tour, Meninga agreed to join the breakaway Super League organisation.

From talking to him, and from listening to his comments in the media, I think it is clear Meninga believes that Super League offers a better alternative for the players of the '90s. However, in the eyes of many fans and critics, Meninga tarnished his reputation during an often fiery meeting at the Cronulla Leagues Club in April 1995, when he was one of the speakers called by that club to discuss the pros and cons of Super League.

INTRODUCTION

That night Mal Meninga made a blunder, one he regrets.

What the Super League critics pounced on was his badly phrased response to a question saying that he had "played the game for 16 years" and had "got nothing out of it".

Meninga did not mean that, as anyone who knows him would realise. He would be the first to admit that, as one of the highest-profile players in the history of the sport, he has gained great rewards out of the game. However, typically, his concern is for the middle-of-the-road players who try their very best but can't make the transition from average performer to very good player. These were the players he was referring to in his answer. Quite often, the game can leave them on a scrap heap when their modest careers are over.

●●●

I have loved my life involvement with rugby league. I am friends with some of the great players and I admire and like the present crop of stars. I've been fortunate to have known some of the great characters of the game — both knockabouts and larrikins, paupers and wealthy men. I have liaised with great officials and worked beside sports-writing legends. But right up there among the very best people I have been associated with is Mal Meninga.

Personally, I couldn't care less if he had never put his foot on a football field again. To me, he is simply a quality person, a man you would be proud to call your friend.

Because when you have Mal Meninga as a friend, you have a friend for life.

MENINGA

1: THE LONG FAREWELL

November 20, 1994 was a very important date in the life of Mal Meninga. On this day I was involved in a football match of great consequence, played at Elland Road, home stadium of the world-famous Leeds United soccer club. But on this occasion Elland Road had been transformed into a rugby league ground. And not just any rugby league ground — it was the venue for the third Test of the 1994 Ashes series, a series that is locked at one Test all. Australia and Great Britain were about to battle for international rugby league's most famous trophy.

For myself, the fact that the Ashes trophy was on the line made this as crucial as any Test match I had ever played. But there was added significance. This was my last Test against Great Britain ... and the last truly big match of my career. Sure, there were games still to be played in France, including a Test match at a place called Béziers. But such is the ordinary standard of French football in the 1990s that few would watch them and only the players, player's relatives and statisticians would remember them.

Unfortunately, the week leading up to the Test had not been a memorable one for me. Personal pressures that I think should have remained a private matter had become public property. Consequently, when I woke that morning I was in an angry mood, the same angry mood I had been in for the previous couple of days. It was not the frame of mind I would have hoped for, or the one I had anticipated when I decided months before that this was the game I wanted to be the final big encounter of my playing career.

The burden imposed on my side by history and media expectations was immense. Australian rugby league teams have not made a habit of losing in recent years. Not since 1970 had an Australian team lost an Ashes series. No Kangaroo side had lost a series in England in 35 years. To our critics (and most of our supporters), nothing less than a decisive win would do.

I was desperate to play well, to leave the centre stage at the peak of my form.

I had been hoping I would have been able to dismiss from my mind the events of the past few days. Not a chance. My day began some time between 10 and 11 a.m., with a hearty breakfast. I ate all the "right" things

Opposite: *Trying to evade Great Britain's lock Phil Clarke during the first Test of the 1994 Ashes series, at Wembley Stadium.*

With Bob Fulton, who coached the Australian team throughout my time as Australian captain, from 1990 to 1994. Bob had a profound influence on my career — no-one could have done a better job as coach of the national team.

— cereal, pasta and fruit — and drank plenty of water, plus the appropriate sports drink. Then I just tried to do all the things I would normally do before a game.

But I couldn't shake the anger; the feeling that someone or something was trying to hijack this important day in my life.

Around noon, our coach, Bob Fulton, gathered us together for a final team meeting. Typical of the man, he had forgotten nothing. On a whiteboard, Bob had written the goals he had emphasised all tour. It was my job, as captain, to talk about them. They all amounted to one thing ... victory. Bob then summarised our opponents' weaknesses and strengths — in that order. We went through our game plan, which had been developed over the past fortnight and discussed in detail at the team dinner the previous night.

We knew what we needed to do.

Meeting over, the butterflies — bane of high-profile sportsmen and women the world over — began. There's no cure for them, and no harm in them either. They just mean you're alert, that the moment matters. But even as the butterflies emerged, I couldn't shake the rage inside me. Frustrating memories of the past few days rebounded around my head.

Kick-off was scheduled for 3 p.m. In the bus to the ground there was precious little talk. Everyone has their own ambitions, their own desires, their own motivation. Experience gathered over a long career told me my comrades were thinking about what they would have to do to perform at their very best ... and what not to do to let the side down. That was what I should have been doing myself. But part of my mind was elsewhere.

It is at this point, about an hour before the kick-off, that a real fear — the fear of failure — can take over the mind of some players. This usually affects senior players more than junior ones — they've got more to lose in terms of reputation.

Throughout my career, coaches, senior team-mates and former champions had told me that I had to have faith in my ability. Never run away from a challenge, they would say. Respond to it. Fortunately, I was able to turn the threat of defeat into a positive motivational tool. I learned that the way to avoid a poor performance was to focus on what needed to be done. Early in my career, I hadn't worried about failure. Perhaps that had been the arrogance of youth. In those days I had just enjoyed the game and played from day to day, game to game, season to season. But, as the number of days before my retirement diminished, the thought of not getting as much out of the game as I possibly could had become a great motivator. In 1987–88 I had broken my arm four times. Rather than these setbacks driving me from rugby league, they had made me appreciate the game and what it had to offer a whole lot more.

As I stepped from the bus to walk to the Elland Road away dressing-room on November 20, 1994, I knew I didn't want to fail. And I knew what I had to do to avoid such failure. I wanted to win the Test, this game that was so important to us all. To achieve this, I knew I had to fight the anger inside me. I needed to concentrate on the task at hand.

The dressing-room was quiet. For me, it was like heaven — suddenly the stresses of the past few days began to dissipate. They couldn't get me in here. Out on the field it would be the same, my only rivals my 13 opponents. Only now did I truly begin to focus on the game. All the emotion of the previous few days began channelling in the right direction. I felt good ... and confident.

Around me, there was the occasional chat. But no more. Everyone was trying to do the things they normally do before a game. Some went out to inspect the playing surface and to stare at the crowd as it slowly grew to capacity. Others preferred to get strapped early. There are players who like to get their kit on as soon as possible, others who like leaving things to the very last minute. Every player's routine is different, and their own. As 3 p.m. approached, the room began to get more rowdy ... the final gee-up. Our coach was quiet; there was nothing more for him to say — it was up to his players now.

Opposite: Acknowledging the many Australians in the Elland Road crowd after our third Test victory in 1994.

I brought the team together, not for a random rave but to be constructive and to relax the boys a bit. A general discussion between the players ensued, the more extroverted leading the way. Then there was time to collect our thoughts.

The team seemed so relaxed and confident. Bob's preparation had been spot-on. As we walked on to the Elland Road pitch, I could tell how well the team was reacting to the singing and buzzing of the crowd. We were ready. It appeared that for all of us the occasion was not intimidating, but inspiring.

The Australian team's performance that day was superb, and ended with a conclusive 23–4 victory. My own performance was satisfactory, though less than the dominant farewell I had dreamed of. I made a few mistakes early on — perhaps the frustration and the anger played a hand — but from that point on, I concentrated particularly well as I became totally absorbed in the Test and did my bit to achieve the victory.

On the field after the game, I savoured the atmosphere, responding to the exuberant waves of the travelling Australian supporters and the joy and celebrations of my team-mates. This was the last big moment of my career in top-grade rugby league, a 16-year adventure that had developed into so much more than I could ever have imagined. At that moment, I thought of so many things — of the many great days of the family, friends and colleagues who had helped my career.

It had been quite a ride.

● ● ●

My final year was a demanding one, right from the time we began pre-season training. The trials began in January, then came the premiership, the State of Origin series, a Test against France, the finals series and finally the Kangaroo tour. By the end of it, I was relieved it was all over. I felt I just could not be bothered playing football any more.

I can now sit back and, for a change, enjoy life as a spectator, watching the game I love. It's funny — when I was playing, I could not bear to watch a game, but now I'm just a smiling, happy person, another face in the crowd.

I feel no frustration that I am not out there. And there is a bonus — I can get out of bed on a Monday morning without the post-match pain that is the lot of the modern football gladiator.

There are a lot of fabulous memories crowded into my final year as a footballer. There are also a couple of disappointments ... and the usual touch of drama ... but, as far as I am concerned, it was close enough to a perfect finale to a career.

The first major event was the State of Origin series in 1994. Queensland, the state I proudly led, were the underdogs. Through the

The Long Farewell

Opposite: Comforted by Raiders team-mate but NSW opponent, Laurie Daley, after my final match at Lang Park, the third State of Origin battle of 1994. I had been desperately hoping to farewell the Queensland faithful with a victory, which would have won us the series, but, unfortunately, Laurie's team were too good on the night. But even though we lost, I was moved by the way the Lang Park crowd went out of their way to acknowledge my departure.

1980s, we had, except for a two-year break in 1985–86, been dominant in inter-state football. Famous names that are now part of Queensland rugby league folklore, such as Wally Lewis, Allan Langer, Paul "Fatty" Vautin, Gene Miles, Chris Close, Greg Dowling, Kerry Boustead, Mark Murray, Bryan Niebling and Greg Conescu, had created a magic Maroon era. But in 1994 the New South Wales team had developed a similar formula to the one that had made us so successful. They had discovered a good group of young players and kept them together for several years, during which time they had gained in cohesion, confidence and respect for each other.

In 1994, Queensland were a team between eras. We were still an excellent team but, in certain positions (notably the front row), we had suffered due to a lack of younger players coming through to replace the recently departed champions. And for the first match of the '94 Origin series, it appeared that that weakness was going to cost us dearly.

However, the celebrated never-say-die spirit of the team, a verve that has been fostered and taken great advantage of by the Maroons right though the history of Origin football, was still very much in place. This spirit didn't always guarantee victory, but it did give us a head start. And in the concluding stages of that wonderful game, the spirit rose to the surface once again.

Five minutes from time, we were down and, as far as the Sydney Football Stadium crowd and most of the millions watching on television were concerned, out — behind by eight points, 12–4. Then our winger, Willie Carne, scored near the posts, a try I converted. 12–10.

Then came one of those magic moments of football that will stay with me for ever. The time-clock was charging towards full-time. We had the ball, but were camped near our own quarter. Time for one last raid. Alfie Langer spread the ball across our back line. It reached Willie Carne, who lobbed the ball to Steve Renouf. He had to stop to catch the ball, and then accelerate over the halfway. The NSW defence, in something of a panic, was madly trying to quell the attack. When confronted by the cover, Steve passed back inside to Mick Hancock. A try was on!

But there was still plenty to do. As Mick was tackled, he passed to our replacement forward, Darren Smith. Darren passed to Alfie, and I positioned myself to Alfie's right. To my right was Mark Coyne, another replacement, but an outstanding player who, in the previous two seasons, had starred with the St George team which had reached both grand finals.

Then I had the ball, but my way to the tryline was blocked. I drew one defender and passed to Mark, and watched with a great sense of joy and relief as he stepped back inside and, as he was tackled, reached out and planted the ball over the line.

I could be wrong but, considering the importance of the game, the

The Long Farewell

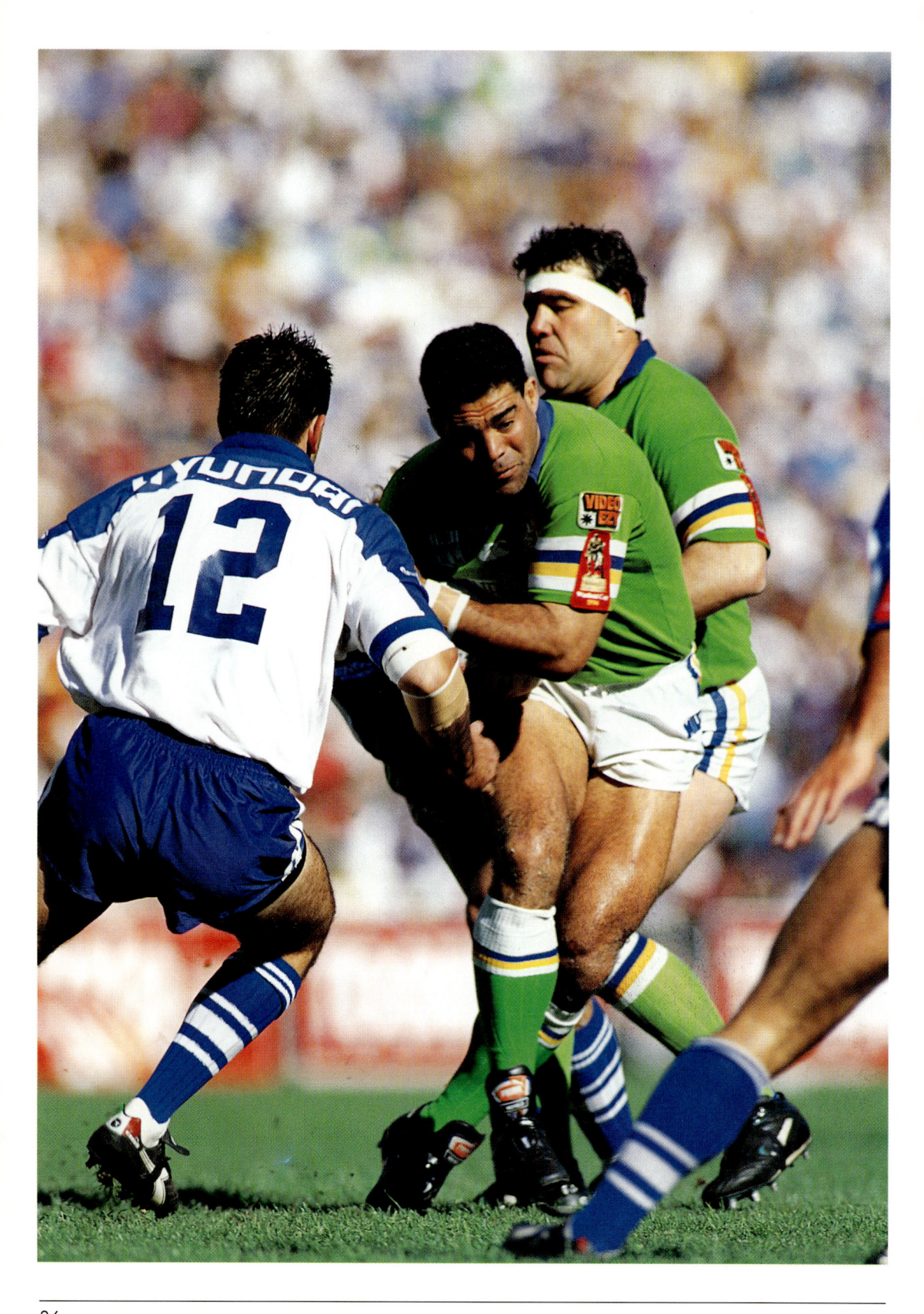

Meninga

quality of the defenders and the time it was scored, that has to be just about the greatest team try ever scored in Australian rugby league.

Afterwards, we acknowledged NSW were the better team on the night, but we didn't care — it was a bonus to be one up after playing in Sydney. It's always nice to beat NSW, but just that little bit sweeter if victory comes on their own turf. We were fully aware that except for the last five minutes we had not played well, but we'd still won, which gave us the confidence to believe we could continue with a win in the second game of the series, which would be played at the Melbourne Cricket Ground.

What a night that was! Over 87,000 people packed into Melbourne's mega-stadium — many of them Victorians experiencing their first game of rugby league. The spectacle was incredible and the opportunity to play in front of a full house there was a once-in-a-lifetime thrill for every player.

Unfortunately, the game itself was disappointing. I think this had something to do with the fact that many of the players were accustomed to the razor-sharp atmosphere that is generated at Origin battles at the Sydney Football Stadium or at Suncorp Stadium in Brisbane. And at both those venues the crowd is right on top of you, whereas the MCG is a cricket and Australian Rules football ground. For a league match, the fans are a long way away. I always liked it when they were just about in your pocket. When you are out there in the big matches, people chanting and screaming gives you a lift and I believe it makes you play better.

The atmosphere at the MCG that night was weird. Reflecting their lack of experience as a rugby league audience, the crowd would cheer at the "wrong" time. Or they wouldn't cheer when they should have done. The best indication that things weren't quite right was that I didn't have to yell and scream to make myself heard!

Mind you, the lack of atmosphere had nothing to do with our defeat. The Canberra Raiders in the Blues team told me that they also struggled to come to terms with the setting. NSW won 14–0 — the first time we had been held to nil in a State of Origin match. It was a frustrating night.

The team's hopes were high for my last match in those wonderful Queensland colours. Our lead-up to the game was very good — we trained hard and prepared well. And there was an air of expectation that we would win. But, sadly, on the night, NSW were just too good.

I don't think we played to our potential. We struggled for most of the game and were beaten by a more cohesive team who seemed to want to win that little bit more than we did. This was an unusual situation — for most of Origin history we always felt we had a slight advantage in the desire department. So it was fantastic to see a return to the old days in 1995, when Fatty Vautin's Maroons won the series, despite the fact that on paper they had seemed outclassed. You could tell from the opening

Opposite: Charging at Canterbury's Dean Pay during the 1994 grand final. Behind me is Paul Osborne, who came into the Canberra starting line-up after first-choice prop John Lomax was suspended, and proceeded to play the game of his life.

My final game at Bruce Stadium came in round 21, 1994 — a 40–22 defeat of Western Suburbs. After the match, I was given the chance to run a final lap to thank the thousands of Canberra fans who had made my time as a Raider such an enjoyable and rewarding experience.

The Long Farewell

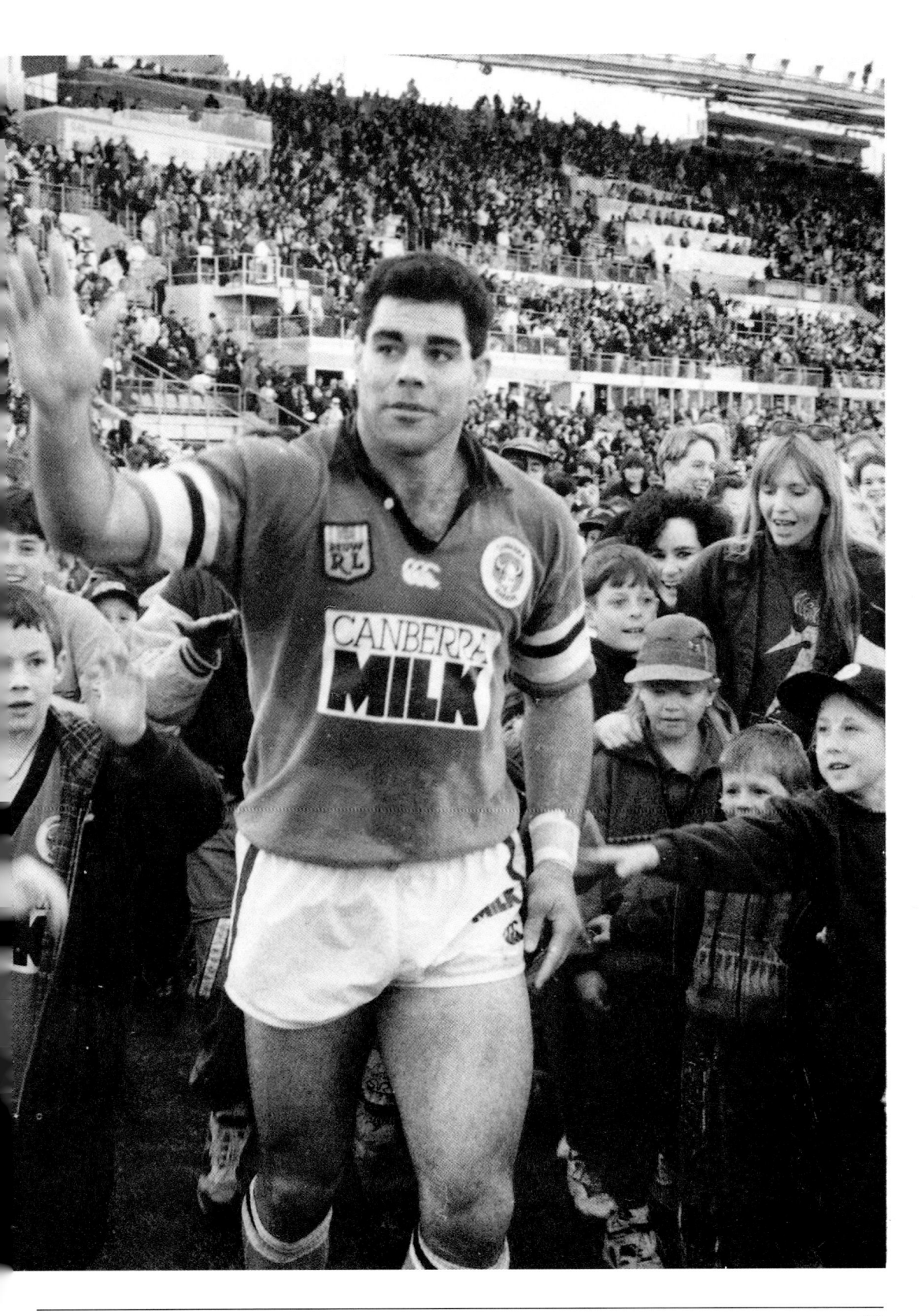

MENINGA

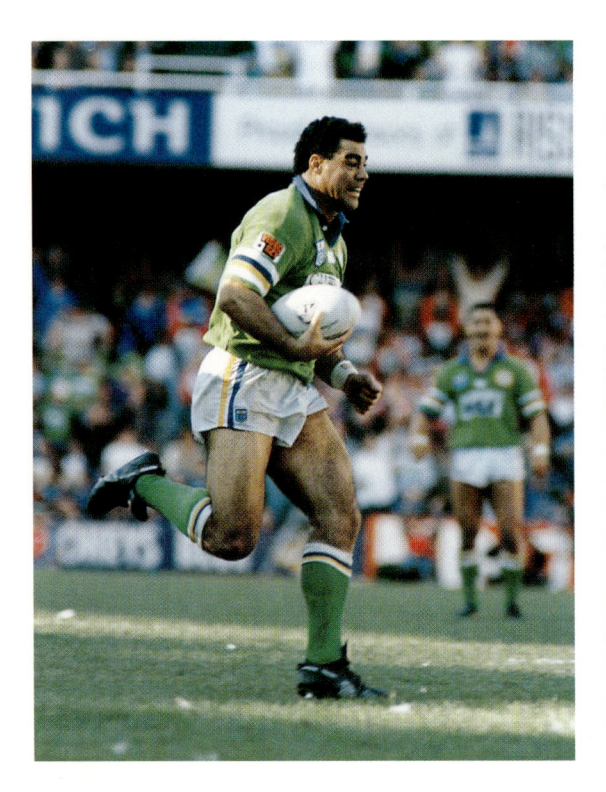

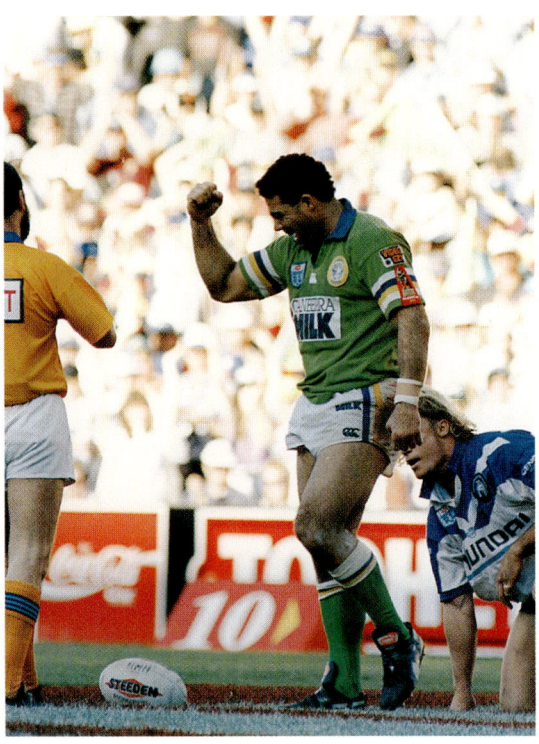

Above and opposite: Late in the second half of the 1994 grand final, I managed to intercept a Canterbury pass and set sail for the try-line. As full-time approached and a Raiders victory became assured, I set my sights on ending my club career with a four-pointer. When it actually happened, I made sure I savoured the moment to the full.

exchanges of that '95 series that Queensland were serious about winning.

I was disappointed with our loss in 1994, but not with my time as a Queensland representative footballer. I had worn the maroon jumper for 16 years and been a part of some amazing triumphs. In terms of my whole career as a member of this wonderful football family, I did not have much to be disappointed about.

As it was, I didn't have much time to mourn the loss. On the following Sunday, the Raiders were at home to the Broncos in a contest many critics billed as a grand final rehearsal. Coming into the game, we were running fourth and, on the day, we played like premiers, winning 29–10, with Ricky Stuart and Steve Walters in brilliant form.

More than anything else, I wanted to win the grand final in my farewell year. As far as I am concerned, there is no greater thrill in rugby league than to win the premiership. It's great to play for Queensland, fantastic to play for Australia and hugely rewarding to achieve team success on Kangaroo tours. However, nothing can beat the feeling when that final siren goes and you are the premiers in the toughest and most demanding rugby league competition in the world — the grand final.

I knew all the Canberra players wanted to send me out a winner. They had said so publicly and things were also said to me privately that convinced me everyone was single-minded about what we as a team wanted to achieve.

The Long Farewell

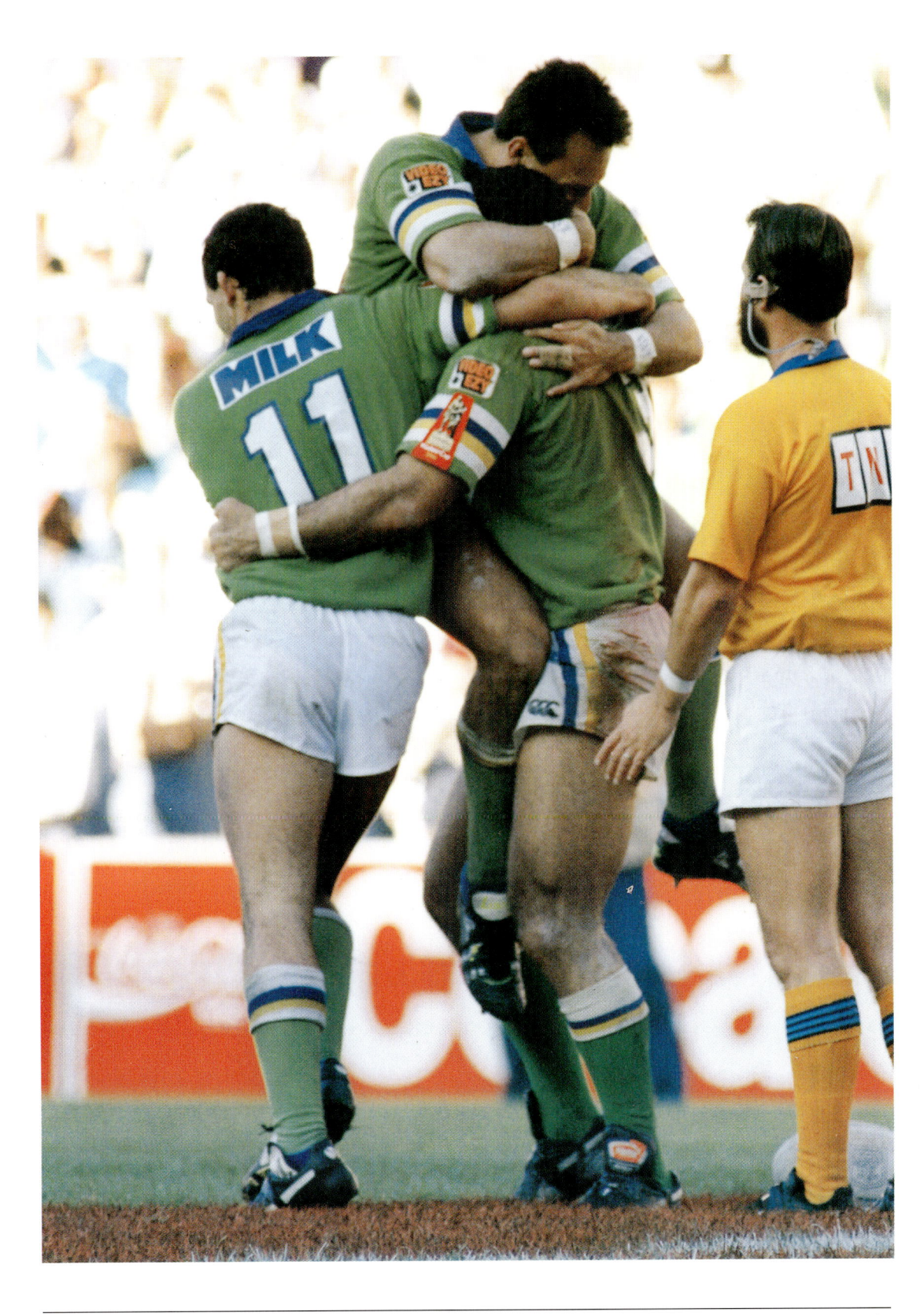

Ken Nagas (no. 2) has just scored the final try in Canberra's 22–9 victory over Norths in the 1994 preliminary final. The other Raiders are Brett Hetherington, Jason Croker, Ricky Stuart, Quentin Pongia and myself.

However, there were some scratchy moments towards the end of the season when we were heading for the grand final. We had played consistently throughout the season, with that defeat of the Broncos the highlight, and finished second on the premiership ladder, two points behind the minor premiers, Canterbury. But, for some reason, we couldn't discover our best football once we reached the end-of-season games. It was crazy, and terribly frustrating. Despite all the effort we knew we were putting in, it seemed we were just going through the motions.

In the major preliminary semi-final, against Norths, we were well clear at half-time, but then went to automatic pilot in the second 40 minutes.

Then we were beaten 19–18 in the major semi-final by the Bulldogs, when their Kiwi winger, Daryl Halligan, kicked a field goal just two minutes from the end of extra time. Canterbury deserved to win that day and should have won a lot more comfortably than they did. We just did not put it together — we made far too many mistakes. Despite our best intentions, our minds were not totally focussed on the tough job we had.

The reasons for our lackadaisical approach were difficult to determine. It was a fact that we had many brilliant individuals in the team, players whose unique individual skills could get a team out of trouble, but somehow this had led to us all waiting for each other to do the job.

Things did not get any better in the final against North Sydney: not even the realisation that if we lost we'd be eliminated from the competition could shake us out of our lethargy. We played terrible football but, fortunately, Norths played even more badly than we did! We bombed half a dozen tries we would normally have scored, took some poor options and struggled throughout. But we got away with it.

Back in the dressing-room after the game, our coach, Tim Sheens, gave the players a blast, pointing out in no uncertain terms just how ordinary we had been. I did the same. We all knew if we didn't improve sharply we'd be out of the race against Canterbury in the grand final.

However, not long after the start of grand final week, Tim and I were both much happier with the players' change in attitude. We trained well and the things that were said in team meetings and at training were the comments of footballers completely concentrated on their upcoming assignment. I was confident we would win.

And so it proved. From the opening minutes at the Sydney Football Stadium, when our replacement front-rower, Paul Osborne, put David Furner over for the grand final's first try, we were in control. "Ossie" had a blinder; soon after, he slipped a pass behind the back of a Bulldogs defender and winger Ken Nagas raced away for 10–nil. Then Laurie Daley produced something special, accelerating through a gap to score in the corner. At half-time, it was 18–6. Then 24–6. Then 30–6.

After the game, the question I was asked most often was the old standard: "How do you feel?" My answer surprised people. I was certainly highly satisfied, but I wasn't excited. In fact, the experience was something of an anticlimax, and I was left with a slightly empty feeling as I looked back on the match. This is why ...

For most of my football life, I usually had to win things the hard way, in the sense that important games or series were rarely won comfortably.

The majority of the grand finals I played in were thrillers. As captain of Queensland or Australia, the third match of the series was always the decider. None of this 3–nil whitewash business for Mal Meninga. But that grand final against Canterbury was probably the easiest big-game match victory I have ever been a part of.

The '94 Raiders were a team overflowing with exceptional players — Ricky Stuart, Laurie Daley, Bradley Clyde, Brett Mullins, Steve Walters, Ken Nagas ... the list goes on. On grand final day, every player performed to the very best of his extraordinary ability. Really, Canterbury didn't have a chance. And, from a personal point of view, the game becomes so much easier when your team-mates are going so brilliantly — all you have to worry about is your own performance.

During the second half, I found myself watching the SFS clock as it ticked its way towards full-time and the conclusion of my last game of rugby league in Australia. I was waiting for the game to finish and the celebrations to begin. There was no tension, desperation or reason to fret. I knew we had it won. It was a long way from the Canberra–Balmain extra-time epic in 1989, or the games against Penrith in 1990 and 1991, which went all the way to the final minute.

I'm sure other players will agree with me about this. What we desire is challenge. If games are won easily, they become pedestrian. The skill and effort are still there, as is the pride in your personal performance. However, the passion — the thing that makes famous sporting contests so memorable — is gone.

I was, I must stress, extremely grateful for the efforts of my team-mates, appreciative of the fact that I was captain of rugby league's premier team and very, very proud of what the Raiders had achieved. Late in the game came a personal highlight as I intercepted an errant Bulldog pass and ran 30 metres to score the grand final's last try. This was something I had wanted to do — it was a nice way to send myself out. I just wish that try had come in the final seconds to get the Raiders to the front. That was the type of grandstand finish I would have written if I had been in charge of the script.

Nevertheless, by the time we had returned to Canberra and the celebrations had begun, the adrenalin was pumping. On the way home, away from prying TV cameras, I had a chance to reflect on our great victory. The decisiveness of our win had established us as one of the best teams of the modern era, and for me this was the fulfilment of all I had dreamed about when I had first come to Canberra a decade earlier. So I felt genuinely excited about the fact that I had achieved one of the goals I had set myself at the start of the year.

That night, while the party was in full swing, the Kangaroo touring squad was announced. I was expecting to be named as captain, though I have learned over the years never to take anything for granted. In 1948, the selectors left the Australian captain, Len Smith, out of the Kangaroos, while in 1967, they somehow managed to leave Bob Fulton and Bob McCarthy behind, so nothing is absolutely certain with these things. So it was still an enormous thrill to hear my name read out. Especially with the magic word "captain" alongside it.

This was my fourth tour, and I never doubted it would be the most difficult yet. The British side had performed admirably in the two years since the last Ashes series in Australia, defeating the Kiwis comfortably in 1993 (more comfortably, in fact, than we had earlier that year). With

The Long Farewell

classy players such as Jonathan Davies, Denis Betts, Gary Connolly, Martin Offiah and Phil Clarke available, I knew retaining the Ashes trophy was going to be a formidable task.

The first Test, at Wembley Stadium, confirmed my opinion. We played badly, but they were superb, especially Davies, who had an inspired afternoon. His try late in the first half was a match-winner, a brilliant run from near halfway that gave Great Britain a 6–nil lead. This had come not long after their captain, Shaun Edwards, was sent off for a high shot on Bradley Clyde.

With our opponents a man down, we should have won the day but, unfortunately, we took some terrible options. Our defence was fine, but in attack we had the blinkers on. We did not utilise our talents and skills, we did not move the ball at all and we did not make the other team run around even though they only had 12 men for much of the game.

Put simply (and taking nothing away from a gallant and very good British side), we played very badly.

However, just a fortnight later in the second Test at Manchester, the Kangaroos produced what I believe to be the best all-round performance by a team that I have been a part of. I say this because of the quality of the

With the help of Wendell Sailor (far left), I try to contain Wigan's former All Black winger Va'aiga Tuigamala during the 1994 Kangaroo tour. We finally won this match 30–20. I needed the headgear after cutting my forehead open earlier in the game.

Confronted by Wales's John Devereux at a rain-swept Ninian Park in Cardiff in 1994. This was the Kangaroos' second match after our first Test loss. Four days earlier, a team made up mostly of players who had missed the defeat at Wembley had humiliated the Sheffield Eagles by 80 points to two. Now we set about destroying the Welsh. By half-time, it was 30–0 after five Australian tries, and only the ever-worsening weather kept the final scoreline to 46–4.

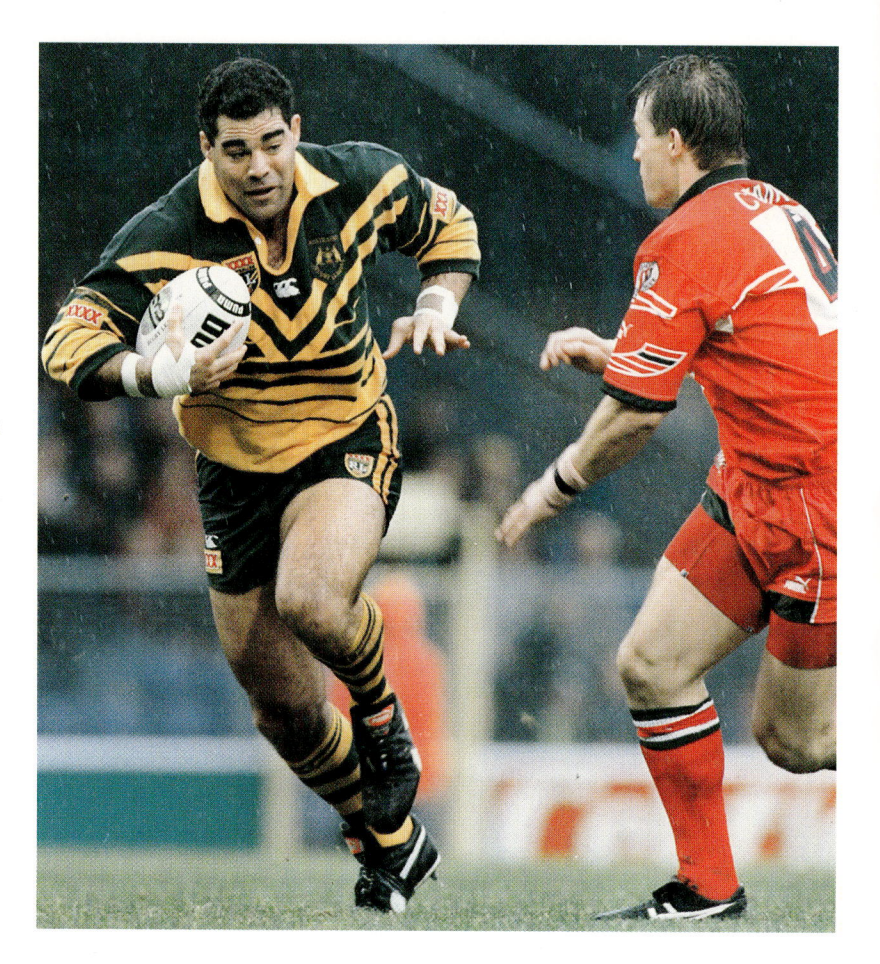

opposition and because of the significance of the occasion. We didn't want to be part of the first Australian team to be beaten in an Ashes series since 1970.

Right from the jump we were magnificent. The first 25 minutes were of an extraordinarily high quality: we attempted to spread the ball as often as possible and Great Britain matched us with some stirring defence work. Fortunes turned, and the home team launched an assault on our line, but our defensive line held. A pair of penalty goals had Great Britain ahead 4–2, and then Bobby Goulding, in at halfback replacing the suspended Edwards, threw an ambitious pass out towards the left wing. I read his mind, dashed into their back line and grabbed the intercept.

There were 80 long metres between me and the first try of the Test. When I snared Goulding's pass, the first thought to flash through my mind was that I would never make it to the line.

Then I thought, hang on a sec ... I'm in with a chance here. But not for long. Feeling like a sprinter running the Melbourne Cup, about 30 metres from home I began to lose speed. The defence closed in. There was no way I was going to get to the line.

I started looking for support and our winger, Andrew Ettingshausen, appeared. Getting the ball to "ET" wasn't going to be easy, as he was snookered in among four desperate British defenders. However, he took the right option, and stayed on the outside. I gave him the ball just as I was tackled from behind, but the try still had to be scored and this was when ET showed what a superb finisher he is. He dived before the line — if he hadn't, he would have been pushed over the sideline — and slid over in the corner.

This try changed the game. For the rest of the first half, we played outstanding, controlled football and led 18–4 at the break. And just after the interval, a typically brilliant Laurie Daley try killed the contest. In the end, we won 38–8 but, in my opinion, the margin between the teams on the scoreboard was an unfair reflection of the commitment and intensity of both sides. It had been quite a Test.

After the full-time whistle, we gathered out on the field and I stressed the point that we didn't need any bigheads, there was still a hell of a lot of work to do. We could all still vividly recall the hurt and embarrassment that had followed our first Test defeat and the pressure that accompanied it.

The national profile of English rugby league has increased in recent years, but with that has come a greater media spotlight, especially from the tabloid press in London. Spotters were camped in our hotel, their brief being to make sure we were always doing the right thing. Any mistakes, and we were back-page or, perhaps even worse, front-page news. That wasn't pleasant.

That defeat, and the consequent threat of a series loss, added to the stress. Personally, I felt these worries as much as anyone — probably more — especially in the days leading up to the third Test. So I retreated into my shell a bit, and tried to ignore the media. I didn't want to be the first captain to lose an Ashes series in England since 1959. I needed to focus on the task ahead ... to finish a winner.

It was in that week before the third Test, despite the personal pressures that threatened to distract me, that I came to understand how much I wanted a successful end to my playing career. Never in my life had I wanted to win so much. And my team-mates did not let me down.

The key to our third Test victory was the strength and quality of our defensive line. We never let up, not for a moment. Our forwards' efforts, with my Raiders comrade Steve Walters leading the way, were quite fantastic. In attack, we took some wrong options and I made a couple of mistakes but, even though the British team produced arguably their best performance of the series, we were always in control.

They did not score one try, even during a period early in the second half when our line was bombarded during a run where the British held

Meninga

the ball for 24 successive tackles. The courage my team-mates displayed was infectious, producing a defensive display the equal of anything any Kangaroo team in my experience has produced.

After the game, I was overcome with an extraordinary sense of relief. It was as if a huge weight had been lifted off me. We still had the French section of the tour to go, but the tour's focus — the retention of the Ashes — had been accomplished in superb style. For Mal Meninga, the 1994 season had become the perfect farewell.

The French section of the tour was very enjoyable, far removed from the stresses of tour life in the north of England. The Australian Rugby League allowed our wives and children to link up with us, so I did a bit more sightseeing than I had managed previously. Bob Fulton and his wife, Anne, and my wife, Debbie, and I took in a number of the attractions together, while our children, Tamika and Joshua, who had been attending a French–English school in Canberra, took the opportunity to test their language skills on the locals.

In recent years, the French leg of a Kangaroo tour has become something akin to an end-of-season trip, where everyone gets on the booze and you play a couple of games. To have Debbie and the kids over was a very enjoyable change from that, and one I appreciated a great deal.

The Test match was a fantastic way to end my career — both rewarding and great fun. We could easily have jogged on to the field, gone through the motions, performed badly and still won the game. But that wouldn't have been the style of this Kangaroo team. Everyone had the same objective in mind ... to win the match by the greatest possible margin.

I was able to do the stuff I really enjoy — running the football — and to round things off perfectly, I scored the Test's final try. It was grand final day revisited. It was everything I could have hoped for, and I felt more elation and more satisfaction just after that game than I had after all the other "farewell" games put together.

I know that sounds strange, considering so much less was at stake. Maybe it was because there had been so much less tension in the lead-up to this game. There was no cloud of disappointment after Béziers, as there had been after the third State of Origin encounter, no feeling of anticlimax, as there had been after the grand final. I didn't feel relief, which was the predominant sensation after our Ashes victory. This time, there was only elation and that glorious feeling of being completely satisfied with my football career. This was the last game I was ever going to play. To go out the way I did, with the team I captained playing so brilliantly as they racked up a record score, and being able to score a try in the last minute of my last match ... what a wonderful way to leave my playing days behind.

Opposite: One of the last sprints of my rugby league career, during the Test against France at Béziers on December 4, 1994.

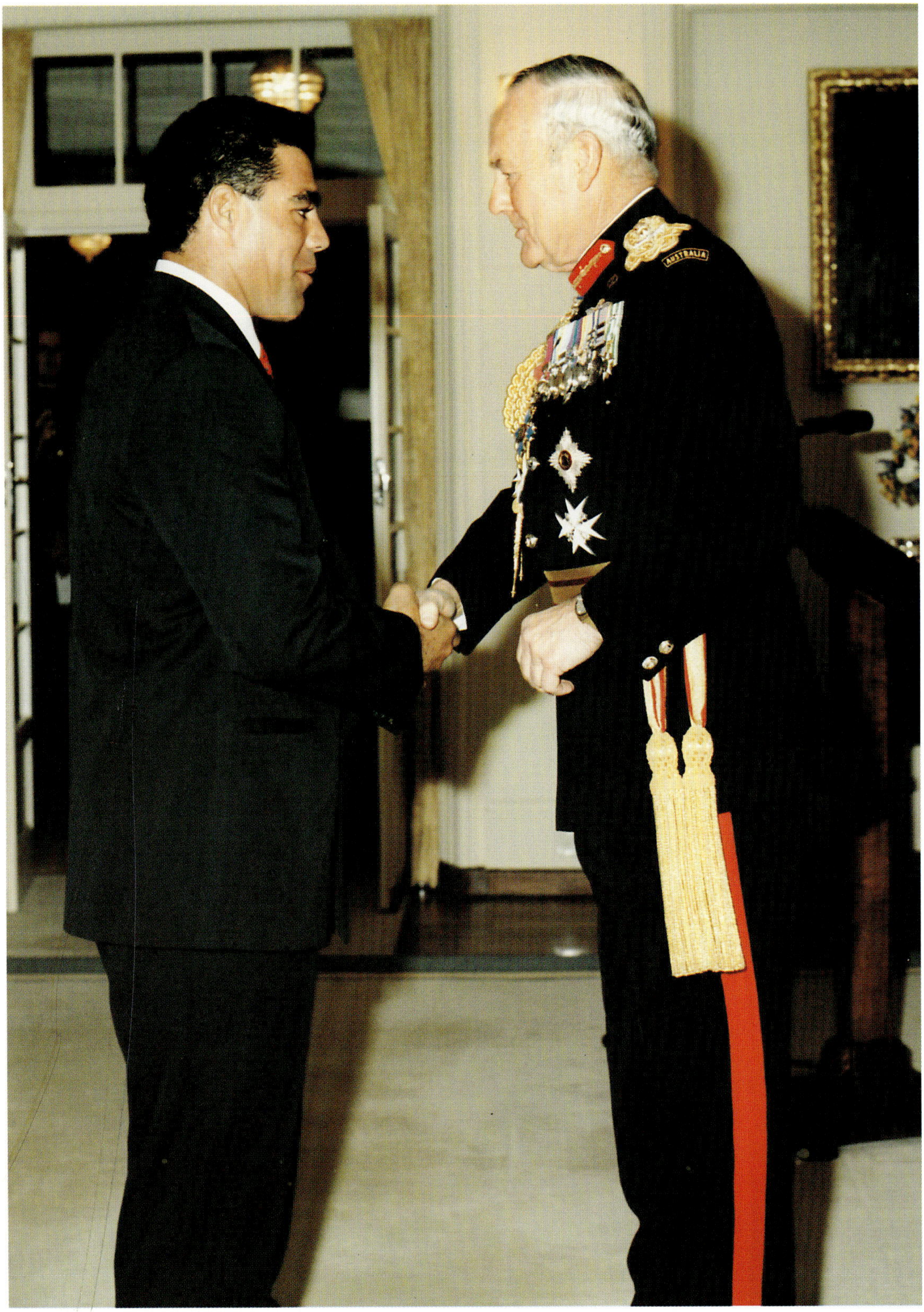

2: MY FATHER'S SON

My father, Norman, has a strong South Sea Islander background and my mother, Lee, is Australian-born of Scottish parentage. To the best of my understanding, from the hazy records we have, my father's family came from an island just near Vanuatu. His ancestors came to Australian shores as slaves, brought to work in the northern cane fields.

One of the mysteries of my life is how we ended up with the name Meninga. Apparently, on the island where my father's family came from everyone's name was Tanna ... there was Joe Tanna and Harry Tanna and Sally Tanna and so on. I understand that under the bizarre laws in those misguided times Island names were taboo in Australia, so they had to be changed.

Meninga is a Dutch name. It is believed within our family that my great-great-grandfather had come into contact with Dutch sailors who came to the Islands. When he was made to choose a non-Islander surname, he remembered one of those ancient mariners, and took his name. However, I cannot be 100 per cent sure this story is accurate, as my relatives just won't talk about anything relating to that tempestuous period in our history.

It's strange to think that for all these years I could have been playing under the name of Mal Tanna ...

My father was an outstanding track and field athlete who had a great passion for rugby league both as a player and as a coach. But the ugly spectre of racism appeared often enough to thwart any grand ambitions he might have had in the sporting arena. Many more times than once he wasn't selected for athletic events, even though he was the best available.

I found similar problems when I was going through school, particularly in athletics. I did well in athletics and I still hold some records in the country areas in Queensland, but never once was I selected to represent my district in the state titles. Through someone in the know we found out that some officials had suggested I couldn't be billeted out. This wasn't because of any past poor behaviour on my part, nor because of any previous mistakes by any member of my family. It was purely because of the colour of my skin. That really made Mum mad, though she was philosophical about it. Dad always said that you couldn't do much about it, so why worry.

Opposite: A proud day, receiving my Order of Australia medal in 1991.

So I didn't worry ... I was just a kid and didn't really understand what racial prejudice and discrimination were all about anyway. Within the bounds of my family, I was taught that it does not matter what colour, race, creed or religion you are, life shouldn't be about discrimination on these grounds.

As a kid, I found it difficult to make friends. I had a couple of close mates but because I was above average at most sports there seemed to be a bit of jealousy in the schoolyard. I used to get into fights all the time. I remember when I was in grade five it seemed the entire school was against me for a while. The inevitable brawl erupted, but after it was over (in a points victory to M. Meninga!) we were suddenly all happy again.

I didn't enjoy being on the outside in this way, but it did help to toughen me mentally.

Despite the discrimination, my father was a footballer of some note in Queensland country areas through the late 1950s and 1960s. His brightest star shone in the Bundaberg competition on the central Queensland coast, from where he represented Wide Bay. That's where I was born, in Bundaberg, the eldest of four brothers.

In all, Dad coached or was player–coach for about 22 years, in a variety of locations in country Queensland. At various points in my upbringing, we lived at Maryborough, Wondai, Monto, Thangool and Maroochydore. His record was extraordinary — only once did a side coached by Norman Meninga fail to reach the grand final.

He was my first coach — one of the most important influences on my career. I enjoyed going to the football with him. I used to go to the training sessions and was in turn mascot and ballboy. As well, Dad would take me to the pub with him. Those country pubs were great. I remember sitting on a bar stool while Dad had his beer; sometimes I used to operate the jukebox and play pool with him.

I loved being at the training sessions and watching what the players did. At times, I would kick the football around but I would always keep watching. Mum told me I was a good watcher and a good learner.

Most of the other kids at training would spend some of their time going around collecting bottles and getting money for them, but I used to sit on the sideline and watch our fathers play football and train. Trying to work out what was happening and why something was happening was more important to me than collecting a couple of bottles.

I started playing football when I was six or seven at Monto, in central Queensland, about 130 kilometres inland of Bundaberg. Dad remained my coach from when I started playing until I went to the Police Academy when I was 15.

He had a lot to do with shaping my life and my football. He was a

The Wide Bay first-grade team of 1966. Back row (left to right): Joe Dewyer, Graham Bertram, Francis Morretti, Merv Hartman, Norman Meninga, John Everinham, Allen Hegarty, Garth Walsh. Front row: Don Golden, Jim Logan, Bret Brickland, Toby Britten, Charlie Kurtz, John Graham, Bill McCoulogh. Ball boy: Mal Meninga.

During his long football career, my father played for Wide Bay against touring sides from Great Britain, France and New Zealand, and might well have been a Queensland prop had he not broken his collarbone in two places during a state trial in the early '60s. The player eventually chosen to fill the vacancy in the Maroons' front row that year was John Wittenberg, who went on to play for Australia and to enjoy a number of successful seasons in Sydney with St George.

In an interview with the Brisbane Sun's David Kiefer in 1989, my mother had this to say about my early relationship with my father: "Wherever Norm was, Malcolm was. He went to training with Norm and to the games. Norm was so mad keen on football — that's all he talked about and that's what Malcolm grew up with. They were always very close. He really looked up to his father."

In the same article in which Mum was quoted, David also interviewed a gentleman called Bill Ovens, then 56 years old, who had played with my father in Bundaberg, and later played against him when Dad played for Maryborough.

"He was a big bloke," said Mr Ovens of my father, "Not as big as Mal, but still a big bloke. And he was a fair player, a good sportsman well respected by everyone. Norm had the potential — he could have been anything if he had the breaks."

My father died in 1982. I will never forget or fail to appreciate all he did to help me in life and in football.

very dedicated person. He was fit, he had a passion for rugby league and he enjoyed being involved in it. At one stage, Dad used to drive three times a week to Thangool to coach and to play. I used to go on those trips sometimes, but I always got very car sick on the bumpy dirt roads. This was a hardship I didn't mind wearing, however. Life with my father was fun, my respect for him was huge and we shared a passionate love of football that made us as close as father and son can be.

However, in 1967 our lives were turned upside down when Dad was badly injured in the sawmill where he worked in Monto to complement his meagre earnings as a football coach. He was a benchman, one of the men who had to pull the logs through the saw. One day, a massive piece of timber log skipped off the pads and smashed into his chest. The left side of his body was shattered. Sadly, physically he was never the same man again. The blow played havoc with his heart, and eventually he had an artificial valve implanted. Though he tried to battle on, his playing career was effectively over. However, he stayed involved in rugby league as a coach and later on, after we moved south to Maroochydore, north of Brisbane on the Sunshine Coast, he helped set up the Junior competition there.

I believe you are born with a talent, but how you utilise that talent is up to you. As a young footballer, I possessed certain skills of the game — I could run and tackle and kick the ball. My father taught me how to develop those skills — things like passing the ball and kicking it further and more accurately. He showed me defensive techniques that complemented my natural ability to bring an opponent to the ground. These were no more than basic skills, but they provided a platform that launched my football career.

My father also taught me how to be a whole person. It did not worry him what his colour was, he did not discriminate between an Aboriginal, a European or an Australian. He made friends with people from a lot of different nationalities and that is the way I live my life. I am not even slightly concerned about my colour. My philosophy on the rights of Aboriginal people is that they deserve no more and no less than anyone else. I do not possess an Aboriginal heritage but, even if I did, I would not see my obligations as a high-profile figure as being solely to advance their cause. I believe my duty is to be a good ambassador for everyone.

When I was 15, I enrolled at the Queensland Police Academy and finished my schooling there. I had been awarded a three-year cadetship that allowed me to complete my Higher School Certificate and also to study police law. I completed my certificate in 1977, but the following year had to get time away from the Force because of Dad's declining health. I became a Luxaflex man, which allowed me to be closer to home.

Left: My father Norman (centre, back), with his parents Edward (centre, front) and Ada (left, front) and sisters Beryl (left, back), Lauretta (right, back) and Florence.
Below: My father, with my brother Geoff.
Below left: My parents Norman and Leona, on their wedding day.

Bottom left: Mum and Dad, and Geoff and me, at our grandparents' place in Bundaberg in the early '60s.

Constable Mal Meninga, at West End Primary School, deep in the heart of Southern Suburbs territory, in the early 1980s.

Then in 1979, I worked in the bottle department of a hotel for six months before rejoining the police force as a probationary constable. I was sworn in in February 1980. In many ways my early years after school were typical of so many school leavers: a range of jobs in a variety of locations, while you decide what to do with the rest of your life.

However, the irresistible attraction for me was the police force. The inclination to become a policeman never left me. Mum was keen on the idea too and eventually I had to make the decision to break away from my home environment and head back to the Police Academy.

At the interviews, I was extremely pleased to learn that the Force was actually looking for men who played rugby league. That, of course, applied to me. By 1980, I had already played one full season of first-grade football with the Southern Suburbs club in Brisbane, and I was a Queensland representative as well. In my first year as a probationary constable, I played for Queensland in the inaugural State of Origin match. And I also played for the Academy team, which I enjoyed a great deal. Like that famous Artie Beetson-led attack which whipped the Blues at Lang Park in July, the police team had a great spirit, and many friendships were forged then that have remained ironclad in all the years that followed. It was like a club — you lived under the same roof, you studied together, you played sport together, you did everything together. A lot of my closest mates today are guys I first met back in the old Police Academy days.

It was at the Police Academy that I first met a man named Wayne Bennett, then a physical education instructor, who was to have a remarkable impact on my football career and my life. I'll never forget our first meeting, back in 1976 during my original spell there. He had just introduced himself to us, his new class, and asked who among us had ambitions to play rugby league. I threw my hand up.

Wayne asked me if I had played any junior representative football. I had. In fact, I had represented most of the districts I had played in. But though he took a strong interest in my football from that first meeting, he wasn't my coach in the first year, because I was then in the under-16s. Wayne Bennett was an ex-international and already a proven coach with Souths in the Brisbane first-grade competition and, naturally enough, he was looking after the Academy's more senior grades.

Even though the Academy under-16s were struggling that year, I managed to graduate to the open Academy side before the year was out. The following year, I started in the under-17s, but was soon elevated to the under-18s ... coached by Wayne Bennett.

Our teams were up against junior teams from the Brisbane grade clubs, in what they called the Super-A competition. I remember in 1977, my team, the under-18s, were beaten in the grand final by Valleys, who were captained by a young bloke called Wally Lewis, who was about to depart on an Australian schoolboys' rugby union tour. A week earlier, we had edged out Paul Vautin's Western Suburbs team by a solitary point in the semi-finals.

Wally wasn't the only rugby league player doing a bit of moonlighting in that other rugby code. There were times when I would pull on my boots for the Academy's union team, for matches against the Armed Services. I also played a bit of soccer and, in the summer, cricket and occasionally basketball.

After I left the Academy in 1978, I went up the coast with my father to Palmwoods, near Maroochydore, where Dad had snared a senior coaching

Meninga

job and I played for the under-18s. From there, I was selected in the Wide Bay under-18 rep. team, a stepping-stone to the Queensland under-18s, where my team-mates included future Test footballers Brad Tessmann and Bryan Niebling. We played against a NSW team which included two more future international stars, John Muggleton and Eric Grothe, and, while we were beaten in both games, it was only 28–25 in the second encounter after the junior Blues scored off an intercept late in the game.

During that season, I suffered from persistent knee problems. But every time the problem recurred, I resorted to pain-killing injections. I didn't know it at the time, but I had a cracked kneecap. My knee used to swell up every so often, but I didn't have a clue what was wrong with it. Getting the offending joint X-rayed didn't occur to me, and I didn't know of any sports doctors in those days. Quite frankly, I didn't have the money to get the best medical opinion anyway.

It wasn't until the following year, after I'd linked up again with Wayne Bennett at Souths, that I finally introduced the knee to an X-ray, which showed there was a bone growth that was rubbing against my kneecap, with the result that it had cracked. I cracked it again in the 1985 semi-final. Eventually, after that season's grand final (or, to be more precise, after an end-of-season trip away with my police mates) I finally had the thing fixed.

Until I left in 1985, I spent my last three years in the Force in the physical education section. The police force were always very good to me. They gave me a nine to five job, Monday to Friday, which meant I had the weekends free to play top-grade football. And they gave me time off when I needed it for football, sometimes with pay, sometimes without.

I have always been grateful for what I was taught at the Academy. It was there that I learned the value of discipline, to stay clear of drugs and be wary of alcohol.

Wayne Bennett played a major role in my development. It was Wayne who put the polish on my football, who grabbed my natural talent and the skills my father had taught me and turned me into a player capable of succeeding in the top grade. How did he do this? One of the ways was by motivating us. I clearly recall one session in which he told a number of the players in the under-18 team that they had the ability to play first-grade football. When Wayne came to me, he told me I could be anything I wanted to be, that I could even go on and play for Australia if I put my mind to it.

That was the moment I decided I wanted to go further in the game. Until then, I had simply been enjoying the game and had no real ambitions about playing for Australia. With Wayne, goal-setting is a very important factor in preparation for football, and in preparing for life as

Opposite page, clockwise from top left: A very early shot of myself (right) and brother Geoff; five of my closest friends from the Queensland Police Academy days: (left to right) Gary Harvey, Bill Turner, John Wacker, Dave Dini and Ash Lumby; the Maroochy Black Swans in 1972; Debbie and me on our wedding day, November 19, 1983. November 19 will always be a very special day for me — it was also my Dad's birthday, and Dad's parents' wedding day.

The 1979 Southern Suburbs first-grade side.
Back row *(left to right): Mal Connell, Mick Gramm, David Gould, Tony Gibson, Brian Weir, Ken Rach (masseur).*
Centre: *Jim Elder (manager), Dave Brown, Bob Kellaway, Peter Ryan, Mal Meninga, Warren Kenward (trainer).*
Front: *Ash Lumby, Allan Bracken, Wayne Bennett (coach), Bruce Astill (captain), John Salter, Steve Glynn. (Inset: Billy Argeros.)*

well. And I was lucky — the first goal I set for myself, I achieved. There was no major injury, biased selector or personal crisis to get in the way. Once I saw that goal-setting worked, I made it a practice I continued throughout my career. And though my playing career is now over, there's no way I'm going to abandon this approach as I attack new fields in my life after football.

Wayne introduced me to the skills work that became an integral part of rugby league training in the 1980s. We worked terribly hard on fitness and, equally as importantly, Wayne was concerned with our mental preparation for matches.

I consider myself lucky that I had my father and then Wayne to guide me and advise me. Their advice, coupled with the discipline of the police force, helped to mould me in those important early years.

In 1978, I set myself the goal of playing for Queensland before the 1979 season was over. And I was confident enough in my own ability to tell people that was what I intended. They laughed at me. Some thought I was being unrealistic. I recall one bloke who was fairly influential in junior football saying straight to my face that I was too big and too slow to play for Queensland. I turned this sort of "encouragement" into a further incentive.

The following year, when I was selected for the first two games against NSW, I often wondered how that bloke felt when he saw me in the maroon jumper. He was just another face in the crowd, but I was on my way.

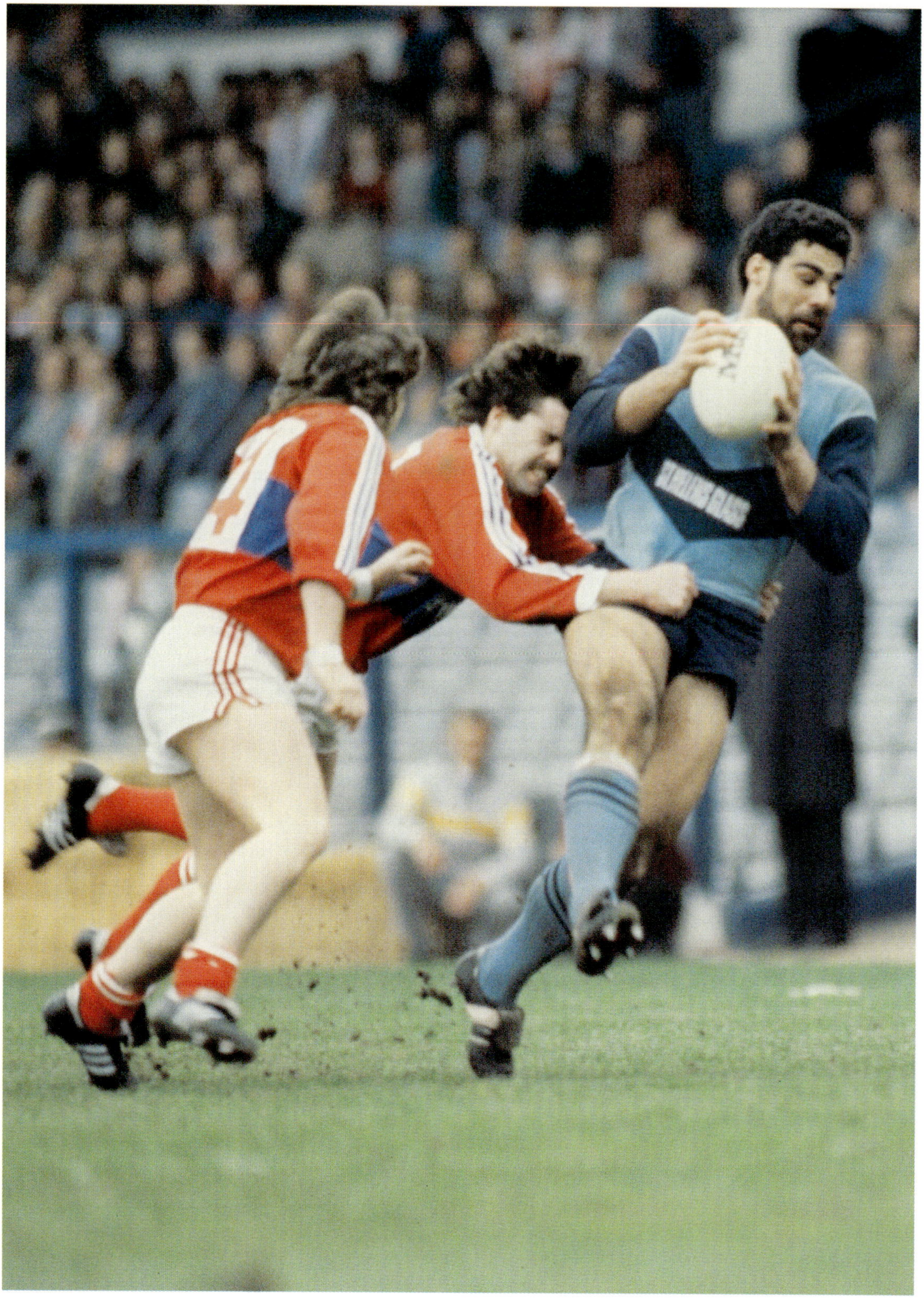

3: SOUTHS AND SAINTS

Wayne Bennett was always keen to get me to Southern Suburbs and, when I finally arrived, in 1979, he didn't hold me back. Straight into the top side I went, fortunately, I'm proud to say, to stay. I never played a reserve grade game in my entire career at the top level, from Sunday, February 18, 1979, the date of my debut for Souths (the Magpies) in a trial against Brothers (we won 19–13), up until Sunday, December 4, 1994, when Australia humiliated France 74–0 at Béziers.

In an interview in 1983, I commented: "My dad played until he was 35 and, if I'm enjoying the game, I want to do the same." At the time, I never realised how many minutes of pain, work and effort — and great satisfaction — there would be in all the days to come.

Things just seemed to click for me immediately in first grade — I felt at home, not overawed at all. Even the reviews after my first game were okay. In *Rugby League Week* the following Thursday, Jack Craig wrote, under the headline MAGIC-MAN MANINGA! [sic]: "The name is Malcolm Maninga. It's a name to remember … a name league fans will read a lot about in the next few years."

Wayne nursed me through those early days. Though he kept me on the first-grade reserves bench for our next two pre-season games, against Easts and Valleys (fearing the hardheads from those teams might enjoy "testing" me out), I still came on against both teams, and nearly gained Souths a draw after the final siren against Valleys, when a long-range penalty goal attempt drifted narrowly wide.

Within a week of my debut, the Sydney scouts were back in touch. The approaches had begun the previous season when the St George coach, Harry Bath, had travelled to Brisbane for a meeting with Dad and me. Harry explained how he would start me in the juniors and bring me along slowly. Dad was keen for me to move south but as I was keen to learn more about the game from Wayne, it wasn't too difficult to knock the opportunity back.

Our first-round premiership match in 1979 was against Wynnum–Manly, with whom I was to have a number of eventful clashes over the years. We won this one easily — 23–8 — and I scored two tries and two goals. The press thought I was a stand-out, but I liked Wayne's comment after the

Opposite: On the attack for St Helens against Hull Kingston Rovers during our win in the 1984–85 English Premiership Trophy final at Elland Road.

Playing for Southern Suburbs in 1979, my first season of first-grade football.

game, when he was asked about my display: "Certainly he had a great game. But centres can't play well unless the forwards have done their job and the five-eighth plays well."

Our forward pack that day included Greg Veivers, a former Queensland and Australian captain, Dave Brown, who would later star for Manly and Easts in the NSWRL premiership and perform stoically for Queensland and Australia, and Bob Kellaway, a future Queensland State of Origin representative. Our five-eighth was a clever footballer by the name of Allan Bracken. I was also fortunate to have an excellent player in Bruce Astill as my centre partner.

We had started with a bang, and this continued through April as we won our first five premiership games. A setback came in round 6, when we were thrashed 25–7 by Valleys, which left us equal leaders with Easts, with our conquerors a point further back. This was the way the table stayed for pretty much the entire year, as we three front-runners battled for supremacy. The previous season, Souths had finished among the also-rans. The club hadn't reached a grand final since 1961 and hadn't won a premiership since 1953, so Souths supporters were revelling in our unlikely success.

My grade career was only a few rounds old when I was selected to play for the Brisbane representative team. However, my excitement at this news was tempered when the coach, a bloke called Henry Holloway, came up to me at the first training session and explained that if he had any say in the selection, I wouldn't be in the team. At least with Henry you knew where you stood, but his remark did little for my confidence.

Fortunately, Henry didn't have the final word in the selection of the Queensland side, and I gained a spot for the first two inter-state games of the season, at Lang Park.

Here, however, we were soundly thrashed by the Blues who were strengthened by a number of Queensland-born players then starring with Sydney clubs. State of Origin was still a season away! Unfortunately, I was dropped for the third match, which NSW won 35–20 before a "crowd" of 4,502 at Leichhardt Oval. Three days earlier, Souths had been thrashed 25–0 by the bottom club, Redcliffe, and I had my worst game to date. It was a salient lesson for a tyro first-grader. Things can change very quickly in football.

Inevitably, after the successful start to my first-grade career, there was a great deal of pressure on me. It is the same for any young player in that situation. The name Meninga began to appear in a few headlines, my picture appeared in the paper from time to time, and I didn't cope with it particularly well. I began by thinking I was going okay, and then I started to get a bit of a big head.

The limelight had come very, very quickly. However, the combination of my good mates at the Police Academy and Wayne Bennett dragged me back to earth pretty quickly and undoubtedly saved me from some embarrassment. I will always appreciate the advice my friends gave me, and the fact I had mates like that in those early years.

I'll never forget what Wayne said to me when I was first chosen for Queensland.

"Congratulations," he said, as he shook my hand. "I don't think you deserve to be in the side, but well done. Get in there and make sure you play well."

Wayne's comment hit home. Perhaps Henry Holloway had been trying to say the same thing. By the end of the regular season, Valleys had

Meninga

marched away with the minor premiership, but we were still safely ensconced in the top four. In round 20, Valleys' highly rated young lock, Wally Lewis, had murdered us with a brilliant display. We led 14–11 with less than 20 minutes left, but then Lewis scored two tries in three minutes and the game was over. I was playing five-eighth by this stage of the season, and with Allan Bracken back at fullback and Greg Veivers out of the side because of injury, we were a very inexperienced team. But what we lacked in years played, we made up for with enthusiasm, and in our coach we had a man ahead of his time.

We eventually finished third, but then defeated Wests and Easts to reach the grand final. I was back in the centres for these games, but it wouldn't have mattered where I was on grand final day, for Valleys were superb and defeated us 26–0. We felt that scoreline was a little lopsided, for the contest was a lot closer than it appeared. We played reasonably well on the day, but the truth was that we were too raw and too inexperienced to cope with their all-round strengths. Lewis, playing at lock forward, was in excellent touch, while their captain–coach, the former Australia halfback Ross Strudwick, was an inspiration.

Even with the setback on grand final day, the '79 season had been a fabulous learning experience for us all. And, most importantly, I had made some good friends in my first year at the club, people whose company I have continued to enjoy in all the years since then. In 1980, our youthful exuberance was complemented by a couple of well-seasoned hard men in the forwards — George Moroko and Chris Phelan. As well, Dave Brown was reaching the peak of his form, and a hooker of great promise, Billy Johnstone, had emerged, so we had a forward pack that was the envy of our premiership rivals. We also had a new coach.

Wayne had transferred to Brothers, and the new man at the helm of Souths was one of the game's legends, Bob McCarthy. The change did us no harm and, despite a wretched run with injuries, we were near the top of the table for the entire season. Valleys were the early pace-setters, but a dramatic late-season decline in their fortunes was matched by a real surge in our form and a brilliant 34–4 thrashing of Wynnum–Manly in round 19 took us to the competition lead. At this point we were definitely the premiership favourites.

It appeared that the young Magpies side who had learned the ropes the previous season would use that experience to run away with the title. We cruised into the grand final after beating Valleys in the major semi, and were very surprised when Northern Suburbs came out the following week and won a dramatic final 15–14. Norths were coached by the New Zealander Graham Lowe, and even though they had some very good players on their side, such as their spirited halfback Mark Murray, hooker

Opposite: Wally Lewis was the best footballer of my time. During the 1980s, when Origin football dominated the Australian rugby league scene and was considered the state of the art, Wally was consistently excellent. How often would his actions change the course of an Origin game? The answer, of course, is many, many times.

In my seven seasons in Brisbane club football, I often played against him and usually ended up on the wrong side of the scoreboard. Early on, he was a rising star with Valleys; later, he transferred to Wynnum–Manly where he was the focal point of a side full of Queensland and Australian players. Wherever he played, he was the best in the business.

Meninga

SOUTHS AND SAINTS

Southern Suburbs, Brisbane's rugby league premiers of 1981. **Back row** (left to right): Graham Kerr (committeeman), Peter Jennings (masseur), Jim McClelland (assistant secretary), Mal Meninga, Geoff Naylor, Ken Rach (masseur), Carlo Costa (trainer). **Middle:** Tony Testa (president), Sel Deed (secretary), Brad Sully, Ash Lumby, Alan Power, Steve Glynn, Bob McCarthy (coach), Jim Elder (manager). **Front:** Darryl Higgs, Bruce Harry, Billy Johnstone, Bruce Astill (captain), Mick Reardon, Gary Thompson, Chris Phelan (absent: Adrian Higgs).

Greg Conescu, New Zealand international forward Mark Graham and a talented young winger called Joe Kilroy, the critics to a man thought we were specials. During the season we had played them three times, for three comfortable wins.

But the final result was Souths 15, Norths 17. It was a very physical game, marked by a wild all-in brawl not long after the start. It was a game we could quite easily have won.

After the game, I received an offer from Sydney's Easts to move south, but I wasn't really interested. The Queensland Rugby League had boosted the money I was being paid by Souths, and I was also keen to further my career with the police.

"I've said all along that my job is important to me," I told *Rugby League Week*'s Tony Durkin at the time, "but I don't think some people believe me. Money now is important, but I don't think it's as important as my future."

As well, I thought my best chance of winning an Australian cap against France the following season was by staying in Brisbane. After Queensland's success in the inaugural State of Origin match, which had been played in July 1980, there was a feeling among the best players in Brisbane that it was no longer necessary to transfer to Sydney if you wanted to play for Australia.

History shows that I wasn't able to win that elusive first Australian jumper until 1982. But I was always going to have to be patient with the champion pairing of Steve Rogers and Mick Cronin established in the side. However, 1981 was still a highly successful year. Once again, Queensland won the season's only State of Origin match and, amid scenes of great jubilation among the Magpies' loyal and long-suffering supporters, we finally won the Brisbane first-grade premiership. It was the club's first premiership in 28 years, and the celebrations went on and on.

The big news in Brisbane before the start of the '81 season was the return of Arthur Beetson to the local club scene, as the captain–coach of Redcliffe. The Dolphins had finished fifth in 1980, but Big Artie's impact was immediate and they surged all the way to the grand final. This was to be his farewell game, and it seemed all of Queensland wanted the great man to go out a winner.

The Souths pack was the smallest in the competition. I'll never forget the way the Redcliffe pack towered over our guys on grand final day. But our forwards' courage and will to win was as big as anything I ever saw in football.

That game was an absolute thriller, not decided until the final 30 seconds when our winger, Mick Reardon, swallow-dived over in the corner to give us the lead. For good measure, I managed the conversion after the siren had sounded, to seal a 13–9 victory.

When we got back to the clubhouse after the game, there were 4,000 to 5,000 people waiting for us. They spilled out on to the ground to enjoy a massive party which continued for a couple of days.

The side we had defeated in the 1981 final had been Wynnum–Manly, who were in the middle of a great resurgence under the coaching of Queensland stalwart Des Morris. For 1982, they had Morris's younger brother Rod, the Test front-rower who had made a big impact with Balmain in Sydney, in their side, to play alongside one of the most promising young front-rowers to emerge in Brisbane for years, Greg Dowling. In the backs was another player of unlimited potential, a centre called Gene Miles, who had made his Queensland debut as a replacement the previous year. Even though we were the defending premiers, right from the start — from before a ball was kicked in 1982 — Wynnum were the side to beat.

Early in the year, I copped a three-match suspension after being sent off in a pre-season match against Valleys at Lang Park. I wasn't impressed at all. All I had done was move in to help our 57-kilo lock forward Billy Argeros, who was being belted by one of the Valleys props. A touch judge came in and I was gone, charged with punching. "It seems okay for a big prop forward to hit a 9-stone lock, but not for two blokes the same size to have a crack at each other," I told one correspondent after the judiciary hearing.

In *Rugby League Week*, Tony Durkin wrote:

Not for one minute am I suggesting that what Mal Meninga did last Friday night was good for the game. But I did see the incident, and I can say I've seen a lot worse happen under the nose of a referee without even the blink of an eyelid. All I would like to see is that all players be given a fair go, by both the referees and the judiciary.

Bob McCarthy was a very angry man after the judiciary hearing. "I could understand the suspension if Mal was a well-known thug," he told waiting reporters. "But anyone who knows the guy realises he's as gentle as a lamb."

This was the first time I had been sent off or suspended in my football career.

Late in the 1982 season, I brought up my 1,000th point in club and representative football. It would have come a bit earlier but for a dislocated elbow I suffered during my Test debut, against New Zealand, in July. That cost me four matches, but the landmark was reached against Easts at our home ground, Davies Park.

Valleys were the minor premiers in '82, with Souths second and Wynnum (who had struggled with injuries) third. But in the minor semi-final, Des Morris's team was awesome, humiliating Redcliffe by 35 points to nil, to re-establish themselves as premiership favourites.

Opposite: Gene Miles playing against the Kiwis at the SCG. Gene was the best centre I played with or against during my entire career. He was a tremendous runner, dreadfully hard to pull down, and he also possessed superb ball-handling skills. I don't think I ever saw another rugby league footballer with the ability not only to run so powerfully with the ball but also when tackled to be able to slip it over the top or around the back of a defender.

In the major semi, we edged out Valleys 10–6 in a gruelling contest, in which Bruce Astill was sent off for the first time in his career, after a blue with Wally Lewis. Bruce was subsequently suspended and, for the grand final, Billy Johnstone took over as captain.

In the final, Valleys were flogged 26–5 to set up the first of three grand finals between two very proud clubs in four seasons (1982, 1984, 1985). The game was promoted as the clash of the birds — Souths (Magpies) versus Wynnum–Manly (Seagulls) — and on this occasion it was the coast-dwellers who prevailed, 17–3. But though the scoreboard might have suggested a one-sided game, in fact the match was a beauty, remaining in the balance until nine minutes from time. Seven minutes before half-time, a try to Seagulls' centre Brett French made the score 7–3 to Wynnum, and that was the way the game remained until we conceded two more tries, in the 71st and 72nd minute. For us, the game was terribly frustrating, for while the score had been stuck at 7–3, we had been camped in our opponents' half. But we could not break through, and after the game could do no more than concede that Wynnum had been the better side on the day.

For me, the game was a very painful affair, and not just because we were defeated. After just three minutes, I tore a rib cartilage, but battled on. Luckily, Gene Miles was struggling with an ankle injury, so in a strange sort of way we cancelled each other out. Certainly, my injury was not a reason why we lost, and the pain for both of us was softened afterwards when we were both named in the Kangaroo squad that would become renowned throughout the rugby league world as the "Invincibles" after we went undefeated through an entire tour of Great Britain and France.

Bob McCarthy had completed his three-year contract with that loss to Wynnum, but fortunately he decided to have one more for the road in 1983. However, before the seasons began, he had to counter suggestions that we didn't know how to win. In the past four seasons we had played four grand finals for only one victory. Then we commenced 1983 with a loss to Wests in the pre-season final — the third straight year we had fallen at the final hurdle in this competition. Such talk was nearly as damaging as the defeats themselves, and was the prelude to an awkward season for me, the only year when Souths failed to reach the grand final while I was with the club.

Early in the year, I was asked whether I was thinking of moving to the NSWRL premiership. "I'd probably like to play in Sydney," I replied, "for the same reason as everyone else — to prove to myself that I can perform in tough competition week after week. But it has never been a burning ambition. I love the Queensland lifestyle, I like my job and I've always been well treated at Souths."

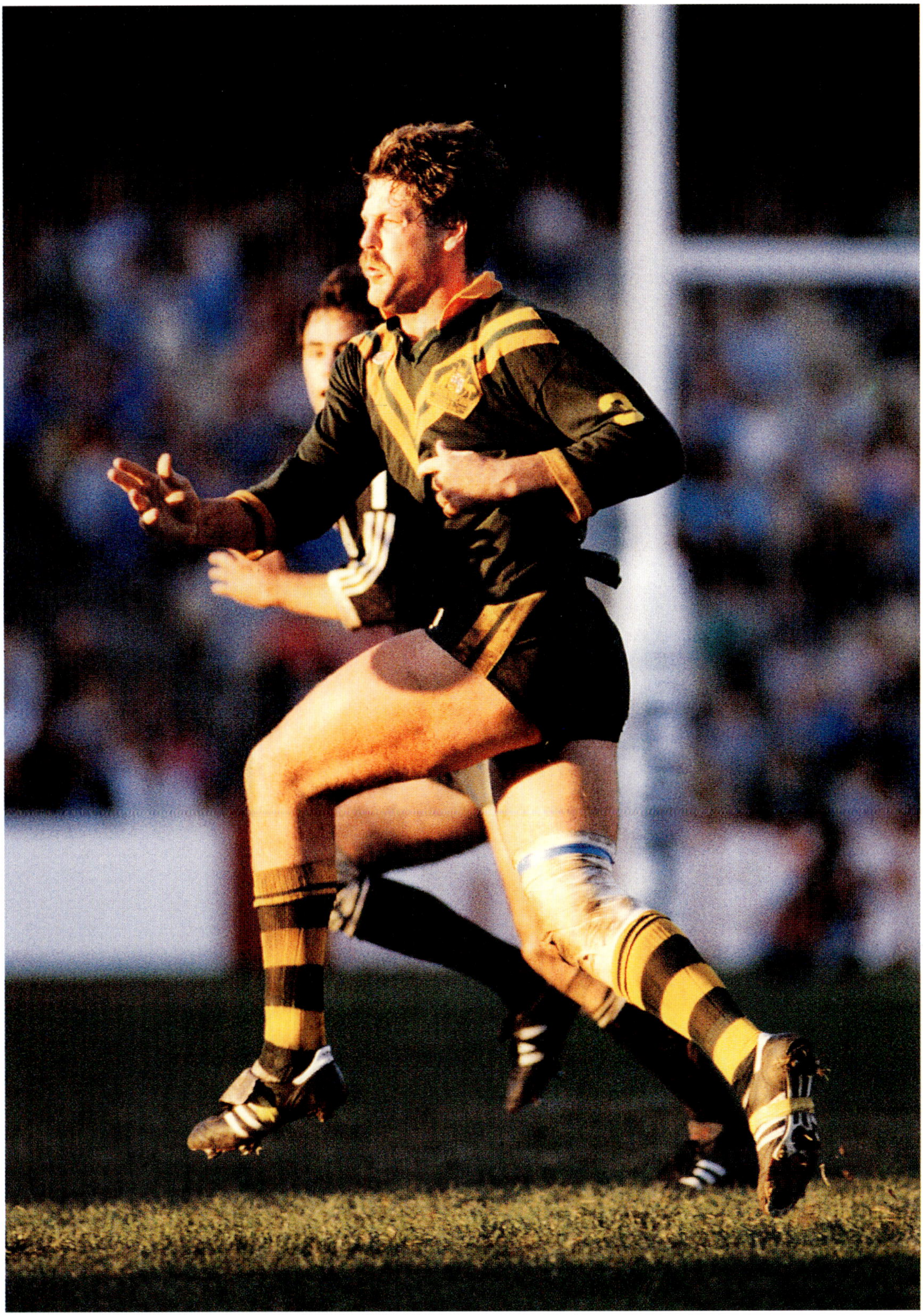

Right and opposite: A consoling pat on the back from Wynnum–Manly's Test front-rower Greg Dowling, after another Seagulls try in the 1984 grand final. This was one of the worst days of my football career, and it needed the wonderful experience of playing club football with St Helens to revitalise my game. My debut for the Saints was against Castleford at our home ground of Knowsley Road, and I managed two tries in a 30–16 win. The photograph here is of my second four-pointer, scored despite the attempted tackle of Castleford's Australian fullback Ron Sigsworth.

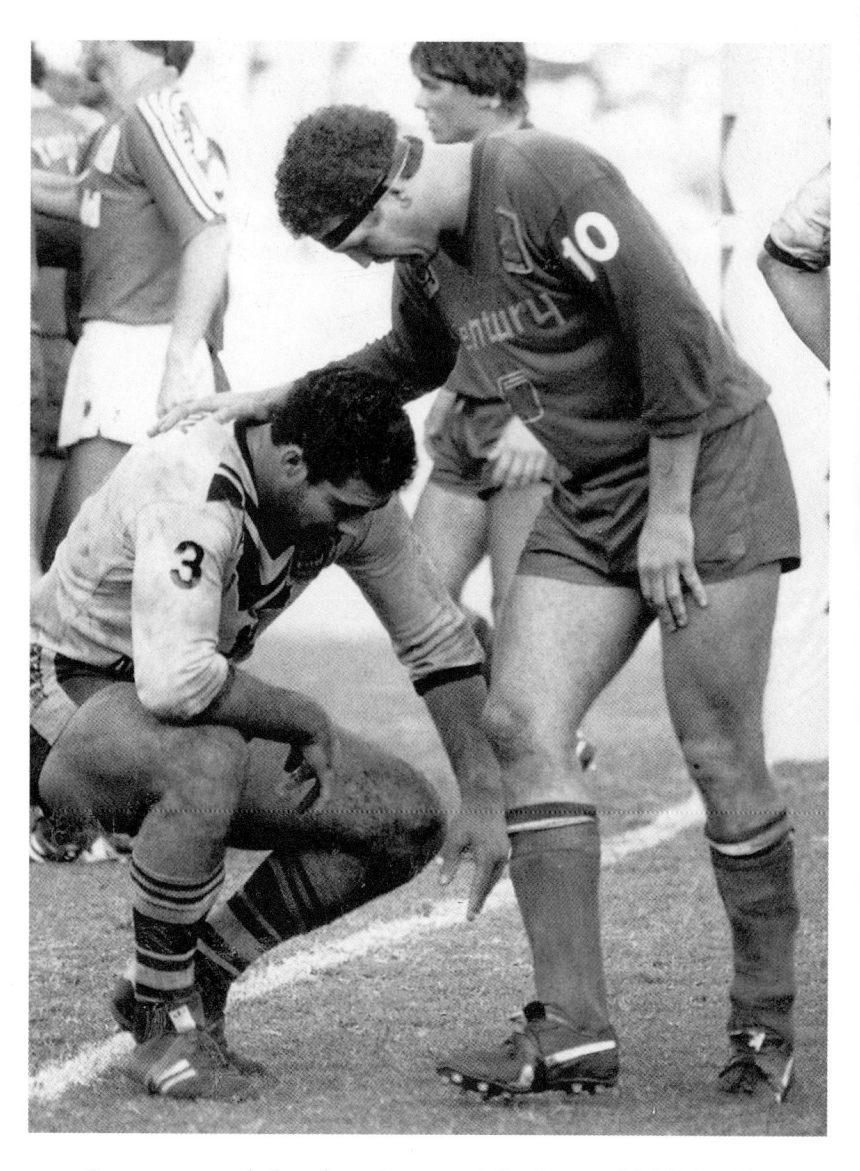

Our season ended at the minor semi-final stage, highlighted by one of Wally Lewis's greatest performances. "We were beaten by a genius today," Bob McCarthy told reporters. "Lewis is the closest thing I've ever seen to Bobby Fulton." The final score was 30–22. I was disappointed to have lost, but after a difficult season coming on top of nearly 18 months of continuous football, I was grateful for the relaxation the off-season would bring.

When a Queensland side was chosen for a post-season tour of England — scheduled as a reward for the Maroons winning the State of Origin series — I was not among the names announced. I had a few reasons for making myself unavailable: I had a few injuries that needed a rest; I wasn't playing well at the time, and wanted to protect the reputation in England that I had developed during the 1982 Kangaroo tour; but, most importantly, in November I was to be married to Debbie, and I was needed to help with all the preparations.

By the new year, my spirits had recovered and I was looking forward to football again. Bob McCarthy had put his coaching cue back in the rack, and although I was disappointed to see him go, I was delighted that his successor was Wayne Bennett. We had quite a few promising youngsters coming through the club and Wayne was just the bloke to bring out the best in them.

Wayne brought to the club Duncan Thompson junior, who had fine-tuned a training program that had first been developed by his father, one of the truly legendary figures of Australian rugby league and

A photographer from the Daily Express *newspaper took this shot of Debbie and me sharing a game of snooker in St Helens in 1984. In an interview, Debbie had this to say of life in the north of England:*

"We were looking forward to coming over here and have found it lovely. What has struck me has been the way people have welcomed us with kindness.

"I'm originally from Taranaki in New Zealand, so the green fields and countryside remind me of home. I don't even mind the rain if it means I can be surrounded by green fields. Some people thought the weather might bother us, but we don't mind it at all."

considered by some to be the greatest halfback of them all. Duncan senior was a footballing wizard (and a native Queenslander, born in Warwick) who had enjoyed some sensational seasons with Norths in the Sydney premiership and with Toowoomba in Queensland's glory days of the 1920s. Later, he became one of the most influential coaches in the game.

His son had clearly listened to much of what his wise old Dad had told him about rugby league. Adopting some of the principles of this training method, we won 13 games in succession in '84. The concept was beautifully simple; its centrepiece was the maxim of keeping the ball alive, of hitting and spinning, of unloading the ball to a support and backing up your mates.

The other key feature was speed: save seconds — or fractions of seconds — whenever you can. Play the ball as quickly as possible. If you pass the ball from dummy half, pass from near the ground instead of picking it up and then passing it. If things are done fractionally quicker, then the opposition has to react that bit more quickly. If they don't, you're in front. Gaps appear, overlaps are created, tries are scored, matches won.

Of course, the system isn't foolproof. You need fitness, football ability, passion and commitment in large doses as well. Sadly, on grand final day 1984 these characteristics weren't there for Souths, and we were slaughtered by minor premiers Wynnum–Manly, by 42–8. This came just a fortnight after we had lost the major semi-final by 46–22. The Seagulls were a sensational combination, featuring a collection of stars who had played, or would later go on to play for Queensland and, in many cases, Australia. Wally Lewis had moved there to join Gene Miles, Greg Dowling, Gary Coyne, Colin Scott and Brett and Ian French. But our side was pretty formidable as well including, as it did, players of the calibre of Gary Belcher, Peter Jackson and Bob Lindner. To get beaten that easily was highly embarrassing!

I was in the doldrums after that debacle, and felt I needed a new lease of life. Fortunately, earlier in the year I had accepted an offer from St Helens in England and although the last thing I wanted after a grand final loss was to go and play another eight months of football, my time in

Emotional scenes after Souths' win in the 1985 grand final at Lang Park. The Magpies no. 12 is hooker Eddie Muller. The winger behind him (with the tattered sponsor's logo on his jumper) is Peter Wallace.

England turned out to be some of the most enjoyable days of my career.

I was able to get time off from the police force, and so I remained at St Helens until the end of their season. There were no obligations to be back in Australia by a certain date, but while I missed most of the pre-season State League, I was back in plenty of time to keep my place in the Queensland State of Origin team.

Playing club football in England was a tremendous experience and I quickly started to enjoy the game again. English football in 1984–85 was played in a very "open" style. There was no great emphasis on defence, which suited me just fine as I have always liked to run with the ball.

We stayed with a marvellous family, the Rainfords, on a little dairy in a place called Eccleston, just 2 kilometres from Knowsley Road, St Helens' home ground. It was so relaxing. We had a lovely room upstairs, from which we sometimes wouldn't appear until about midday. But as soon as the lady of the house, Margaret, heard us walking around, she set to work, and by the time we got downstairs, breakfast ... or perhaps it should have been called brunch ... would be waiting for us.

Debbie and I grabbed every chance to have a look around the place. One weekend when the pitches were frozen out, we went to North Africa — to Morocco — where Deb, being a shrewd bargain hunter, bought a couple of rugs. They were great buys because today they are worth about 12 times what we paid for them, a fact which confirms what I have always maintained ... Deb is a very, very smart shopper.

St Helens had a lot of success that year. We scored a season's record of 1,267 points, including 215 tries. In the championship alone we scored 156 tries, also a record. Our wins included thrashings of Hunslet 68–7, Workington Town 62–0 and Keighley 60–8. I managed 28 tries, fifth best in the League but only second at St Helens behind Barry Ledger, who scored 30. We were both a long way behind Bradford Northern's impressive Ellery Hanley, who put the ball down over the opponent's try-line a remarkable 52 times.

On October 28, St Helens won the Lancashire Cup for the first time in 16 years. It was a great victory over Wigan, and I was able to play a major role, scoring two tries and setting up two more. We had the match in control at half-time, when we led 24–2 and, though Wigan made a comeback in the second half, the result was never really in doubt. The final score was 26–18. This was St Helens' first trophy of any kind in seven years, and served as a good comeback to those English critics who had been insinuating that I was lazy and overweight.

I was not the only Australian on the field that day. Also wearing the St Helens colours that day was my Southern Suburbs team-mate Phil Veivers (a younger brother of Greg), while Wigan's line-up included Mark

Cannon, who played in the Sydney premiership with St George and later Norths, and John "Chicka" Ferguson, a brilliant winger who played for Newtown and Easts and would later play a prominent role in the Mal Meninga story when he transferred to the Canberra Raiders.

In fact, there was an extraordinary number of Australians playing in the English championship in 1984–85. Some were there for just a brief stint, others stayed for the entire season. In the case of Phil Veivers, he played out the rest of his career with the Saints. Other Australians in England that season included Paul Hamson (St Helens), Bob Kellaway (Bradford Northern), Ron Sigsworth (Castleford), Chris Anderson, Paul Langmack and Michael Hagan (Halifax), Peter Sterling and John Muggleton (Hull), Tony Currie, Eric Grothe, Trevor Paterson, Neil Hunt and Wally Fullerton Smith (Leeds), Paul Taylor (Oldham) and Brett Kenny (Wigan).

In the Challenge Cup we were knocked out in the first round by Hull Kingston Rovers. Playing on a quagmire at home, we led 3–2 with eight minutes left, but Rovers' star Aussie import Gavin Miller set up a try for winger Garry Clark which was converted from the sideline and we were out. It was only the second time in 50 years that Hull KR had beaten St Helens at Knowsley Road.

In the championship, we finished second to Hull KR, but we reversed that finish in the premiership. The championship is decided in much the same way as the Australian season's minor premiership; then the top eight teams play off in a knock-out series to determine the winners of the premiership trophy.

The championship was not decided until the final weekend, when Rovers won at Barrow and we lost at Leigh. We had needed the opposite to happen for us to be champions. Still, second place was the club's best result in eight years.

In the premiership trophy play-offs, we comfortably handled Widnes and then Wigan, to result in a match-up with the champions, at Elland Road. The contest produced 10 tries, seven of them to St Helens (two of them intercepts to Mal Meninga) and we careered away in the end to win 36–16. It was a fabulous way to end my time with the club, although there was a negative touch, as the Rovers' fans booed me from the field when I was replaced with four minutes to go. They were objecting to a tackle I had made on their replacement, John Lydiat. I felt my shoulder charge was definitely legitimate, but the referee judged it to be a fraction late and awarded a penalty. The fans were carrying on as though it was a high shot, but the video later confirmed what I already knew — the hit was never higher than the chest.

I will never forget how well I was received in St Helens. Right from the start the atmosphere generated by the fans was excellent. It didn't

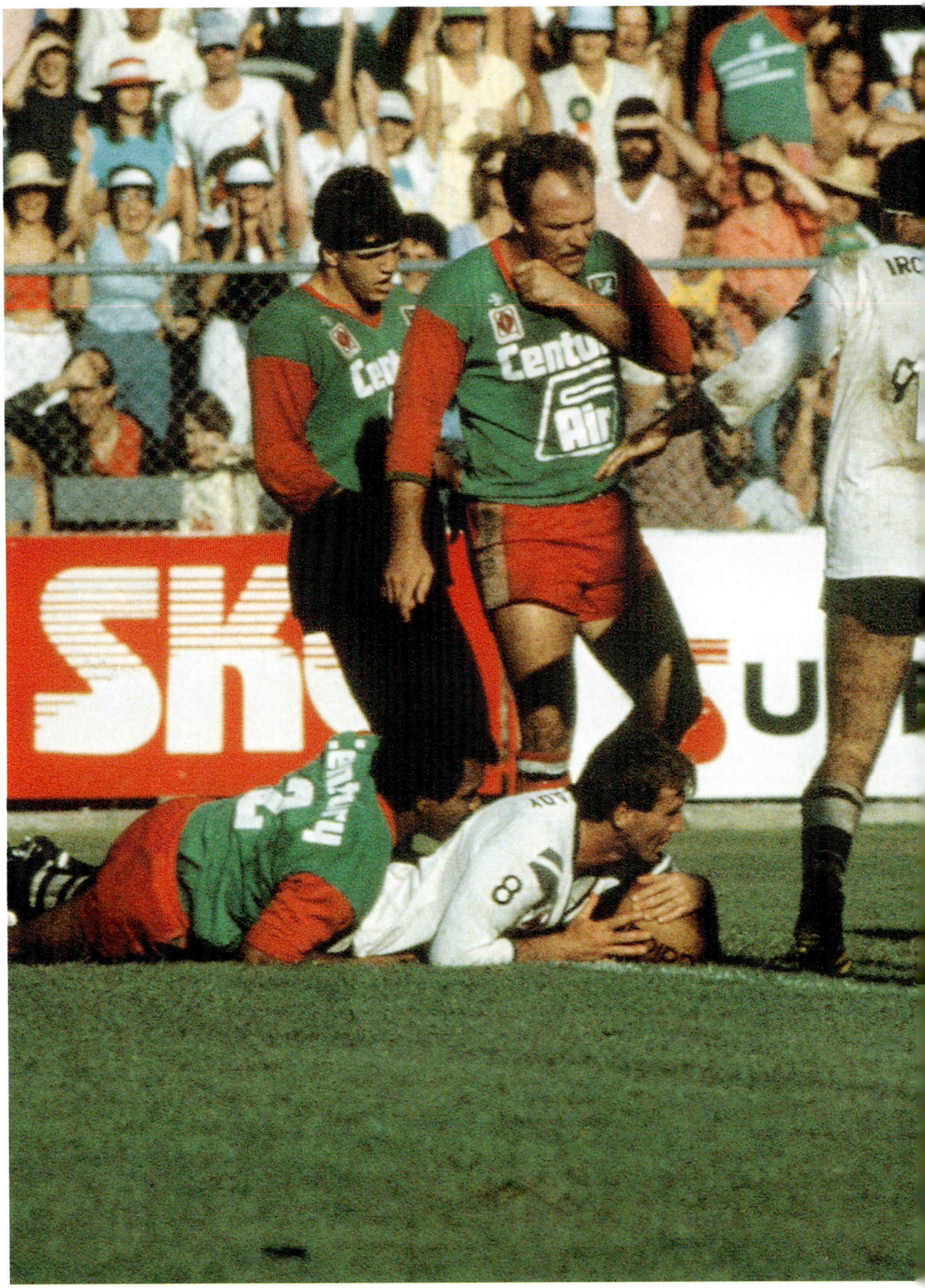

Souths and Saints

Captain Norm Carr has just scored his crucial try in the '85 grand final, to give us a significant 10–2 advantage over Wynnum–Manly, and I'm off into the in-goal area to celebrate. Despite a gallant comeback from the Seagulls late in the game, and the fact that more than one of my team-mates were battling through injury, we held on to win 10–8 — one of the most memorable days of my career.

The Wynnum no. 2 whose tackle could not prevent Norm getting over the line is Terry Butler. The other two Seagulls are their captain, hooker David Green, and Wally Lewis. The Magpies no. 12 is Eddie Muller. The referee is David Manson.

matter whether there were 5,000 or 50,000 people singing, clapping and chanting — it was fantastic.

I appreciated the fact that the club had given me the use of a car — a Ford Escort — but I wished they hadn't gone to the trouble of adding the name "Mal Meninga" to both sides. Whenever Deb and I jumped in that car, the entire town knew where we were going! However, I felt very welcome and very much at home as people would wave, and shout their hellos to us.

I remember once parking in a "No Parking" zone and coming back to find a parking officer waiting by the car. As I tried to remember my best excuse, he shot out a hand. "'Allo, Mal," he said. "Very nice to meet you." And then he began asking me a few questions about how the football was going. I couldn't even talk him into giving me a ticket!

St Helens will always be special to me. It is one of the regrets of my career that I never returned to play another club season there. I actually signed a contract to go over in 1988–89, but my broken arm put an end to that agreement. Then, in 1991, I was very tempted by a substantial offer at a time when the Canberra Raiders were in severe financial trouble.

What has been most rewarding for me has been the reaction I have received every time I have played for the Kangaroos against St Helens. Banners appeared in the crowd — I remember one that read, "Waltzing Meninga" — and the fans repeated chants I had heard often in 1984–85. They truly are great people. And, like the fans, the committee always treated me magnificently, presenting plaques or crystal in recognition of my time at the club.

When this happened, I felt more than a little inadequate as I had only played there for one season! But, frankly, I appreciated and enjoyed the gesture. To be held in such esteem by the fans and the club makes me feel extremely humble.

The success I had with St Helens was a confidence booster for me, coming as it did straight after the hammering we copped in the 1984 grand final.

I came home in May for what would be my farewell season with Souths. Wayne was again the coach, and once more we reached the grand final, where our opponents ... again! ... were Wynnum–Manly.

Before I could play in the grand final, I had to find a place in the side. On my return to Brisbane, I learned that Peter Jackson had been Souths' star in the season to date. So for my comeback match, the semi-final of the State League against Brothers (which we lost), I played in the second row, with Hubie Abbott partnering "Jacko" in the centres. But for my next appearance, against Wynnum–Manly, I was back where I liked to be, as Jacko's partner. It was the start of an allegiance that lasted the rest of the

'85 season (we were reunited in Canberra in 1987).

I didn't get to play too often with the Magpies in 1985. First, not long after I returned from St Helens, I was involved in the State of Origin series. Then I was off to New Zealand for a tour that included two Test matches. After the third Origin match, which followed the Kiwi tour, I decided to have a fortnight off, to rest a nagging groin injury. So I wasn't really involved in things at Davies Park until late July, by which time the boys were entrenched in the top four.

With one dramatic round to play, Souths, Wynnum and Brothers were locked in a three-way tie at the top of the ladder, with 14 wins and six losses each. We were on top, with easily the healthiest points for-and-against difference, and needed only to win our final match, against Wests at Davies Park, to clinch the minor premiership. This we did, 25–4, and I was delighted to farewell my home ground of the past seven seasons with a three-try performance.

In the minor semi-final, Wynnum–Manly were too good for Valleys, and after we defeated Brothers 14–8 in the major semi, Lewis's men outclassed the Brethren 35–16 in the final. This was, I must admit, the grand final match-up I wanted — the perfect finale to my club career in Brisbane. And, though I was in some doubt for the game because of a hairline fracture of the kneecap (I needed a pain-killing injection to get me through), I was primed to give the Souths fans a grand farewell.

The game developed into a classic, which we were able to win narrowly, and bravely, 10–8, after Wynnum had scored a converted try 12 minutes from time to set up a very nervous finish. I'll never forget the sight of veteran prop Chris Phelan, in those final minutes, his right knee badly damaged but his other "good" leg still propelling him towards the Wynnum attackers. The courage our blokes displayed was infectious, and we clung to our precious two-point advantage until the siren. This really was one of the most satisfying wins I have ever been associated with and a tribute to the team spirit that Wayne Bennett had fostered throughout the club.

After the grand final, Wayne was asked what he'd found to be the most rewarding part about the 1985 season.

"That's easy —" he replied, "— turning a disaster into a victory."

Twelve months earlier, we had been publicly humiliated by Wynnum–Manly. Many thought the Seagulls to be invincible. But not Wayne Bennett. He set about getting the entire Souths club focused on the path to reversing that catastrophe. Now we were premiers. Such a triumph, against all the odds, was the perfect way for me to bid farewell to the mighty Magpies, a club that will always retain a big piece of my football heart.

MENINGA

4: MATE AGAINST MATE

The stepping-stone from first-grade football to Test football is the State of Origin series. Launched by League officials in 1980 as something of an experiment, Origin football has become, to many followers of the game, just about the major highlight of the rugby league calendar. It is an event that marketers and advertisers fall over each other to be a part of. Unfortunately, these promoters have grabbed the "hate" aspect of the contest, and pushed it to the fore. "Mate against mate" was their theme. By the end of my career, I was wondering whether these promoters had developed a monster, still full of the atmosphere and skill of days gone by, but lacking the enjoyment that is so important to those who play the game.

When the concept was first mooted, back in the late '70s, there was doubt in many people's minds as to whether it would work. Some doubted whether players would go in hard against their club-mates. This pessimism was most prevalent in New South Wales, where officials and players were a little apprehensive about the idea and did not take it seriously.

We in Queensland did. We believed, provided we played well, that it would lead to a resurgence of the game in Queensland. Which, of course, is exactly what happened. Before the Origin revolution, interest in interstate football had been on the wane. NSW, usually reinforced with a number of Queensland-born players, were winning matches against their hopelessly outgunned Maroon opponents as a matter of course. The Origin concept gave Queensland a chance, the Lang Park crowds were loud and colossal and, within two years, Origin football was here to stay.

Playing for Queensland was very important for us. In the early '80s it was a great buzz to represent our state on the Origin battlefield. I will never forget the thrill of playing in the inaugural State of Origin game in 1980 alongside famous names such as captain Arthur Beetson, Rod Reddy, Kerry Boustead and Rod Morris. These men had travelled to Sydney to make a name for themselves in rugby league. Now, they were back.

Arthur Beetson had travelled south in 1966 to play with Balmain and had quickly made an impact. That season he starred for Australia in the third Ashes Test, which Australia won before a full house at the SCG to seal the series. Later, he moved to Eastern Suburbs, where he captained successive grand final winning sides in 1974 and 1975. Big Arthur, a Test

Opposite: Trying to break through the tackle of NSW's Paul Sironen (in headband), with Brad Fittler moving in, during my final State of Origin match, at Lang Park in 1994.

regular for much of the '70s, also captained Australia to a World Series triumph in 1977. By 1980, he was in the twilight of his wonderful career, struggling to find a place in the Parramatta first-grade pack. But he was still a legend, and on the night of the first Origin he was at his inspiring best.

Rod Reddy was another of the game's greats, a man who in the late 1970s with St George was just about the most dominant forward in the game. Originally from Rockhampton, he first played with the Saints in 1971 as a raw teenager, and won premierships with that famous club in 1977 and 1979. Like Beetson, he had gone to Sydney before he had the chance to play for his home state. But for the State of Origin concept, they would never have had that privilege.

The other Sydney-based players in the side were winger Kerry Boustead, who had moved south after making the Test side from Innisfail as a teenager in 1978, the tough international prop Rod Morris, five-eighth Allan Smith, who had scored four tries in the inter-state clash I missed in 1979, Johnny Lang, the outstanding hooker-forward who had played most of his league in Brisbane before moving to Sydney's Easts in 1980, and Greg Oliphant, a very strong halfback who had won two Test caps while playing for Redcliffe in 1978 before transferring to Balmain.

Despite some concerns in the southern press, the intensity was always going to be there as far as the Queensland players were concerned. I remember three days before the match saying to myself: "Everyone is serious ... we are going to be fair dinkum in this match." We had not been training too hard but we had got to know each other. Any fear I had that the Sydney-based players were only up for the ride had been totally quashed. Instead, an extraordinary determination and cooperation — the Queensland spirit — had developed.

All the players who returned from Sydney had a ton of enthusiasm, which served to inspire the locally-based players. As far as I was concerned, to be part of the occasion was tremendous, as was the opportunity to share a dressing-room with such men. I was just happy to be there and I remember playing much of the game with a smile on my face because I was so proud to be involved.

The final score was 20–10 to the Maroons, before a happy and vibrant crowd of 33,210. And to make things even better for the Meninga clan, the game was played on my 20th birthday. I could not have received a better present than my seven goals from seven attempts which helped to get us over the line.

There were a number of flare-ups in the game, many of them involving our leader but, as far as fighting is concerned, I am a very good peacemaker.

Queensland coach Arthur Beetson is good enough to pour me a cup of tea on the morning of the first Origin match of 1983.

I did do a bit of pushing and shoving and a bit of grabbing (which had absolutely no impact on the proceedings at all!) but around me there was some pretty fearsome stuff going on. This aggression worked in our favour — I don't think NSW ever recovered from the early fire we put into the match.

The Origin story had begun. In 1981, as in 1980, there was only one Origin match, and Queensland won again, 22–15, despite the fact we trailed 15–0 after 25 minutes. My major contribution was a penalty try awarded late in the game after the Blues' Steve Rogers had tackled me without the ball. I liked a comment Rogers' centre partner, Michael Cronin, made seasons later, when asked about the game by Bret Harris, the author of *State of Origin 1980–1991*.

"That comeback set the standard for Queensland which they have maintained all these years," Cronin told Harris. "They are never beaten. Whenever they are down, they get up again."

The following season was the first to have a three-match Origin series, and Queensland won it, two matches to one. In the first game in 1982, played at Lang Park, I was named Man of the Match after having a pretty successful night during which I set up a try and kicked five goals. However, NSW won the game 20–16. We levelled the series one match all with a win in the second game (again at Lang Park) and then, with Wally Lewis dominating the game, we wrapped up the series with a 10–5 win at the Sydney Cricket Ground. That third win stunned league

Meninga

With Raiders team-mate but NSW opponent Ricky Stuart after the Blues had won the 1992 series. The jumpers may be the same, but the shorts are different (I had swapped jumpers with NSW's Brad Fittler).

followers south of the border. They thought that our success had been due to the passionate support we'd been receiving from the people at Lang Park. It took this victory to prove we were a football team with the ability to match the quality of our supporters.

The biggest story of 1983 was the Les Boyd–Daryl Brohman clash in game 1 that led to Boyd being suspended for 12 months and left the Queensland forward with a shattered jaw. From Daryl's point of view, this was a terrible personal misfortune. He was one of those gifted players who seemed to have time to do magic things with the ball, and he had gone into the match playing the best football of his career. There was talk of an Australian jumper ... until he was taken from the field and into hospital. He was never the same player after the incident.

But I must say that I like Les Boyd. He's a good bloke but, unfortunately, on the rugby league field there was a bit of the Jekyll and Hyde about him. He probably received more notoriety than he deserved, and there were definitely times when he was victimised. He could play remarkable, explosive football, but then he would do something stupid; during the second Test of the 1982 Ashes series, for example, we were comfortably ahead, but he got himself sent off for kicking one of the British forwards.

Despite the loss of Daryl, we still won the first match in '83, lost the second at the SCG but swamped NSW 43–22 in the third.

In those early years of State of Origin, playing in the games was a massive mental and physical drain. Everyone involved found it difficult to get fully motivated for their club match the next weekend. It was in many ways a no-win situation. If your state had won, you were on such an emotional high that there was inevitably a letdown when you played for your club the next weekend. But, if you lost, it was such a disappointment that it was hard to get yourself back in the right positive frame of mind for the next club round.

That was in the early days. Gradually times changed, and by the end of my career things were working in reverse. For me, club matches with the Raiders became the number-one priority. Instead of concentrating solely on the Origin contest, in the back of my mind was the thought that I had to get through the game so I could help Canberra win two critical premiership points on the coming weekend.

The marketing gurus knew they were on to a winner when they came up with that infamous promotional line of "state against state, mate against mate" to describe State of Origin matches. In those early years, mate against mate wasn't part of the equation for me. I lived my life and played my football in Brisbane so I was not playing against my club-mates in Origin rugby league. My opponents were from NSW — "cockroaches" we called them — and it wasn't difficult to develop an intense dislike for them when it came to football. This attitude was strictly professional: having played international football with many of them, I knew they were good blokes — but on the field, it was different.

However, then I moved to Canberra and it became a burden to line up against Raiders comrades. My first season down south, 1986, was okay — the only other Raider involved in Origin football was Queensland fullback Gary Belcher. But from 1989 on (I missed 1987 and 1988 because of my broken arms), club-mates such as Laurie Daley, Bradley Clyde, Glenn Lazarus, John Ferguson, Ricky Stuart, Brett Mullins, Jason Croker and Ken Nagas were in the NSW team at different times. I didn't like playing against them because we were good

Opposite: NSW captain Steve Mortimer (left) and a drenched colleague try to arrest my progress during game 1 of 1985, at Lang Park. The NSW no. 12 (right) is Benny Elias. The Blues won 18–2, and two weeks later clinched their first series with a 21–14 victory at the SCG.

mates. Whenever you go on to the field you always try to do your best and play the jersey (which I certainly did, and I'm sure I never let the Maroons down) but I confess I did not enjoy playing against my Canberra colleagues. And I also don't mind admitting that when Laurie Daley was running towards me, I wouldn't tackle him as hard as I would someone from another club.

That's just me. I know other blokes think differently and enjoy it. But I never did, and neither did many of the others. Winning is great, but survival is critical. When a State of Origin game was over, the first questions we asked each other as we walked off were, "Have you been hurt?" and, "Will you be right for the next club game?"

I don't have good memories of the second State of Origin match in 1984, which was played in atrocious conditions at the Sydney Cricket Ground, even though we won the game to clinch the series. Rain belted down all night and the field was a quagmire. All I had with me, boot-wise, was a pair with moulded soles — hardly the right footwear for the occasion. And to make matters worse as far as I was concerned, I had been chosen on the wing, with Gene Miles and Chris Close in the centres. Now, I'm not complaining about the selection — both Gene and Chris were outstanding Test footballers — but I hated playing in that position.

There I was, out on the wing, supposedly one of the speedsters in the team, and I could hardly keep my footing because of those ugly moulded soles on my boots.

The highlight of the game for us (but not, I imagine, for the saturated crowd) was an incredible catch by Greg Dowling — he grabbed a kick-through that had rebounded off the cross-bar and dived into a pond over the goal-line to score. He made the catch with his fingertips, just centimetres from the ground. No-one had any right to hold on to the ball like that, given the conditions. It was as good as Fatty Vautin's cricket catch ...

Then poor Noel Cleal mis-kicked a line drop-out and the ball failed to travel the necessary 10 metres. It was ridiculous — he dropped the ball to the ground and it stayed there, stuck in the mud. From the resulting penalty, I managed to kick my third goal of the night, which was a pretty good trick, considering the ball seemed to weigh a tonne.

Season 1985 was one of controversy for the Australian team, and it all boiled over in the third Origin match. NSW had won their first Origin series by winning the opening two matches, but on the national team's tour of New Zealand, which followed game 2 and ended a fortnight before the final Origin game, then Australian coach Terry Fearnley (who was also the NSW Origin coach) had brought the wrath of Queensland down on his head by dumping a number of Maroons from the team for the third Test, in Auckland. Out of the Test side went Greg Dowling, Greg Conescu,

MATE AGAINST MATE

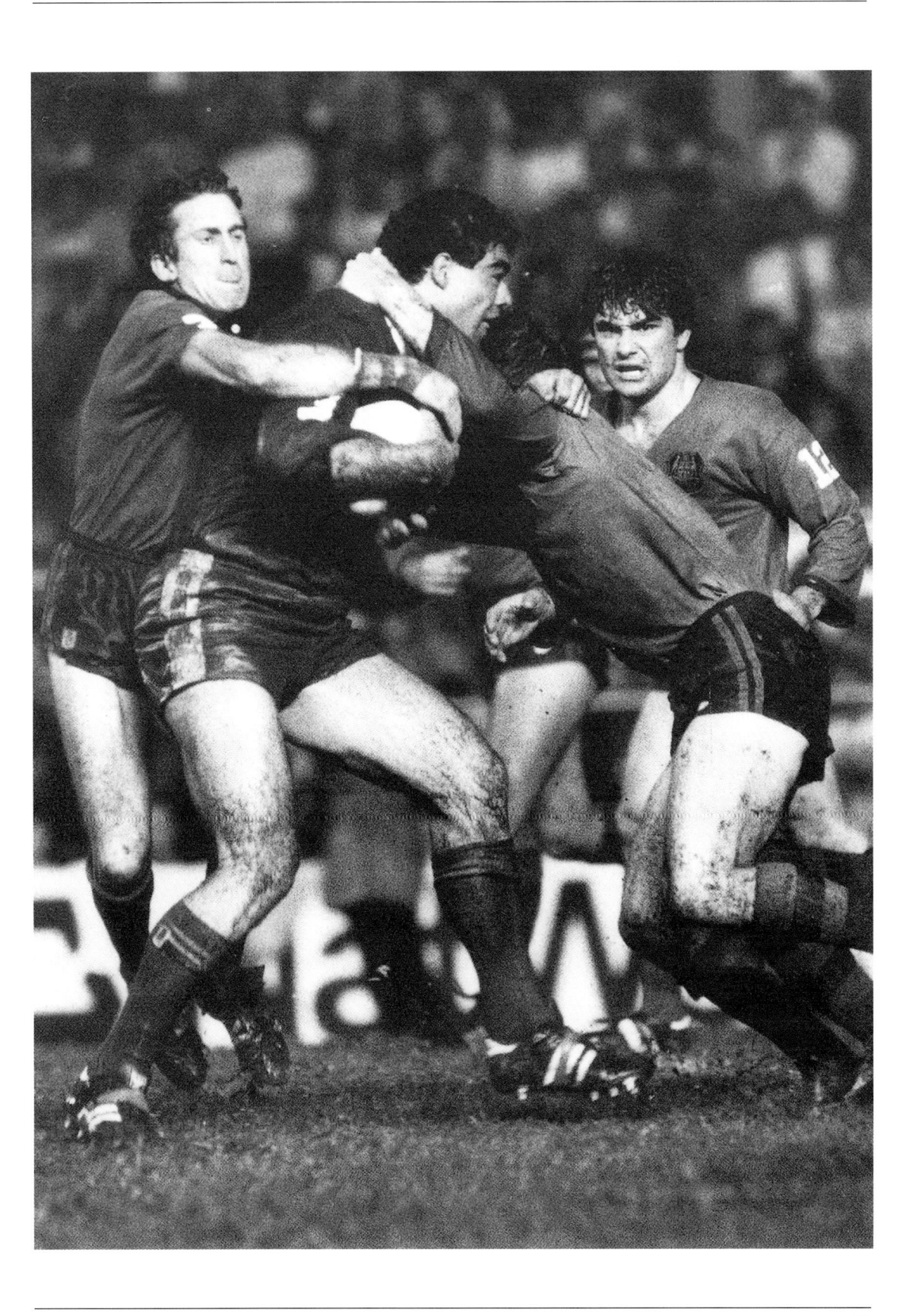

Mark Murray and Chris Close, to be replaced by Peter Tunks, Ben Elias, Dessie Hasler and Steve Ella.

The storm that followed, with allegations of anti-Queensland vendettas and the like was, in my opinion, a little over the top. I was disappointed I allowed myself to be caught up in the drama because I had been looked after very well during the tour. However, I don't think Terry did himself any favours by failing to inform the sacked players of their omissions privately, before the team meeting when the side was read out. This error of judgement by Terry created a tremendous amount of animosity within the squad and in the third Origin there were a number of Queenslanders who wanted to prove something.

That anger and desire to prove a point were infectious, and by kick-off time the Queensland side was in an extremely hyped-up and vengeful mood. We were pretty mean that night and weren't going to be beaten.

The final 20–6 scoreline was an indication of how dominant we were. Often in a State of Origin match the play switches from end to end, like a wave flowing from one side of a pool to the other, but this night we took control from the jump and never relaxed our hold on the game.

The Blues retained their newly-won Origin crown in 1986 by achieving the first clean sweep of a series. However, there were only a few points separating the teams in the three matches: 22–16 in the first, 24–20 in the second, 18–16 in the third. If the ball had bounced a fraction differently, we would have won.

This was Gary Belcher's first season in State of Origin football. In previous years and for the opening game of 1986, Gary had been in the shadow of Colin Scott, but Badge's move to the Canberra Raiders and the intensity of the Sydney premiership had allowed him to blossom into a really superb fullback.

We were out for dinner on the night the teams for the second state game of the season were announced. Most pundits had Badge in their teams, but selections are something you can never be sure about. We were all a little nervous, Gary more than anyone. I was given the job of making the call to see if the team had been selected. It had. I put on my grimmest face, and walked back to the table, trying not to look Gary in the eye. I must have done a good job, because when I finally glanced at him, he looked downcast, like a student who has just discovered he has failed his exam. "Badge ..." I said slowly, "... you made it!!"

From this moment, through until 1990, Gary was unchallenged as Queensland's fullback. However, for 1987 and 1988 because of my broken arm, I had to watch his marvellous play from the sidelines. Consequently, I was keen to make up for lost time in the opening State of Origin match in 1989 where I scored a couple of tries and kicked four goals in a 36–6

I played with Gary Belcher at Souths, in Canberra, for Queensland and for Australia, and right through this time I had an extraordinary on-field rapport with him. We could have been twins, so closely did we think and move together on the football field. Many was the time "Badge" made me look like a good footballer by being there when I needed him.

If I had to use one word to describe his play it would be "class". Everything he did in football had that special quality about it. That he was also a top-quality bloke off the field just made the package even more special.

Despite the fantastic football his successor at Canberra, Brett Mullins, played after taking over the fullback job in 1994, I still rate Gary Belcher as the best fullback I ever played with.

Looking the worse for wear during one of Queensland rugby league's greatest nights — game 2 of the 1989 series. Despite a string of severe injuries suffered by various team members (including my fractured eye socket), the mighty Maroons fought their way to a phenomenal 16–12 victory.

blitzing of NSW. We then kept the momentum rolling with two more strong wins for a clean sweep of the series.

The first match of the series, as well as being a performance right up there with Queensland's best in Origin history, was also Laurie Daley's interstate debut. As the score mounted, he became more and more downcast.

After another Queensland try, Laurie picked himself up off the Lang Park turf and I heard him muttering to himself, "What can I do?" I remember muttering back to him, "Just keep going." Despite the hype, and the different-coloured jumpers, he was still my mate.

Our second win, at the Sydney Football Stadium, was one of the most heroic in Queensland rugby league history. I was one of four Maroons to be injured and replaced at half-time. My problem was a fractured eye socket, Alfie Langer broke an ankle, Fatty Vautin damaged an elbow and Michael Hancock a shoulder. Near the end, Bobby Lindner was carried from the field as well to leave just 12 gutsy men to defend our 16–12 lead.

While our '89 side produced some of the classiest performances by a Queensland side, it is hard to say whether it was the best Maroons team that I was a part of. Even in the '90s, our playing talent was among the best we've had. It was a little like a rugby league *Who's Who* with footballers such as Gary Belcher, Dale Shearer, Wally Lewis, Allan Langer, Kevin Walters, Steve Renouf, Peter Jackson, Steve Walters and Bob Lindner involved.

If you go back to 1985, when we lost the series, we had players of the calibre of John Ribot, Chris Close, Dale Shearer, Wally Lewis, Mark Murray, Paul Vautin, Wally Fullerton Smith, Dave Brown and Greg Dowling in the team. This was nearly an all-Australian team! And the following year, when NSW completed their only clean sweep, in game 1 we had only one player in the starting XIII who had never played for Australia, (second-rower Gavin Jones).

The truth is that every year the Queensland team has been, at the very least, outstanding. The events of 1995, when a nondescript Maroon side won the series 3–0, confirmed that yet again. The only trouble has been that sometimes the NSW side has been even better. We've never liked that, but occasionally we have to admit that it can happen.

After we lost the series in 1990, every member of the team vowed to do their utmost to get the title back the following year. This was a season of much emotion, for the king of Origin football, Wally Lewis, had announced that this would be his farewell series.

We won the first match, 6–4 (in which Canberra players scored every point — Meninga a try and a goal for Queensland, Daley a try for NSW), but lost the second 14–12. This set the stage for a nerve-wracking finish to Wally's Origin career.

Appropriately, the send-off was at Lang Park, scene of so many of his finest triumphs. The game was a thriller, with the scores tight all the way. Twenty minutes from time, we were behind 12–8, but you could sense the entire team lift in that final quarter. Dale Shearer scored the crucial try with 13 minutes left, and I managed the conversion, the only successful kick at goal all night. The feeling afterwards, as the Lang Park crowd waved and cheered their farewells to Wally, will long be remembered by all who were there that night.

Some people like Wally ... others don't. However, no-one can ever question his contribution to rugby league in Queensland and Australia, or his ability as a footballer. He has been one of the greatest of all time, probably the most dominant player in the long history of inter-state rugby league in Australia. He deserved to go out of Origin football a winner and the entire team busted themselves to make sure he did.

In 1992, I was named the Queensland captain, a privilege I was to keep until my retirement. I had captained Australia before my appointment, but this was a new honour for me and I was nervous about it. I probably put a bit too much pressure on myself because one of my major goals was to win a series as captain. Unfortunately, it was not to happen, which I regret. I would have loved to have led Queensland to a series win.

The reasons why are difficult to quantify. Certainly one of the major causes was that NSW during this period was an excellent young team, expertly coached by Phil Gould. But there were other factors, which I think have a little to do with the evolution of the Origin concept.

There can be no doubt that State of Origin football has been one of the great success stories in the code's recent history. It remains a wonderful advertisement for the game worldwide. However, I believe the inordinate pressure that was applied to the players during my last few seasons took a lot of the enjoyment out of the event. Most of the Queensland team had been through the Origin build-up many times, and to an extent the novelty had worn off. For me, the whole thing was getting a bit stale.

Losing an Origin series in the 1990s did not worry me as much as it had done in the mid '80s, when a defeat to the Blues was devastating. I was not alone in having this feeling. I knew of many players who, while wanting to perform well for their state, placed as much, if not more, importance on winning those critical premiership points on weekends.

This is something I touched on earlier in this chapter, and I'd like to come back to it again. Club football is a vital concern to all players, and to many, especially those who have been in the game for a number of years, it is the most important. They are playing and training with all their mates and enjoying close friendships that have been developing for many seasons.

I have said it many times — to win a premiership is the greatest thrill in football. There is more emotion and more exhilaration in a grand final victory than any other single event the game can offer. Something you and your closest friends have been working towards for the entire season (or, in some cases, many seasons) has come to fruition. Making that slow walk around the ground when it is all over is an extraordinarily rewarding moment in time, the true worth of which is not totally apparent until it has been experienced. You, and your team, are champions!

The fire and brimstone of Origin football is really made for young players who still have time to climb the many mountains the game of rugby league can offer them. This was clearly shown in 1995, when we saw a return to something like the old Queensland days, courtesy of the exuberant, intensely patriotic performance of coach Fatty Vautin's side. The "Queensland spirit" was there in a big way. Most of that Maroons side were untried in Origin football, and clearly responded to what — for them — was a new experience. And their passion rubbed off on the senior guys, who played accordingly. The State of Origin needed something new, and Fatty's young team were it.

Queensland appeared to want to win more in the 1995 series. NSW were always the favourites because on paper they appeared to have the better players and the more experienced team. NSW expected to win but seemed to lack the urgency and energy of their opponents. Perhaps the enjoyment has gone out of the game for them and their feeling is, just get the game over and done with and be free of injury.

When Fatty's Queenslanders were continually written off and given no chance in any of the matches, even after they had won the series with victories in the first two matches, it just fuelled the fire in their bellies and they produced where it mattered, on the field. Sometimes the media inadvertently helps a coach when they criticise a player or a team. Footballers love to prove their critics wrong!

The third game in 1995 was a great match, certainly one of the best games I have seen for a long time. There was plenty of excitement, as the teams took it in turns to score and it wasn't wrapped up by the Maroons until very late in the game.

The Lang Park crowd was at its raucous best on the night, inspiring their team to a superb performance. It was the same back in 1992, for my first home match as captain. This was another thriller, not decided until the final moments, when Alfie kicked his first ever field goal in a big match to give us a tense 5–4 win. However, that was our only victory of the series.

In 1993, we again lost 2–1 which was especially disappointing because the entire squad wanted to send another great Maroon stalwart, Bob Lindner, out a winner. Bobby deserved a similarly victorious send-off to the one given to Wally Lewis but, unfortunately, it was not to be. We lost the first two matches, but at least we were able to give him a decent farewell by taking the final match of the series, by 24 points to 12.

I would put Bob in my best-ever team because he was such a magnificent competitor. His work rate was enormous, his mental approach to the game was second to none and he was very consistent, particularly in representative football.

We might have won the second game in '93 had I not taken the wrong option late in the game. With time ticking away, and Queensland trailing, I made a dash from inside our own half. Across in cover came the Blues captain, Laurie Daley, and I decided to prop and pass the ball. Soon after, the ball was fumbled, the opportunity lost and the game over. I should have taken Laurie on — I knew it almost as soon as I had passed the ball. It's funny, that was probably one of the best games I played for Queensland. But while my performance has been forgotten, I'm still

Bob Lindner, with Queensland's long-serving manager Dick "Tosser" Turner after the final Origin encounter of 1993 during Bob's farewell to inter-state football. I played with few better footballers than Bobby Lindner, who was a colleague at Souths in the early 1980s, an Origin regular for 10 seasons from 1984 and a lock or second-rower in 23 Test matches. Perhaps the highlight of his career came in 1990, when he was considered by most critics to be player of that year's Kangaroo tour. I was always glad to have Bob Lindner on my side.

reminded from time to time about that incorrect option.

When I reflected on my Origin career after my farewell game in 1994, the thing that stuck with me was the pleasure I took from being a survivor. Rugby league is a tough game at this level. Especially in the early days, as a tyro coming from the Brisbane premiership, it was a big step up in class. Those games sorted out the men from the boys.

Along with the big hits and controversies, the wins and the defeats, I made some good mates through Origin football. In the latter years, when my career was winding down and I realised it wasn't long until I retired, I started to think about the great friendships I had made in the game. I have no doubt that in the future, long after our deeds on the football field have been forgotten, we will all remain friends.

While the 1995 State of Origin players were battling it out at Lang Park during the final match of the series, the players who had committed themselves to the Super League gathered in Sydney for a big party. In one corner was a big television screen, showing the Origin match in all its glory. Inevitably, a big crowd collected around that area. And, just as inevitably, the house was divided straight down the middle. The Super

League footballers and officials from NSW were cheering for the Blues; those from north of the border were yelling for the Maroons. The banter during the match was good natured and after the game, as the Queensland guys were collecting their winnings and everyone was commenting on just what a good and exciting game it had been, I realised that here was a classic example of the comradeship of rugby league.

In these highly competitive days, when the game is so intense and much of it is more like a business than a sport, I believe it is imperative that the players don't become too serious about the whole thing. As the game becomes more and more professional, and the demands on players continue to increase, the footballers of this and future generations have to realise no matter what happens, footy is still footy. When the match is over, you have to get together and enjoy the game of life. That's the way things have been for decades. It is something we cannot afford to lose.

Above: With St George and Queensland centre Mark Coyne, after the final match of 1994.

Next page: A final wave for the crowd at Lang Park, after my farewell appearance in the Maroon jumper.

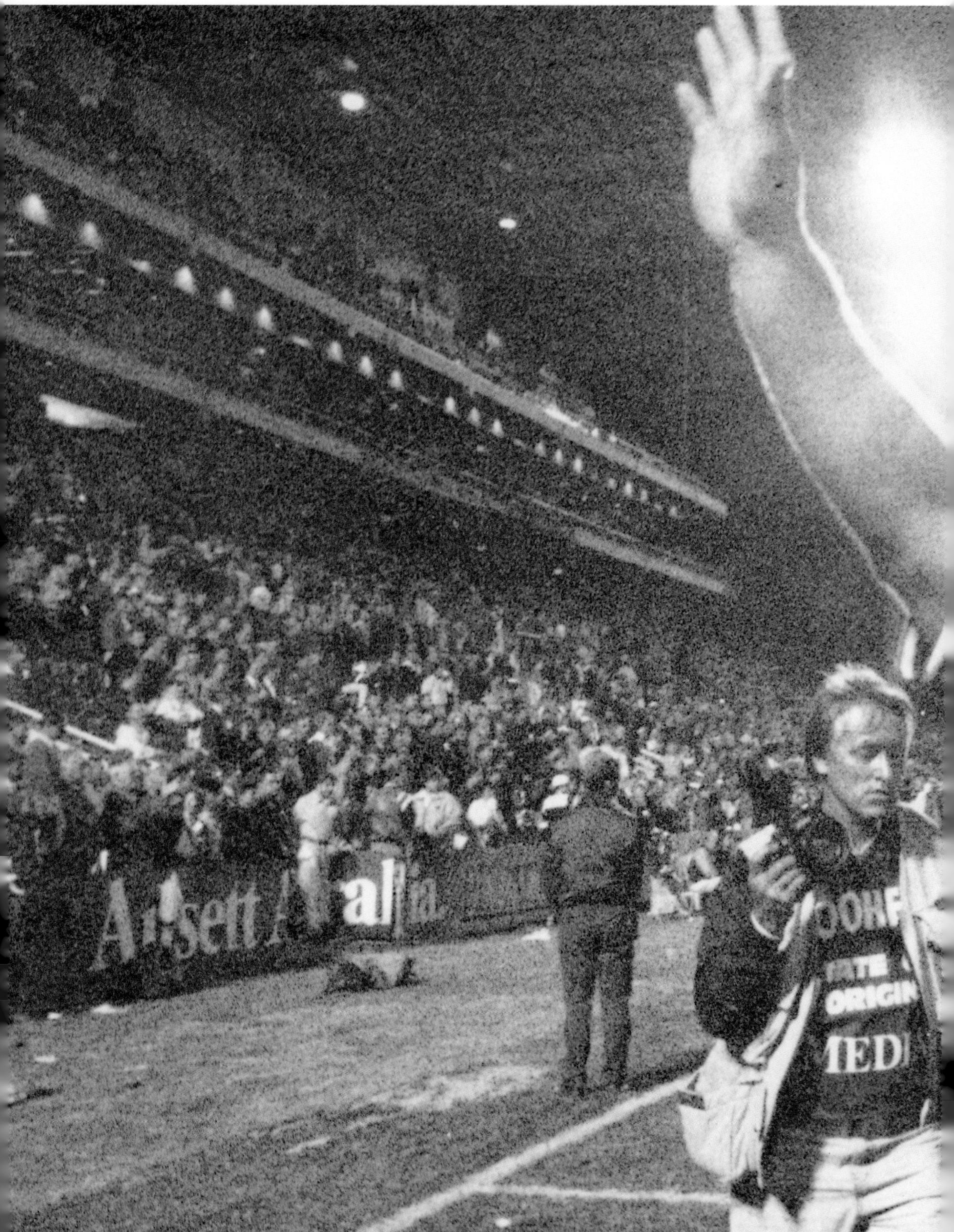

Mate Against Mate

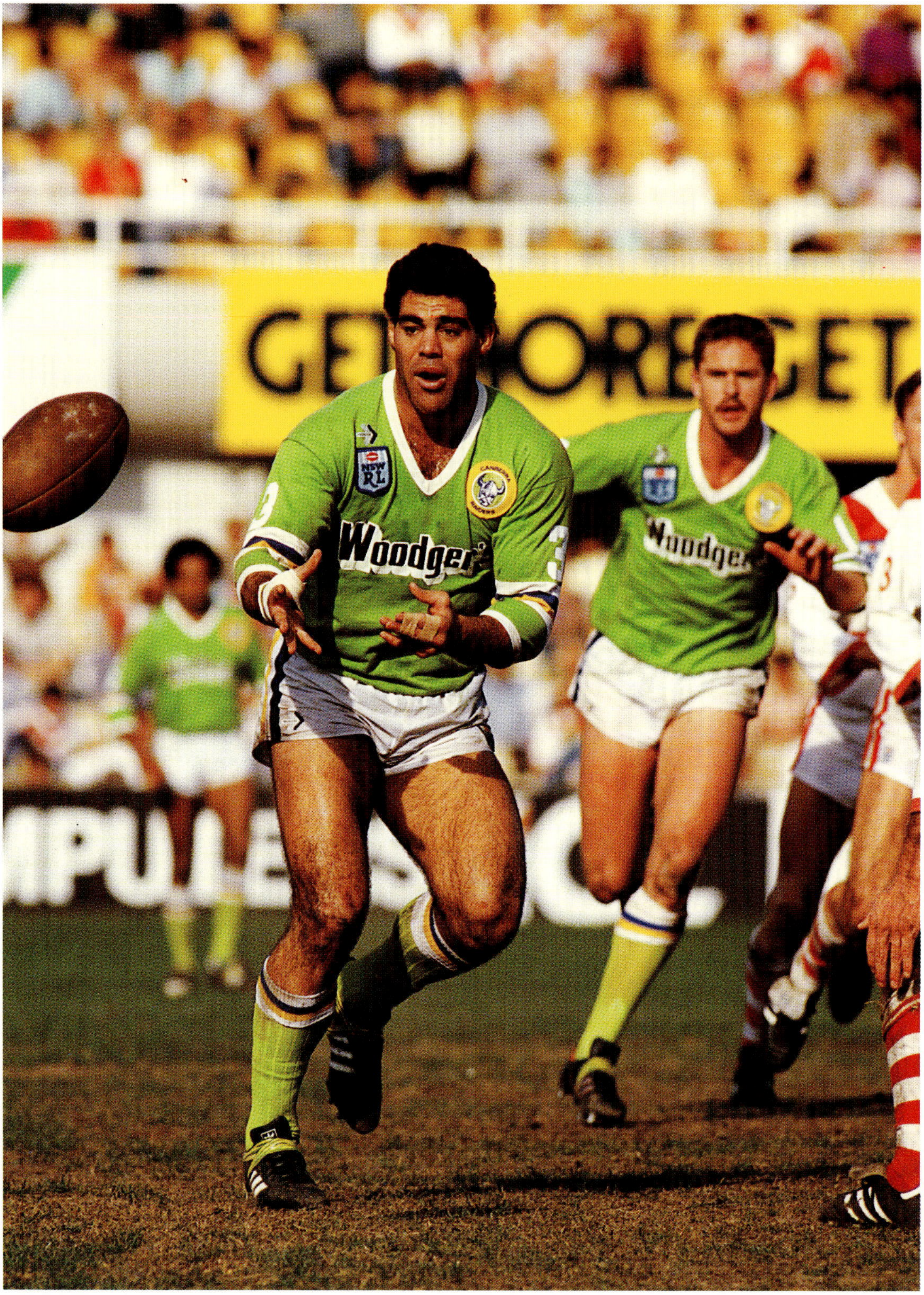
NSW RL
Woodgers

5: TRAVELLING SOUTH

In July 1985, the Canberra Raiders approached the Queensland Rugby League, officially seeking permission to negotiate with me regarding a possible move into the NSWRL premiership. They were not alone — Manly had also made a move, and other clubs were rumoured to be thinking along similar lines. At this time, the QRL had in place a transfer system, which stipulated set amounts that had to be paid to managements if players moved from club to club. The system was designed, more than anything else, to keep the best players in Queensland (the amounts laid down for international and State of Origin players were automatically doubled if the move was to a NSW-based club), but Ron McAuliffe, the chairman of the QRL, had decently said that the body he ran would not object if I chose to head south. There would be no huge transfer fee put on my head.

"Mal Meninga first represented Queensland in 1979 and has done so for the past six years," McAuliffe said. "He has also been a marvellous servant of Souths. We will not stand in his way."

I appreciated the chairman's attitude and his generosity. He was not always so charitable. At the same time as I decided to travel south, another Brisbane-based Test player, Wally Fullerton Smith, was complaining publicly about the QRL's transfer system which, he claimed, was stifling his ambition to move to Sydney. Wally eventually did move south, to St George, but not until 1987.

By late August 1985, I was still not sure which way I wanted to go. The decision of where I was going to continue my football career was not one Debbie and I were going to be rushed into. Easts had come in with a firm offer as well, but I favoured Canberra. All I knew at this time was that I wanted to play in the Winfield Cup. I knew it was the best competition in the world, and I wanted to prove to myself that I could handle the week to week stresses of playing in such a competition. I also wanted to become a better player and heading south seemed the best way for me to achieve this.

After a lot of discussion, Debbie and I agreed we did not want to go to ultra-busy Sydney. I liked the idea of playing in a one-team town. That was one of the things that really appealed to me about rugby league in England and was one of the factors that made the Canberra approach so

Opposite: Playing for Canberra against St George in round 22, 1986, a match that ended in an 18–all draw. The other Raider in the photograph is fullback Gary Belcher.

The Rugby League Week *cover for their September 5 edition, in which I explained why I decided the Canberra Raiders would be my "Sydney" club.*

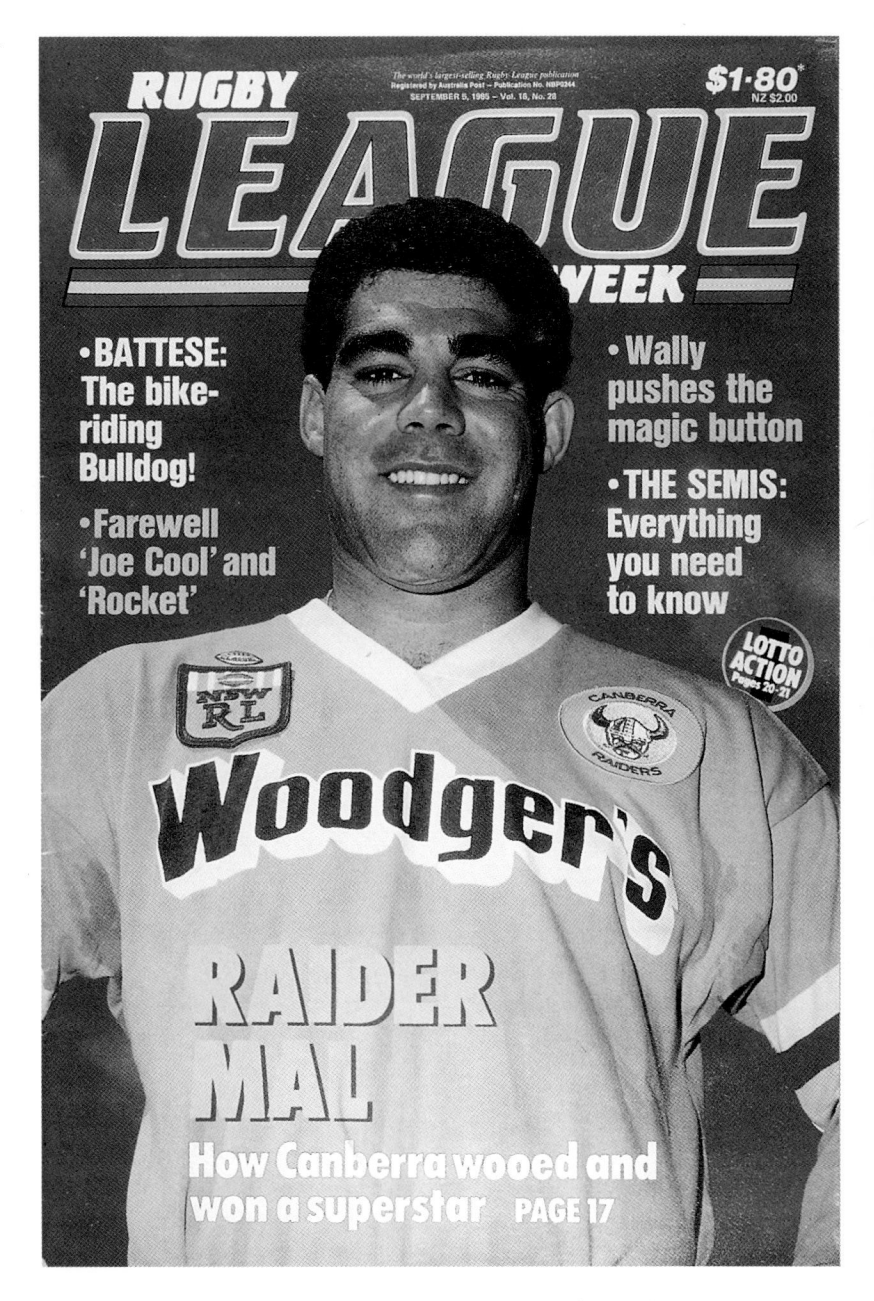

attractive. Finally, on September 4, I settled my future by signing a two-year deal with the Raiders.

The whole concept of the one-team town is fantastic. Give the townsfolk a successful side and entertaining football and they'll get behind you, often fanatically. I genuinely believed at that time that one-team towns would gradually come to dominate the league scene in Australia. This was because of the advantages they held over clubs based in the Sydney metropolitan area, who are obliged to compete with their near-neighbours for corporate and spectator support. The years since 1985, with the success of the Raiders and the Brisbane Broncos, have proved this theory to be correct.

In an interview with *Rugby League Week*'s Brisbane correspondent Tony Durkin on September 5, I went through the reasons why I was journeying to Canberra.

"I'm very impressed with Don Furner [the Raiders' coach]," I explained. "He strikes me as being genuine in everything he says and does. He struck me as something of a father figure. I like the man very much. [When Don was told I had described him as a 'father figure', he remarked: 'Tell him I can be a very hard father!'] And I also like the idea of living in Canberra. In this situation I can still play in the tough Sydney competition, yet live in the country-type atmosphere of Canberra."

And there was a third reason. "The money is good," I told Tony. "I can't deny that."

I compared my decision to sign with the Raiders to my choice of St Helens rather than the more glamorous Leeds club.

"[Then] it was a toss-up between Leeds, a team stacked with internationals and near the top of the ladder, and St Helens, with just a couple of name players, who were struggling. On that occasion, I believed I'd be more happy trying to help a struggling club. I'm proud to say that's the way things panned out.

"I just hope I can lift the Raiders in some way."

There was an interesting sidelight to that *RLW* story by Tony Durkin. The *RLW* managing editor, Ian Heads, wanted a shot of me on the front cover of the magazine, wearing a Raiders jumper. But this wasn't as simple as it sounds. There wasn't a shop in Brisbane that stocked one ("Not enough demand," one sports shop owner explained), so a jumper had to be flown up specially from Sydney. That was 1985. The Raiders' national profile has improved quite a bit since then.

Wayne Bennett was a major behind-the-scenes influence in my decision to move so far south. He had worked with Don Furner in the past and consequently knew the way he operated. The one thing I didn't want from a coach was a regimented approach to the way our team played and trained.

Wayne thought Don would get the best out of me. He was very aware I can get bored easily. His skills-oriented approach to training sessions suited me fine — he always had something different happening. I wanted to keep improving, and to do that I had to concentrate on sharpening my skills. The club I played with in the NSWRL premiership had to have a coach who approached the game in the same way as Wayne Bennett.

Canberra had narrowly missed the semi-finals in 1985, falling to

Opposite: John "Chicka" Ferguson was one of the best wingers I played with. He had exceptional speed off the mark, great evasive ability and could score magic tries, as he showed in the 1989 grand final when he sidestepped past a pack of Balmain Tigers to obtain the try that sent that match into extra-time.

He was quite an enigma. In the dressing-room before a Raiders match, some players would be getting all revved up, others would be having a rub down, a couple might be going over their match notes. At first glance, Chicka was nowhere to be seen. But then you'd spot him in the corner having a nap, or he might have ducked out to the toilet for one last cigarette.

Nothing ever worried him. But what a player and what a crowd pleaser! In our home matches in Canberra, the crowd wouldn't be yelling for Ricky, or Laurie, or Bradley, they'd be shouting, "Get it out to Chicka!" He had the ability to bring the fans to their feet before he even had the ball. Not many other footballers have that gift.

Souths in a play-off for the fifth spot in the semis, while their reserve-grade side had been desperately unlucky to lose to St George in the grand final. Based not in Canberra itself but in Queanbeyan on the Australian Capital Territory border, and playing out of the Seiffert Sports Ground, the Raiders had only entered the premiership in 1982, at the same time as the Illawarra Steelers, and were an ambitious club destined for much greater things. Their playing staff was dominated by a collection of hard-working, low-profile footballers, such as tough little halfbacks Chris O'Sullivan and Ivan Henjak, dependable hooker-forward Jay Hoffman, the tackling dynamo Dean Lance and big, no-nonsense front-rower Sam Backo. And the quality of the squad was increasing by the year. Joining me in the club's green jumper for 1986 were my classy team-mate from Souths, fullback Gary Belcher, plus two other likely prospects from the Brisbane premiership, hooker Steve Walters from Norths and second-rower Gary Coyne from Wynnum–Manly. Also coming to town was one of football's most remarkable characters, the Test winger of 1985, Chicka Ferguson.

The Raiders' buying program during the mid '80s, spearheaded by Don Furner's astute judgement, was unbelievably successful. For every dud, they landed a dozen men who helped the club to the very top. The thing Don concentrated on in those early years was to buy players who would develop into important components in the football club machine. He was always looking to the future.

There were no semi-final appearances for the Raiders in my first year but, even though we finished down the ladder (11th of 13), we did provide some encouraging signs in the last few matches of the season. We started badly, winning only four of our first 16 matches (the first in round 4, against Cronulla, when I scored my first try for the club), but in the last eight rounds we managed four wins and a draw, to finish the year on 21 competition points (which included four points from two byes). Probably my best performance was against the eventual premiers, Parramatta, in round 25, when we defeated them 19–12 at home.

To be honest, I felt my form throughout the year was okay, even though I wasn't picked for any of the three Tests against New Zealand (Gene Miles and Brett Kenny — not a bad pair at all — were the centres). My performances in the Origin series had been satisfactory, if not startling, and I was always fairly confident of winning a spot on that year's Kangaroo tour (though never certain — there was a host of excellent three-quarters around at the time). This was a tour I wanted for many reasons, not least of which was the honour of being the first player from the Raiders to become a Kangaroo. As things turned out, I was happy to share this honour with Gary Belcher, who played excellent football all

TRAVELLING SOUTH

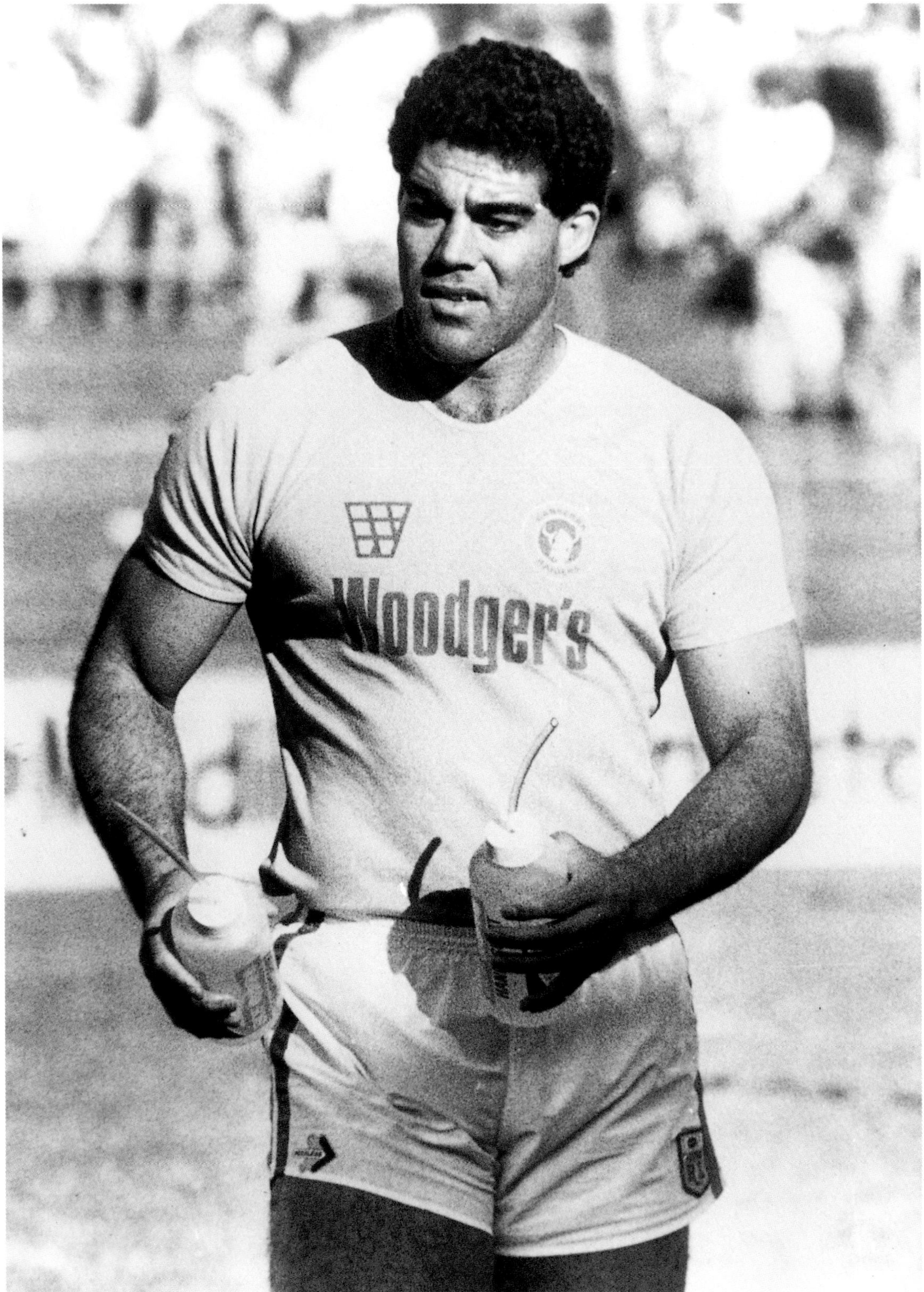
Woodger's

season with Canberra, Queensland and then on tour with the Australians.

In early September 1986 came an announcement I was extremely pleased to hear — that Wayne Bennett was coming south, on a two-year deal, to be Don's co-coach of the first-grade side. This was an innovation of great vision by the club and Don Furner and led to a remarkably rewarding season for the Raiders in 1987. And, of course, it was the best of both worlds for me. Wayne's input was of huge significance: he brought in fresh concepts, put much thought into developing the players' skills and stressed the importance of setting goals. We were basically the same team, bolstered by the addition of my former Souths comrade Peter Jackson, a young utility back from Ipswich, Kevin Walters (the younger brother of Steve) and an uncompromising Kiwi prop, Brent Todd, yet we charged up the competition ladder, from third last in 1986 to third in 1987. We then continued on through the semi-finals to reach the club's initial first-grade grand final.

We began 1987 in sparkling form, with victories over Cronulla and Illawarra interrupted by the bye in round 2. By round 8, when we thrashed Wests 46–11, we were entrenched in the top five, two points off the competition lead, with five wins. But then came two setbacks, the first frustrating and inexcusable, the second a personal disaster for me. In round 9, we led Parramatta 22–0 at half-time, but lost 30–22, a revival without precedent in the premiership's long history. Then, in round 10, against Manly at Seiffert, I smashed my left arm in an infamous collision with a goalpost.

The match against Manly took place on a cold wet day in Queanbeyan. I tried to tackle the Sea Eagles' Darrell Williams, but in the slick conditions couldn't control my momentum. From the sickening shock of the impact, I knew straightaway I was in huge trouble.

A quick trip to hospital confirmed the break. A few days later, doctors inserted a plate into the arm, to assist in the recovery process. Such a procedure, I was told, would limit the time I would be off the paddock.

Ten weeks later, I made a comeback, against Penrith. Just a week after the team had been thrashed by Balmain 28–0, we saw off the Panthers 24–6, and I managed a try and four goals. For 78 minutes things went perfectly but, just as I was mentally beginning to rehearse my post-game interviews, I moved in to tackle Penrith's young replacement winger, Michael Moss. My arm hit the top of his head as he fell to the ground, and soon after I was stumbling from the ground, clutching the injured limb.

As far as I was concerned, the season was over. Ivan Henjak was brought into the team, and he and Kevvie Walters alternated as Jacko's centre partner (with the other playing halfback). This was a system that worked extremely well, and a Raiders' semi-final berth was never really in doubt.

In the weeks leading up to the final series, Wayne made the decision

Opposite: Helping the Raiders out at Lang Park in May 1988, a match the boys won easily, 36–16. It had been 15 weeks since my arm had been broken for the third time, in the inaugural pre-season Sevens tournament; my third ill-fated comeback was still a month away.

Opposite: Doing it tough during the preliminary final in 1987, my first game back after breaking my arm for the second time.

that he wanted to go back to Brisbane. He had twin motivations — family reasons and a desire to coach the Broncos, one of the premiership's new clubs. But could he get an early release from his contract with the Raiders?

The Broncos, along with clubs from Newcastle (the Knights) and the Gold Coast (the Giants) had been granted admission to what would be a 16-team competition in 1988. Wayne's decision to leave created an atmosphere of uncertainty within the club. There were rumours that many of the Queensland-born Raiders, myself included, would follow him back north of the border to be part of a team some critics suggested would be akin to the Queensland State of Origin side.

While Wayne's second reason for wanting to leave didn't matter much to me, the first one certainly did, so I went along to Les McIntyre, the man who had virtually founded the Raiders back in the early '80s, and told him I was prepared to stay in Canberra and would sign for five years if Wayne was released from the last year of his contract. And that is exactly what happened: I signed for another five years and the club allowed Wayne to go to the Broncos. When I had originally moved to Canberra, I had signed for two years only.

A funny incident evolved out of this drama. Not long before the semi-finals, Wayne got the players together and told them he was going back to Brisbane. "You have every right," he solemnly told us, "to ask me to leave right now, before the end of the season."

The players gathered together. To a man we wanted him to stay until the finish, but we thought we'd have some fun. Peter Jackson was appointed spokesperson for the group.

"Wayne, we've had a serious discussion," he started, "and because you've decided to go to the Broncos we don't want you to coach us any more. We'd rather you took off straightaway."

Wayne's face fell: in an instant, he had aged 100 years. He had really thought the boys would stick by him.

"Okay, then," he said slowly, "if that's the way you want it ..."

He dragged himself off his chair and made for the door. And it wasn't until he got there that we yelled out as one: "*Gotcha!!!*"

The Raiders' semi-final campaign started badly. We played poorly in the major preliminary semi-final against Eastern Suburbs, to be beaten 25–16. Afterwards, Wayne did not mince words. He refused to acknowledge there had been any bad luck associated with the loss, but pinpointed the team's poor performance as the primary reason for the defeat.

A week later, the boys took on Souths in the minor semi-final. Fortunately, the lessons from the previous week's defeat had been absorbed and the Rabbitohs were blown away. Sixteen unanswered Raiders' points came in the first 15 minutes, and the final scoreline — a

TRAVELLING SOUTH

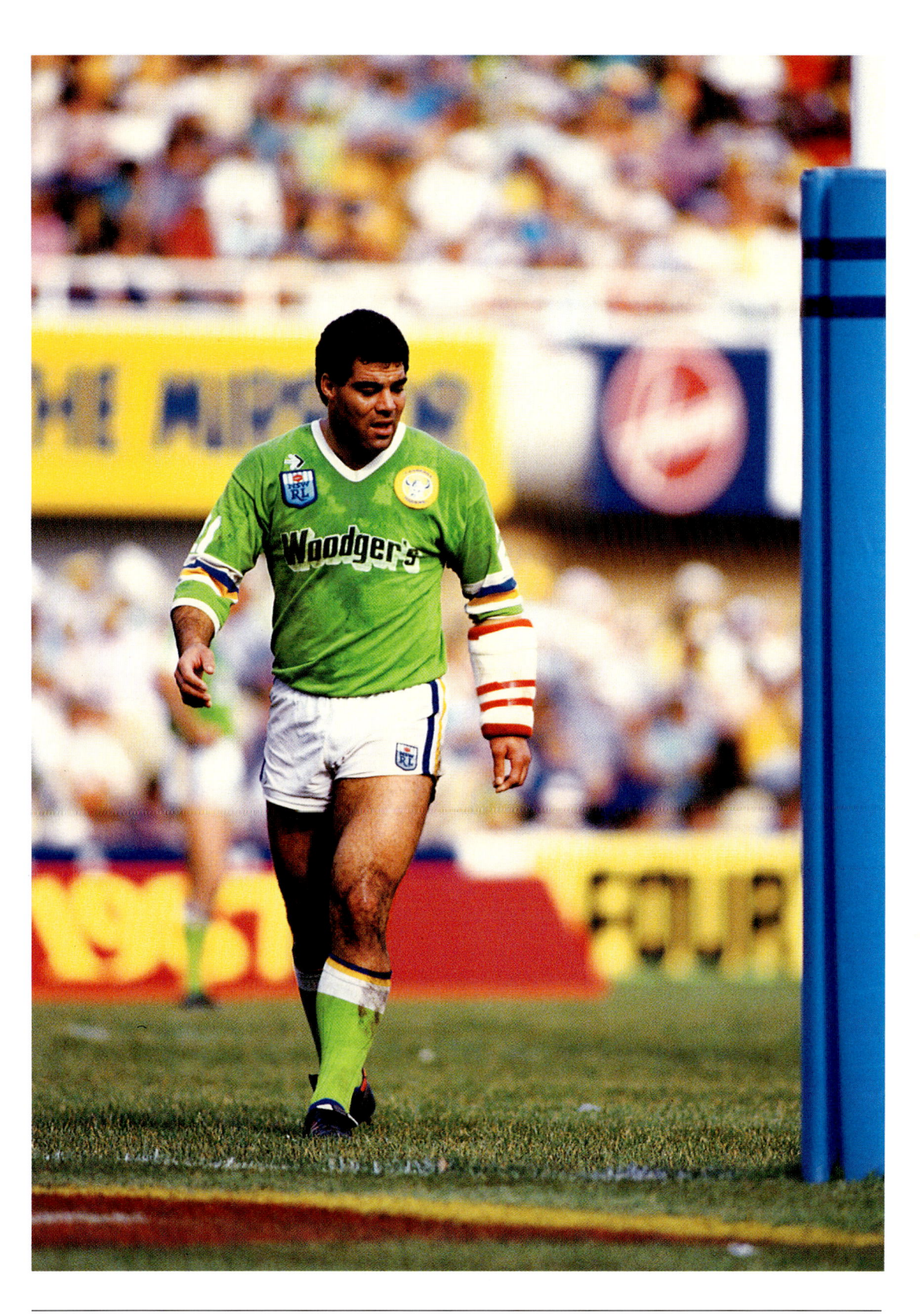

devastating 46–12 — reflected the domination of the Green Machine, as the press were beginning to tag us.

This was the match that finally had our supporters back in Canberra realising we really could play football. I think before this game, even though the team had done so well to reach the semi-finals, there were still a great many sceptics. I remember watching the annihilation of South Sydney from the comfortable surroundings of a sponsor's box. The other guests enjoying the food and drink on offer were genuinely surprised by just how good a side the Raiders were. I wasn't.

This was not the first time I had enjoyed the sponsors' hospitality since my second break. After all, my season was over, so why not have a drink and a sandwich? My playing weight was but a distant memory, something to be regained before the start of the '88 season.

Or so I thought! Wayne brought me back to earth and on to the training track in a hurry when he warned me there was a chance I could play in the final against Eastern Suburbs the following week. He, it had transpired, had been paying more attention to the doctors' reports on my arm than I had. The medicos believed I could play if I had my arm heavily protected by a colossal arm-guard. At first, I was hesitant, but Wayne convinced me I should give it a go, so I trudged out on to the training paddock once more to work as hard as I possibly could. My biggest problem was trying to fit into my shorts and jumper. It seemed in the weeks since my injury they had shrunk a little!

The actual decision to play me was left to the last moment, when I was put into the side to replace Kevvie Walters, who went on to the reserves bench. Initially, Wayne had planned to put me on the reserves bench, to be used a shock weapon late in the game, but in the end I was in at the start, the idea being to get as much out of me as my less-than-well-primed body would grant me. I wore jumper no. 21 and a massive guard on my injured arm which looked like a cross between a rubber beer-can holder and the padding that's wrapped around the bottom of goalposts. Before we went out on the field there was some controversy. Although I had been given the medical go-ahead to play, Arthur Beetson, who was coaching Easts, decided he wanted the guard checked to make sure it was legal. We weren't worried in the slightest — to us, this was just another of old Artie's psychological ploys.

Arthur said he thought the guard was too big and too hard, but the authorities disagreed with him and out I went on to the field.

As things turned out, I scored a try and kicked a couple of goals on the way to our 32–24 win, playing for 64 minutes before being replaced. We were through to the grand final, an achievement not many people would have believed possible a few short months before. The critics in Sydney were having a tough time coming to terms with the fact that a club from outside the Sydney metropolitan area was going to play-off for the premiership.

Meanwhile, supporters in the ACT were going berserk. This was the time when the ultra-close link between the club and the city was first forged, never, hopefully, to be lost. Our fans were clearly very proud of what we had achieved, particularly as they enjoyed getting one over on their cousins from the big smoke! Celebrations in the week leading up to the grand final were overwhelming, and we got caught up in ticker-tape parades and the like which, with hindsight, should have been left until after the big game. Still, this was a lesson that served us well in the years ahead.

As it was, on the day, we were beaten 18–8 by an excellent Manly team, which included names such as Paul Vautin, Cliff Lyons, Noel Cleal, Des Hasler and Kevin Ward. They were much the better side, and though we fought as hard as we could, the trophies should probably have been won by an even bigger margin than the eventual 10 points.

After the grand final hangovers had cleared, I decided to give the arm the entire off-season to heal. As part of this process, I had the plate

Opposite: I've just scored the Raiders' second try of the '87 preliminary final, and my team-mates share my excitement. The other players are (left to right): Ivan Henjak, Dean Lance (obscured, in headgear), Gary Belcher (no. 1) and Gary Coyne.

My favourite comment about Gary Coyne came from my wife Debbie, who once described him as "the only Wynnum–Manly player I ever really liked". I appreciated his decision to join the Raiders in 1986, to become a team-mate rather than an opponent of mine, as it was the beginning of a close association that meant a great deal to me. Throughout my football career, Gary was as loyal a comrade as there could be, and remains a great mate today. I'm sure our friendship will continue for many, many years.

The fourth and final break. Australian team doctor Dr Bill Monaghan (left) and team manager Peter Moore examine my damaged arm after I left the field early in the Australian team's match against a Rest of the World XIII at the Sydney Football Stadium in July 1988.

removed and, by the time the trials began, I was primed for a huge comeback. An Ashes series was part of a packed itinerary for this bicentennial year, along with a celebration match between Australia and a Rest of the World team, the first ever Test against Papua New Guinea on Australian soil and the World Cup final (the first since 1977) in October.

The season began with a "Super Sevens" tournament at Parramatta Stadium in the first week of February. We were now coached by Tim Sheens, the former Penrith player and coach who had taken over after Wayne's departure and Don's retirement. However, I was to have precious little direct experience of Tim's methods in his first season.

Our first opponents in the Sevens were the Broncos, who were making their Sydney debut. They were a star-studded outfit — including Wally Lewis, Gene Miles, Allan Langer, Greg Dowling, Greg Conescu, Chris Johns, Michael Hancock and Joe Kilroy among others on their playing roster — and their opening performance was eagerly awaited. But not long into our clash, I was wishing I'd never heard of them. Gene Miles took the ball up, I moved in to tackle him, he ducked, my left arm caught the top of his head and I knew instinctively the bone had gone again.

Peter Jackson who, like Gary Belcher, was a mate of mine in Souths, Canberra, Queensland and Australian teams. Jacko has always been and will always be a bit of a joker. He was also a good friend, a good trainer, a very good player and a great thinker on the field.

The first time I met Jacko was at the business premises of the then Souths first-grade coach, Bob McCarthy. Jacko was just 18, up from the Gold Coast, but he explained how much he was looking forward to being my centre partner that year. I liked his confidence, and soon grew to enjoy his football ability (and sense of fun) as well.

Meninga

I couldn't believe it. My first reaction was to curse the great injustice of it all. But soon self-pity gave way to determination, and I set about concentrating on getting back on the field.

In the meantime, I helped our new coach in any way I could, and at the same time studied the way he went about things. I couldn't help but be impressed. Tim was in a no-win situation when he first came to the club in 1988. We had made the grand final for the first time the previous year and the only way up for our new coach was to go one better. He was under enormous pressure and, to make matters harder for him, it seemed the Raiders' camp was blighted by a dreadful run of severe injuries.

However, for a while things were looking good. The boys' 39–15 round 14 defeat of Balmain was their ninth of the season. This was the first occasion a Raiders' first-grade side had ever beaten the Tigers. I made my return the following week, against Newcastle at Seiffert, and from the opening kick-off, when the Knights booted the ball straight to me and I brought it back to the halfway line, things went smoothly. I scored a try and kicked five goals in an impressive 30–12 victory. The following week, we defeated the Illawarra Steelers 31–22 in Wollongong, in a game most significant for the first-grade debut of a gifted young halfback recruit from rugby union called Ricky Stuart. In round 17, I won all the Man of the Match awards in a decisive 24–8 win over St George in Queanbeyan, and then Souths were humiliated 35–2 at the Sydney Football Stadium. Rugby league experts were unanimous — the Canberra Raiders were seen as *the* team to beat.

I had missed the entire Ashes series, but such was my comeback form that I won a place for the PNG Test in Wagga on July 20, partnering Peter Jackson in the centres. The game was a great promotion for country football, but more a light-hearted romp in the park than a Test match as we piled on 14 tries in a 70–8 cakewalk. Our winning total and margin were both world records. I was just happy to be back in the green and gold, and happy to score two tries. This had been the first time I had started a Test match in the backs since the third New Zealand Test of 1985.

The following Sunday, in what many saw as a grand final rehearsal, we were beaten narrowly by Canterbury in one of the most intense club matches I have ever played. The final score was 23–16 to the Bulldogs, after we had led 12–2 just before half-time. We had to go into this game without Peter Jackson and Ivan Henjak — their injuries were a portent of things to come. Never from this point to the end of the season were we able to play a full-strength side.

The following Wednesday night, Australia played against the Rest of the World. I was in the centres, and desperate to make the most of what I saw as my genuine return to the big time. But the night was a disaster, as

Opposite: If you measure the quality of players by their enthusiasm and courage, then the Bulldogs' Terry Lamb has been one of the best players to ever lace on a boot. He's definitely the best back-up merchant I've ever seen, and he's also just about the most competitive bloke I ever ran into. He never gives up, and has always been prepared to do the work of the bigger guys as well as his own. Yet, despite this, he has played more first-grade premiership games than anyone in the history of the code.

I've always reckoned that if a player can survive in top-grade football for a long time, then he must be doing more than a few things right. This is why I reckon Terry Lamb is entitled to be ranked with the very best footballers of the modern era.

my left arm was broken again. On this occasion I moved in to tackle the tiny PNG winger Dairi Kovae, he ducked into my arm and ... I was gone. Out for the season.

I was under a deal of pressure (again!) from outside sources who pressured me to retire. The intentions of these people were honourable, even compassionate, as they believed this was for my own good, that I would do no more than keep hurting myself. Another comeback, they told me, would be foolhardy. But I never had the slightest doubt that I could make a successful return. However, I acknowledged I had to be conservative about the time I should allow the break to knit and heal. One of the major reasons I kept breaking my arm was that I was always in too much of a rush to get back into the game.

In hindsight, after the first and third break (and perhaps the second as well!) I should have given the injury another two or three weeks to heal. Had I done that, I would not have had to go through all the trauma I did.

The reason my arm broke in the same place a couple of times was because of the pressure on the screwline of the plate. After the fourth fracture, I decided to give the healing process more time. I wanted to keep playing rugby league, and felt sure my best playing days were in front of me.

Sitting beside me in the grandstand for the last few weeks of the '88 season were Ivan Henjak and Chris O'Sullivan, also finished for the year, while Jacko and Sam Backo were carrying the effects of a long, hard season. As well, a new teenage sensation, Laurie Daley, was out, injured and unlikely to make it back before the beginning of the semi-finals. Despite these hardships, the boys rallied to finish third on the competition ladder, level on points with Manly, Penrith and Balmain, but with a much superior for-and-against. In fact, the Raiders had scored 596 points during the 22 rounds, easily the most in the premiership.

Canterbury went on to win the grand final in 1988, with a 24–12 win over Balmain. However, I firmly believe that had we beaten Canterbury in the major preliminary semi-final (instead of going down to a Terry Lamb field goal kicked seven minutes from time) we would have taken out the premiership. Instead of playing Cronulla in the major semi-final, we faced a very committed Balmain team in the knock-out match. The Tigers were on a roll, having beaten the Panthers in the play-off for fifth spot and then the Sea Eagles in the minor preliminary semi. With their late-season import, Great Britain's captain Ellery Hanley, playing some extraordinary football, we knew they would be extremely difficult to overcome. And so it turned out: even with Laurie back on our side, they were too good for us, winning 14 points to 6.

Few people realise just how battered our side was by the end of that long season. The last thing I want to do is take anything away from the achievements of Canterbury and Balmain (especially the Tigers, whose gallant drive from the play-off to the grand final was quite remarkable) — however, I must acknowledge the commitment and courage showed by my club-mates.

The 1988 premiership was the one that got away. Tim Sheens maintained that the title that year was the one above all others that the Raiders should have won. Dean Lance, one of the great stalwarts of the Canberra club as a player and now as a coach, has always said that the 1988 team was the best football side he played in. When you consider he was a crucial member of our premiership-winning teams in the following two years, that speaks volumes for the quality of the '88 combination.

For 1989, Peter Jackson and Sam Backo returned to Queensland to play for the Broncos. But on the other side of the ledger, Laurie Daley and Bradley Clyde, two teenagers with precocious natural gifts, would have a year's more experience and Ricky Stuart would be more used to the ways of the professional game. And I was determined to make 1989 a personal triumph. Most people believed that as long as I survived the season without another broken arm I would be doing well.

But I wanted much more than that. I knew I had a lot to offer. Right through my football career, what I wanted above all else was to be the very best player I could possibly be. If there was a chance I could become a great of the game, then that is what I wanted to be. Despite my setbacks, nothing had changed that philosophy. Luckily for me, 1989 would be the year things began falling into place.

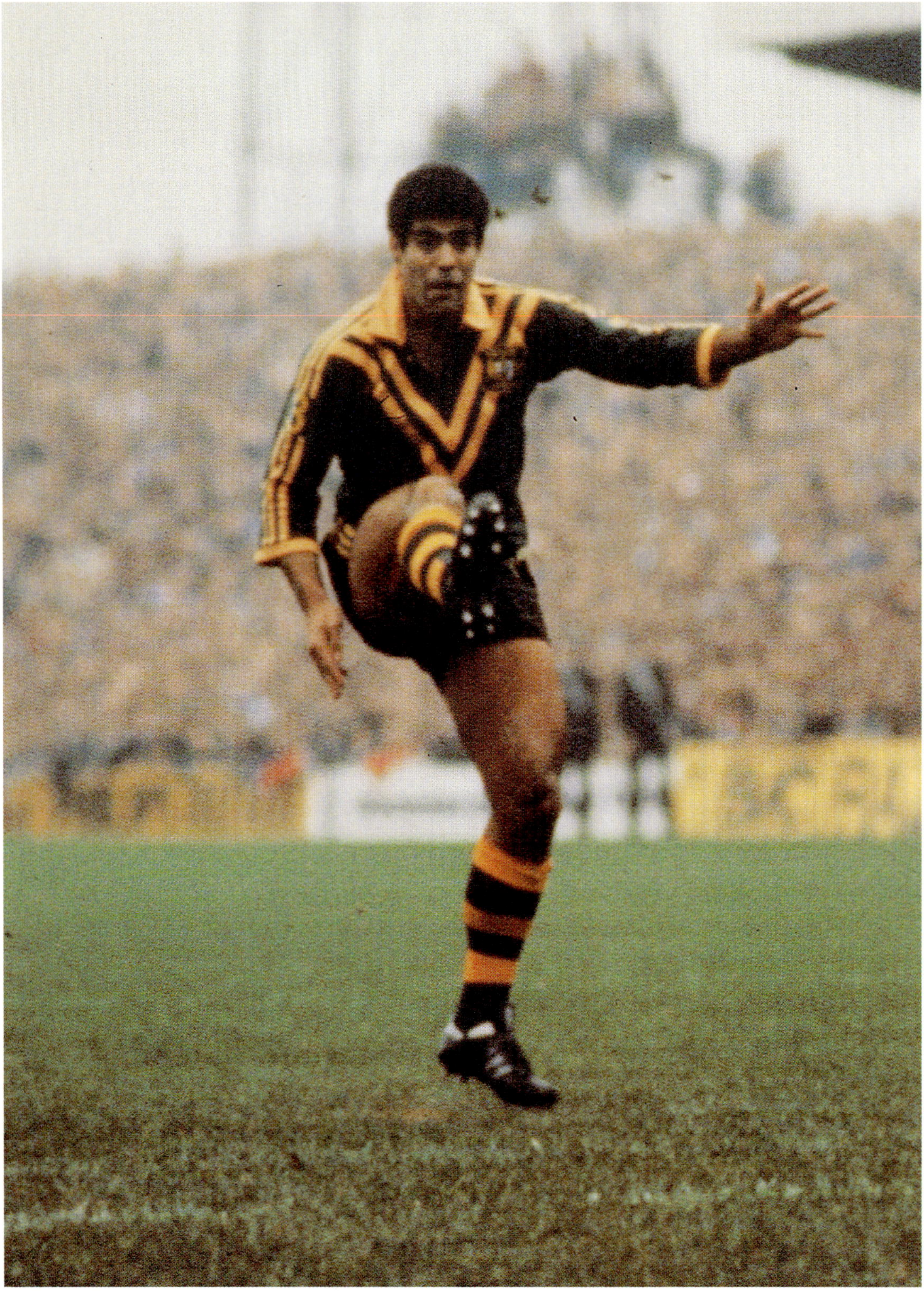

6: GREEN AND GOLD

I can still recall the thrill I felt when I was first named in an Australian Test squad. The year was 1982, and my selection as the reserve back for the first Test against New Zealand had followed Queensland's victory in the inaugural three-match State of Origin series, which we Maroons had won, two matches to one. I was one of four Queensland-based players in the 15-man squad, the others being Wally Lewis (Valleys), Rod Morris (Wynnum–Manly) and Rohan Hancock (Toowoomba). Being the reserve did not reduce my excitement at all. I appreciated being recognised, and now knew that I was on the selectors' shortlist for the Kangaroo tour scheduled for the end of the season.

The Australian centres for the first Test were two of the greats, Michael Cronin and Steve Rogers. I did not get a run in the first Test which was played in Brisbane. It was a tight match, with Australia winning narrowly 11–8, and I realised it would have been a gamble for coach Frank Stanton to put me on in such a tight and intense match.

However, a fortnight later I had my chance, after the selectors decided to give both first Test reserves — me and Parramatta's John Muggleton — an opportunity in the starting XIII. Steve and Rohan were relegated to the role of substitutes, a choice that inspired a deal of controversy in the Sydney media. Some commentators suggested that to give me a chance at the expense of such a great player as Steve Rogers was tantamount to cheapening the Test jersey. For my part, I didn't care what they thought. I was simply delighted to have the chance to play rugby league in a fair dinkum Australian Test jumper.

Unfortunately, my Test debut lasted a mere 15 minutes, when I suffered a dislocated elbow and had to leave the game. Steve came on as my replacement and played a major role as we went on to win by 20 points to two.

My ambition after this setback was to get back on the field as quickly as possible. I had my sights set on selection in the Kangaroo team, so I worked hard to get the injured elbow right. Within four weeks, I was back training and Bob McCarthy, my coach at Souths, gave me a run on the first-grade wing. He reasoned that such a move would place less stress on the elbow, and at the same time it would provide an opportunity for me to regain my confidence and get me match fit.

Opposite: One of the 21 goals I kicked during the 1982 Ashes series in England.

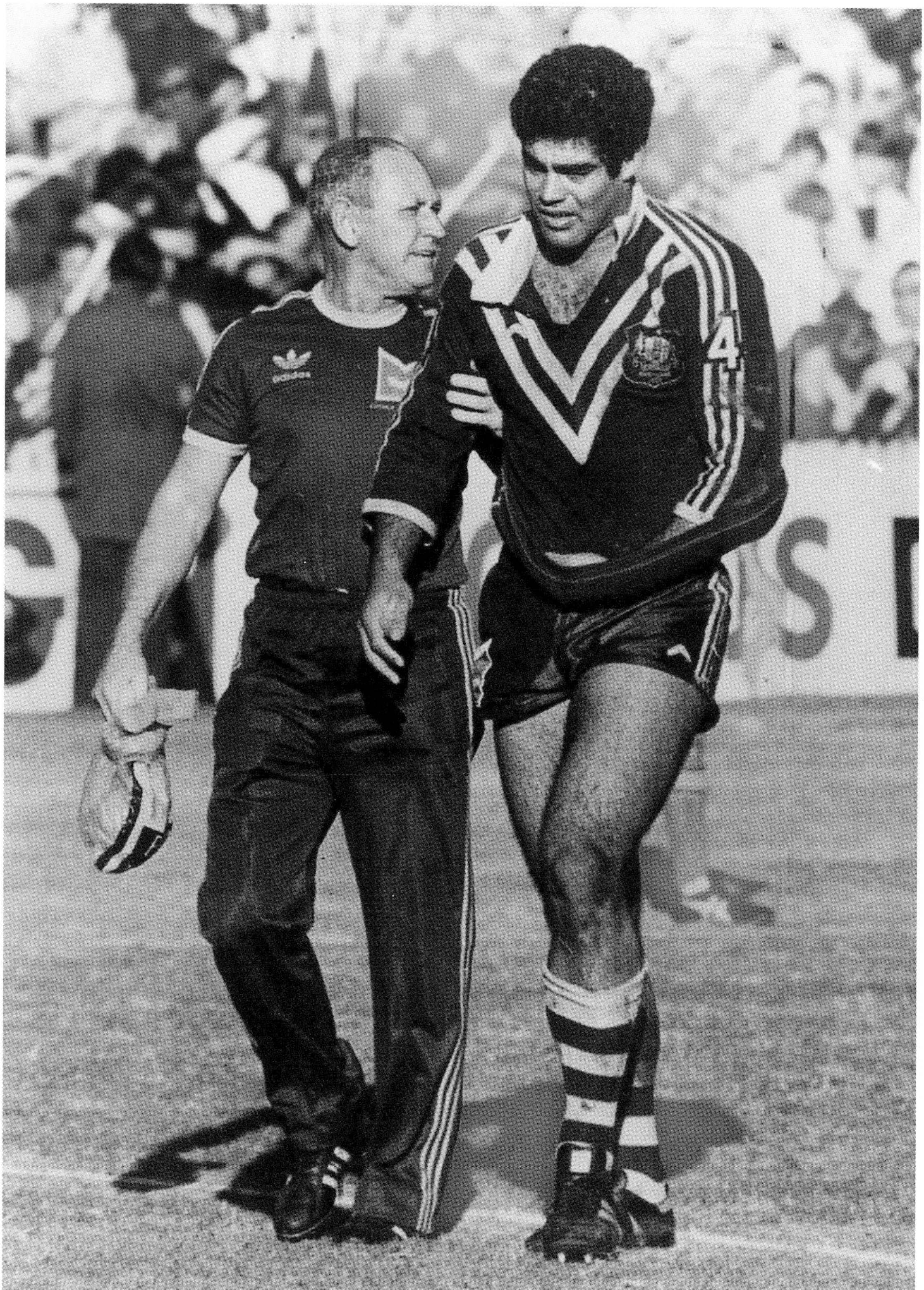

Opposite: Escorted from the SCG by trainer Alf Richards after dislocating my elbow 15 minutes into my Test debut, against New Zealand in 1982.

Left: Congratulated by the great Steve Rogers after being selected (in Steve's place) for that Test match. Later in the year, on the Kangaroo tour, I partnered Steve in the three Ashes Tests and also roomed with him throughout the trip.

Souths went all the way to the grand final in 1982, so I had every chance to regain my top fitness. Ironically, I damaged a rib cartilage in the big game (which we lost to Wynnum–Manly), but I think this actually helped my chances, because I stayed out on the field, played reasonably well and showed people I could battle through some pain. The following weekend, on the night the team was announced, there was a party at Bob's place where we had to sit out a nervous wait until the team was announced. When the names of the tourists were finally revealed, and I had been included, it was a toss-up to decide who was the most excited — Macca or me.

That great gentleman Mick Cronin had declared himself unavailable for the tour, which meant that, if the selections for the New Zealand Tests had been a guide, I was now the front-runner for the job as Rogers' centre partner, but I had plenty of opposition from class acts like Steve Ella, Gene Miles and Brett Kenny.

The Kangaroo coach Frank Stanton gave me my opportunity when he put me in the team for the one-off Test match against Papua New Guinea in Port Moresby. While half of the squad, skippered by tour vice-captain Wally Lewis, headed to Perth for a game against Western Australia, the rest of us (under the admirable and inspiring leadership of tour captain Max Krilich) were involved in the Test. With Wally away, Brett Kenny played five-eighth against PNG, with Steve Mortimer at halfback, which proved a portent of things to come in England. Frank would end up preferring the Parramatta halfback combination of Kenny and Peter Sterling in all of the Tests on tour, bar the first in France (when Wally played five-eighth, Brett moved in the centres, and I went out to the wing). This selection policy was handy for me, as it took arguably my chief rival for the second centre spot out of the equation.

As well as being my centre partner throughout that Ashes series, Steve Rogers was also my room-mate. I put "Sludge", as he is known, right up there with the best roomies of my entire career. I owe the guy a lot. He saw me as something of a young kid on the way up, and took it upon himself to look after me, on and off the field.

So I knocked around with Sludge more than anybody else on the tour, and he kept me under his wing. In those days, I was nervous and shy in the presence of the greats of the team, and I didn't know what to expect from my adventure in England. But Steve reassured me, and told me to keep my feet firmly on the ground. I'm very thankful that he did and for the fact that we've remained good mates to this day.

The Ashes Test series was a fabulous experience, but disappointing in the sense that, frankly, the quality of the opposition was not up to scratch. The British team really wasn't a great challenge, and we won the Tests easily, by 40–4, 27–6 and 32–8. France was a little tougher, if only because we were a little run-down after such a long season, but we still managed to win the two Tests comfortably, 15–4 and 23–9. After that second French Test, we had five more matches, and we won the lot, to become the first Kangaroo side to complete a tour without a defeat. Despite the often ordinary standard of our opponents, this was still quite a feat. It remains one of my proudest achievements in football that I was a member of the side that is now known as the "Invincibles".

In 1983, we had a two-Test series against New Zealand. We won the first in Auckland fairly convincingly, 16–4, but then in the return we were belted off the ground at Lang Park in Brisbane.

Looking back on the brutal second encounter, I am glad the blood bin wasn't operating in those days because at one point we would have been hard put to have even one player on the field! I'll never forget being on the ground and looking up just in time to see a flying Kiwi boot heading in the direction of my lower jaw. It didn't miss. After the game, I had stitches inserted in my chin, to complement an ugly broken nose which had been smashed by the errant elbow of an infamous New Zealand forward.

I was left out of the first Test side for the series against Great Britain in 1984, a huge disappointment after being part of the Test squad for the previous 10 internationals. This was Wally Lewis's first Test as Australian captain. The selectors preferred Brett and Gene in the centres, and picked the Canterbury and NSW goal-kicker Ross Conlon for the wing. However, this was the only Test I missed until 1986, a run that included the last two

Tests of that Ashes series and three Tests against New Zealand in 1985. We won all but one of those five games; in the last, against the Kiwis in Auckland, we played disgracefully and were embarrassed 18–0.

That Test was the occasion coach Terry Fearnley made headlines in Queensland for all the wrong reasons (for dropping four members of the Maroons State of Origin team and replacing them with players from NSW, who were then coached by Terry Fearnley). I have talked about the tension that decision caused in chapter 4, so I won't go over it again here, except to say that on that tour I wasn't a witness to any problems between the players. Most of the tension evolved from an apparent feud between captain Wally Lewis and the coach.

In the next three years, I was involved in just five Test matches (out of a possible 14), and only in two of them — against Papua New Guinea in Port Moresby in 1986 and Parkes in 1988 — was I picked as a starting centre. I missed the three Tests against New Zealand in 1986 (Brett and Gene were back and playing well), but was chosen for the PNG Test, presumably because Brett was still feeling the effects of the

Peter Sterling runs away from the scrum-base during the 1986 Kangaroo tour. Although he wasn't recognised for his running game, I saw him score some superb tries. In many ways, Sterlo was ahead of his time in the way he was able to run a game from halfback. He had astute tactical kicking abilities, and a great sense of timing.

Parramatta–Canterbury grand final that had been played a few days before. I remained the third-choice centre throughout the English leg of the tour, but (after coming on in the first two Tests as a replacement) managed to snag a second-row position for the final Ashes Test.

Manly's Noel "Crusher" Cleal and Redcliffe's courageous warhorse Bryan Niebling were the selected second-rowers for the first two Tests but, during a match against Hull six days before the third Test, Crusher broke his arm. I did have some second-row experience — both Bob McCarthy and Wayne Bennett had used me there occasionally at Souths — and I had replaced Noel and played in the forwards during the second Test. So when our coach, Don Furner, asked what I thought about starting in the second row, I jumped at the opportunity.

Noel Cleal's role was that of a mobile forward runner, working out wide or on the blind side. As a natural centre, I was equipped for that role though, ironically, Don later told me that I probably stayed too close to the centre of the action, rather than scouting wide as he would have liked. Defensively, I found it easier, but more tiring. Out in the three-quarters, in a one-on-one situation (which you very rarely get in the forwards), it is more difficult to stop your opponent effectively. I believe it is difficult, if not impossible, to put a forward in the back line and expect him to do the work of an experienced back. But what work you're expected to do in the forwards! In this respect, the life of a rugby league back is a whole lot more pleasurable.

I remember feeling a little apprehensive in the lead-up to that third Test. We had in the squad quality young forwards such as Balmain's Paul Sironen and Les Davidson of South Sydney who were aching for an opportunity to prove themselves. I must admit, after the opening ruck of the game, when I received a painful blow, I felt they were welcome to it! I had raced into position to take the first pass. Into the British forwards I charged and ... whack! ... someone or something came over the top and belted me in the head. I wasn't sure where I was, and gazed out towards the safety of the reserves bench. Get me out of here! I remember thinking, as one of the Poms yelled something to me which (roughly translated, and with expletives deleted) meant, "Good afternoon, Malcolm. Welcome to the pack!"

That was a fantastic Test match, the best Ashes clash in many years, which we finally won 24–15, to seal another 3–0 result and another undefeated run though Great Britain. Like the '82 Invincibles, the '86 side would continue their unbeaten run through France, but I have a few unhappy memories of the football side to that leg of the trip. I don't know what I did wrong as far as the tour selectors were concerned, but I didn't even get a reserve spot for either of the Tests in France.

The team management wanted me to play in the first game of the French leg of the tour, but I had to withdraw with a groin strain. Perhaps that was held against me. But even though I scored four tries in the game before the second Test in France, I could not get a look in. However, there was one advantage of being on the outer: a group of us set off to see the glamorous side to the French Riviera, including the casinos of Monte Carlo, the delights of Cannes and the style of Nice.

The highlight of my tour in 1986 had nothing to do with football. It was a phone call I received from Mum at about 11 o'clock on the night before the third Test. Deb had just given birth to our first child, a daughter, whom we named Tamika. I was so excited. As I put the phone down, I blurted out my news to my roomie, Brett Kenny. "This," he quickly decided, "is cause for celebration." News travels fast. From across the hallway came Wally Lewis and then Gary Belcher. We opted for a bottle of Blue Nun — just the right thing to toast this great event.

When that bottle was gone (and perhaps another), I decided I wanted to expand the party. Without thinking, I knocked on the nearest door, and it wasn't until our coach stuck his weary head out into the night that I realised that this might not have been the cleverest thing I had ever done. But what could I do?

"G'day, Don," I whispered. "Deb just gave a birth to a baby girl. I'm a dad!"

"Yes, well, that's great, Mal," replied the man who had brought me to the Raiders earlier in the year. "But we have a Test to play tomorrow. Get back to bed."

We did eventually go back to bed, but only after the party had continued on for a couple more hours. The next morning, I woke up a little the worse for wear from the unofficial celebrations, but still as proud as one can possibly be.

I wasted no time getting back to Australia once my football commitments were completed. While the rest of the team stayed over in Singapore, I arranged my own flight back to Australia. I wanted to see my family.

By 1989, I had become a father for the second time. Joshua was born in 1988, easily the best thing to happen to me in that two-year period when my football career was almost totally stifled by my arm injuries.

When I made it back into the Australian team that year, I appreciated the privilege more than I had in the past, and was determined to make an impression. Our rivals in '89 were New Zealand, and a whole lot of pre-series hype surrounded the clash between myself and the big Kiwi centre Kevin Iro, who had made a huge impression with the champion English club side Wigan. This was also the first opportunity for many of us to play

Above: Playing second row in the third Test in 1986. The two Australians are the men who beat me for the Test centre positions during the series, Brett Kenny (no. 3) and Gene Miles.

Opposite: There was something special about the way "Bert" Kenny played rugby league. He was one of those players who never appeared to be running fast, yet he was almost impossible to catch. Off the field, he was a really good bloke and I enjoyed rooming with him in 1986.

under the new Australian coach, Bob Fulton, and I don't think there was one player on the tour who didn't enjoy the experience. It was, without a doubt, one of the happiest Australian teams I was ever a part of.

There had been some doubt about my going to New Zealand because of a medial ligament injury. Had I been required to play as soon as we arrived, I would have been in trouble, but my first match (the first Test, in Christchurch) wasn't until 10 days into the trip, by which time I was sufficiently recovered to get through the 80 minutes, albeit with the aid of a pain-killing injection.

That Test, which we won comfortably, 26–6, was a great experience. It was played at the city's 1974 Commonwealth Games venue, the QEII Stadium, so the playing field was surrounded by a 400-metre athletics track. The combination of a bright sunny day, the crowd being a long way from the action and a dominant performance by our forwards made us backs feel as if there were plenty of wide open spaces out there. Iro tried hard to make an impression, but we were in control of the game from just about the opening whistle.

GREEN AND GOLD

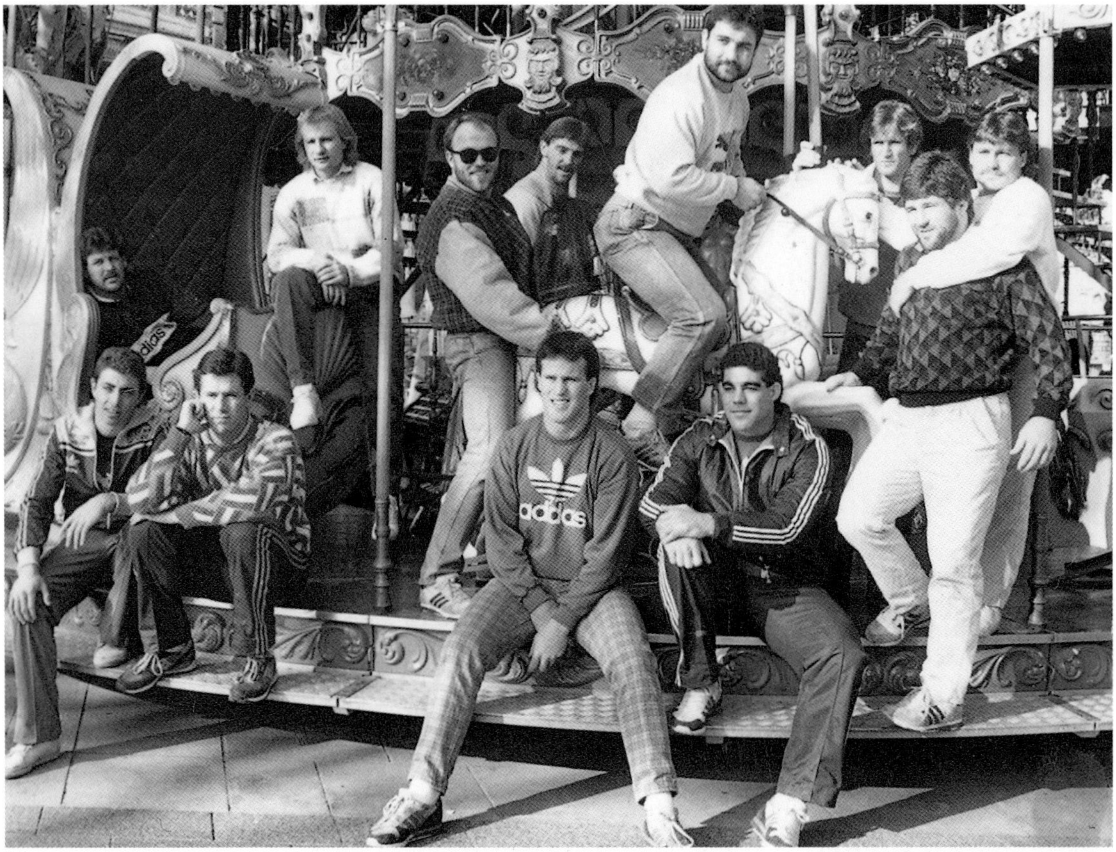
adidas

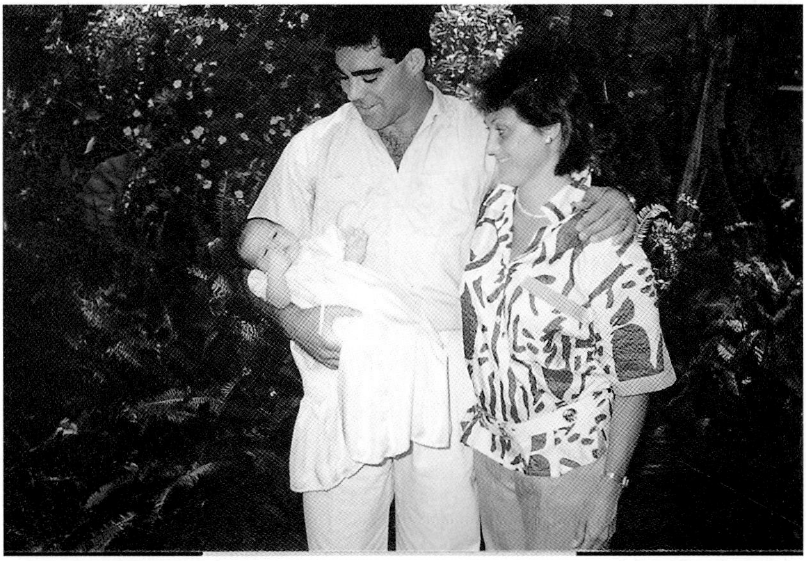

The second Test, played a week later in Rotorua, attracted a 26,000 crowd and was a very different experience from the first. The day was overcast, the field muddy and the fans were right on top of us. Strangely, there were many in the crowd who wanted an Australian victory. But then, Rotorua has a large Maori population and there were a lot of Pakehas in the New Zealand team.

It was a pretty ordinary game, and replacement halfback Des Hasler's entry into the game after half-time proved the difference. We won 8–0.

Before the third Test, Bob Fulton asked me to play in the second row. Paul Sironen had a damaged ankle. Fortunately, things worked out okay. I scored the first try and then, with eight minutes left, set up the match-winner for Bradley Clyde who, at just 19, was making his first Australian tour. Brad's try made the final score 22–14, and was the last instalment in a fabulous trip for the young Raider, who was later judged the player of the tour.

After the game, there was a confrontation of sorts in the Australian dressing-room after the former Australian lock forward Ray Price ventured into the room. Ray, who was working for the media, had had some pretty negative words to say about the Australian forwards. So when he was spotted in the room, one or two of the boys were quick to point out that the series had just been won 3–0 (the first time an Australian side had swept a series in New Zealand). It was a bit crazy, really. Having been a great player himself, Ray should have known better than to bag footballers in the way he did.

That third Test in New Zealand was the last time I would play for Australia without the responsibility of the captaincy. My international record to this point amounted to 22 Tests, each one of which I was extremely proud. At this stage in my life I could have had no idea, or any expectation, that in fact my Test career was not even half over. Or that I would soon be elevated to the captaincy. Wally Lewis was entrenched in that job. But then, in a Broncos' match against St George in late June 1990, Wally shattered his left arm. A Test against France was less than a week away — the match in which Wally was scheduled to equal the legendary Clive Churchill's record figure of 24 Tests as Australia's captain. With our captain suddenly unavailable, I was called into the void, fully aware of the great irony of a broken arm being the reason for my elevation. At this point, I saw myself as a stopgap, to keep the job only until Wally's return.

However, in rugby league, as in life itself, things do not always turn out the way we expect them to.

Opposite: Two photos from 1986: (Top) With a collection of Kangaroos in France. The other guys are (left to right): Greg Alexander (in front), Gene Miles, Steve Folkes, Peter Sterling, Wally Lewis, Brett Kenny (at back), Paul Langmack, Bryan Niebling, Des Hasler, Royce Simmons and Terry Lamb. (Below) Debbie and me with our daughter, Tamika, who was born while I was in England, on the eve of the third Test.

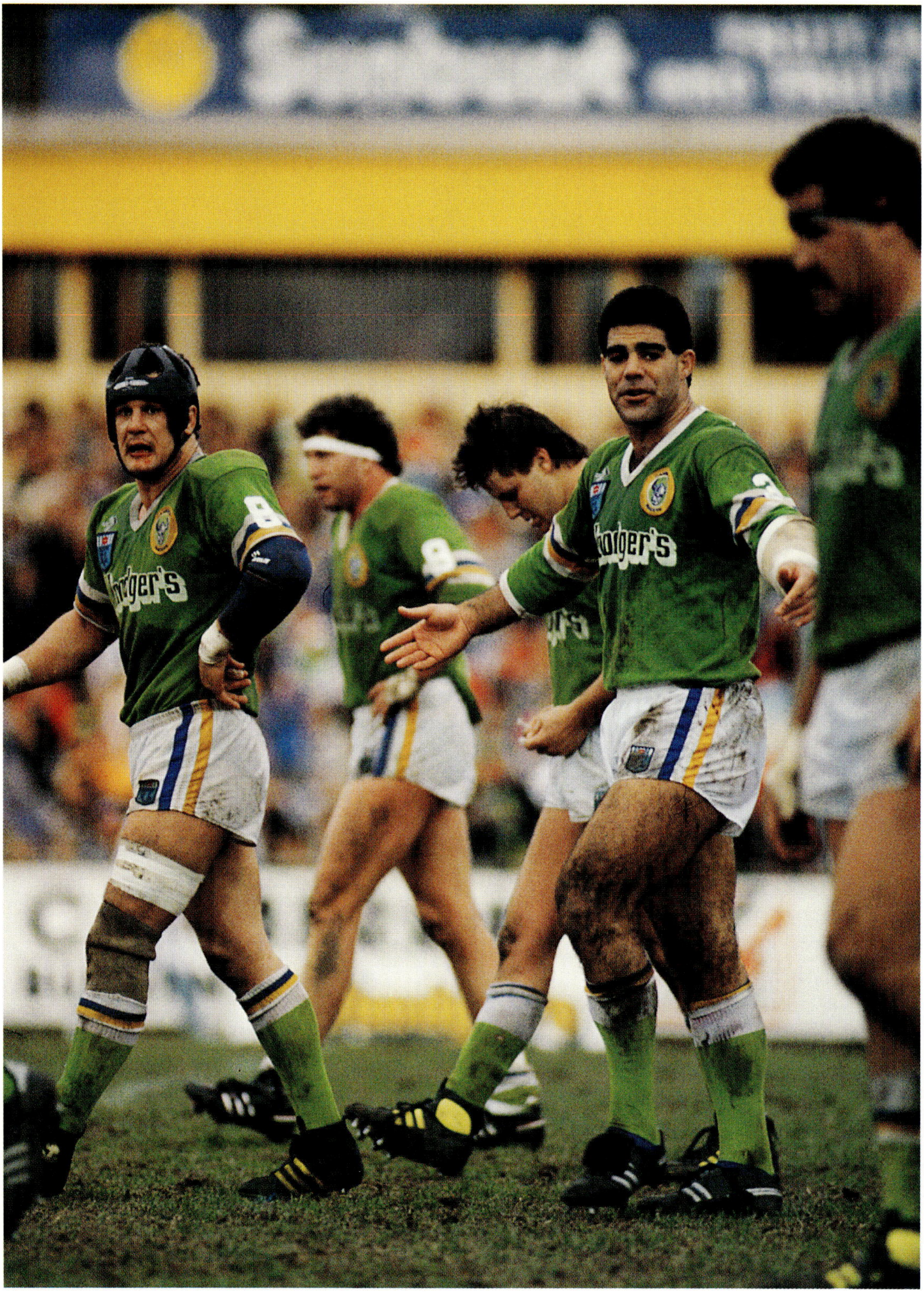

7: CHAMPIONS!

My comeback to football in 1989 did not begin until the sixth round of the premiership, and then as a fresh reserve. I really wasn't supposed to be playing in that round either but our scheduled Sunday meeting with Illawarra was postponed because the Wollongong Showground was waterlogged. Officials decided to transfer the game to Seiffert on the following Tuesday (Anzac Day), and I decided this was the time to take my place on the subs' bench. The plan was to give me something like 20 minutes at the end, but Laurie Daley was hurt and had to come off after 32 minutes, so I ran on and stayed almost to the end, when I was replaced by Chris Houghton. It wasn't a bad Raiders reserves line-up that day. Sitting next to me in a tracksuit was Gary Belcher, who had hurt himself in the opening round and hadn't played since.

We thumped the Steelers 44–8 — our fourth straight win (including a 34–4 thrashing of defending premiers Canterbury in round 5) after a poor start to the season. I feel sure there was more than one cynic expecting me to stagger to the sideline at some stage clutching at my arm, but I didn't let such a thought enter my head. I was nervous, sure, and more than a bit apprehensive. But I knew that I'd taken every single precaution possible this time and my doctors had assured me that the chances of the bone breaking again were remote, so I just forgot about it and headed for the heat of the battle. From that time on, I have not had the slightest problem with my arm.

Our next three games brought three more wins, over Saints, Manly and Parramatta, before the Knights beat us at Newcastle (always a difficult place to play), just five days after the first State of Origin match of the season. That inter-state clash, a resounding 36–6 victory for the Maroons, had been my first Origin match since 1986. I was one of seven Raiders involved in the match; Gary Belcher, Gary Coyne, Laurie Daley, John Ferguson, Bradley Clyde and Glenn Lazarus were the others.

After that defeat at Newcastle, Dean Lance lost his first-grade position to Craig Dimond, son of the former great Test winger Peter Dimond. Tim handed me the captaincy for our next game, against Penrith at Penrith Park. This was the first time I had ever led the Raiders, and I started with a loss, 16–6 in dreadful conditions.

The cheekbone injury I suffered in the second Origin match kept me

Opposite: A rare shot of me wearing a Raiders jumper in 1988 (because of my arm problems, I played a grand total of five matches). The other players are (left to right): captain Dean Lance, Grant Ellis, Glenn Lazarus and Sam Backo.

Above: In the dressing-room with Gary Belcher after surviving my first game back after the fourth broken arm.

Opposite: Post-match interviews completed, I head up the Sydney Football Stadium tunnel after the Raiders' 32–16 victory over Souths in the '89 preliminary final.

out of the Raiders' next match so, with Dean still in reserves, Gary Belcher took over as skipper. I was back for the next match, a shock loss at home to an Ellery Hanley-inspired Wests, but I missed the next game because of injury. With Badge and me, as well as Bradley Clyde and Brent Todd in New Zealand for a three-match Test series, Tim brought Dean back into first grade, as captain. However, when we returned home, I was given back the job, even though Dean was now back to playing at his best and as such assured of his place in the forward pack.

The representative season, with several key players missing, almost brought us undone in 1989 and people were starting to call us the Canberra Faders. Between May 23, the date of the first Origin fixture, and July 23, the date of the final Test of the series in New Zealand, the Raiders won only two of eight matches! And one of those was against Brisbane, the one club which had suffered as much as we had from the demands of inter-state and international football. We needed to win our last five matches to force our way into the finals and, fortunately, we did.

Champions!

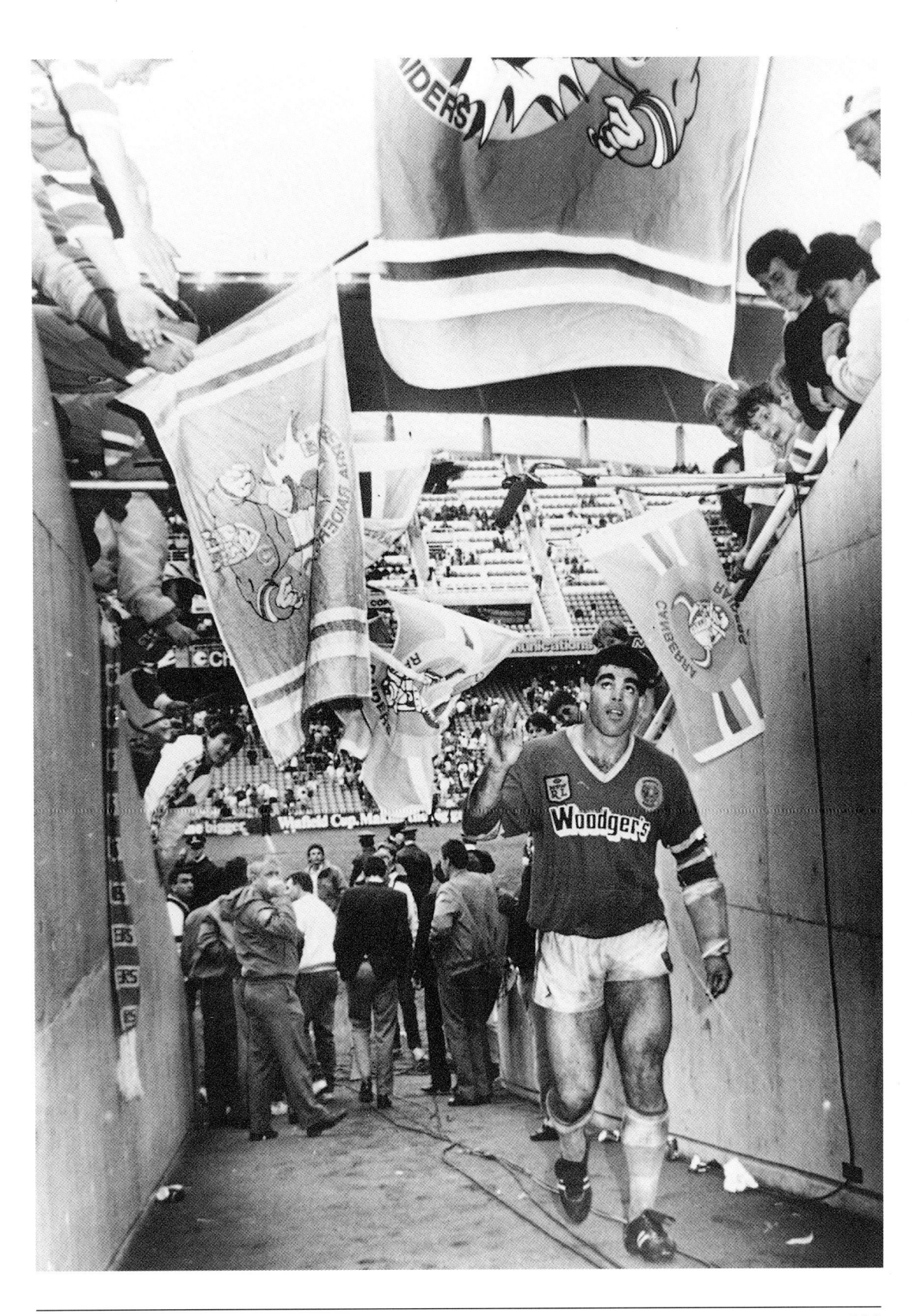

However, on top of these wins, we still needed to achieve four consecutive knock-out matches if we wanted to be premiers. This had never been done since the semi-finals had been expanded to include five teams in 1973. In fact, no team had won from fourth since the mighty Souths had achieved what was thought to be impossible in 1955. Looking on the positive side, we had played some terrific football in the final few rounds, and were highly confident we could go all the way. We were never cocky, but we all shared an inner belief that the Raiders could win the premiership.

In the minor preliminary semi-final we defeated Cronulla 31–10. (The Sharks had knocked the Broncos out of the premiership in a play-off for fifth four days earlier.) Then we edged out Penrith 27–18 in the minor semi-final, in what was probably our worst performance of the final two months of the season. We led 10–2 midway through the first half, and then 11–2 after Ricky Stuart snapped a field goal just before half-time. However, instead of killing the Panthers off, we went to sleep, and they fought back after the break to lead 12–11. Fortunately, this turnaround sparked us into action, and we piled on 16 points in 22 minutes to seal our spot in the final.

Our opponents there were Souths, a young side who had responded magnificently to the urges of their coach, the Rabbitoh stalwart George Piggins, and won their first minor premiership since 1971. For this famous club it was a return to the glory days. However, in the major semi-final they had gone down narrowly to our nemesis of the year before, Balmain. The clash (and the grand final a week later) was a reflection of the way modern rugby league was heading — the proud old team, representing a tiny part of the inner-city of Sydney and with traditions dating back to the very birth of the game, up against the young punks from out of town with little history to speak of but bearing the support of an entire city.

The game was a beauty. We led 10–0 after just six minutes, but by half-time the Rabbitohs had clawed their way back to 12–all. A Chris O'Sullivan converted try made it 18–12, then Souths captain Mario Fenech crossed for 18–16. A place in the grand final was in the balance, a place we wanted desperately. With eight minutes to go, Badge Belcher crossed for his 16th try of the season. Three minutes to go ... and Glenn Lazarus scored. The final score was 32–16. For only the third time since 1973, a side had reached the grand final from fourth or fifth position on the final competition table.

After our experiences over the previous two seasons, we felt we had every right to be there. The disappointments of 1988 had sharpened our focus. And after what happened in the lead-up to the '87 decider this time we made sure there wasn't too much razzamatazz. We completed the bulk of our media commitments early in the week and made sure that when we trained, we trained properly.

The hours before kick-off on the big day were a revelation. I remember vividly that when we went out on the field for the coin toss to decide who would kick off, about an hour before the 3.00 p.m. start, Tigers captain Wayne "Junior" Pearce was palpably nervous. I was amazed at how apprehensive he was. In contrast, I was very calm and confident. I knew we were going to play well.

I thought to myself, we've got these blokes. If their captain is this jittery, how must the others be feeling.

At half-time we trailed 12–2, yet I felt we were the better side. Their first try, to winger James Grant, had come from an intercept. Their second was a superb four-pointer to Paul Sironen, but had featured a wicked bounce of a kick-through that sent the ball in just about the only direction Gary Belcher didn't have covered. Despite the scoreboard, I believed we had a great chance of winning.

Tim Sheens was very calm and positive when he addressed the team at half-time. He stressed that if we stuck to our game plan and continued to play as well as we had, we would wear them down. He told us we had been playing excellent football, and that we were going better than our opponents.

The last thing he said to us before we went out was that we would win the game. I did no more than back up what Tim had said. This grand final, I told the team, would come down to commitment and self-belief. This was a game where a player would either make a name for himself or not.

The individuals who get out there and perform under these circumstances are the ones I term champions. For the remainder of that famous afternoon, as we brought ourselves back into the game and finally won in extra time, the Canberra Raiders proved beyond the slightest doubt that they were an unbeatable combination. In the long history of NSWRL premiership grand finals, no team had fought back from a 10-point deficit and won. Until 1989.

We played brilliant football in the second half. We also had that little bit of luck that had deserted us in the first 40 minutes. This was never more evident than with just six minutes remaining in normal time. With the score 14–8 to the Tigers (Badge had scored a converted try in the 55th minute, and the Tigers' English import Andy Currier had landed a penalty not long after), Benny Elias, the Balmain hooker, tried to kick a field goal. But it bounced off the cross-bar and dropped back into the field of play. What's the width of a cross-bar? That's how close defeat was!

Our biggest moment of inspiration had come earlier in the second half. Balmain's outstanding Test prop Steve "Blocker" Roach rampaged

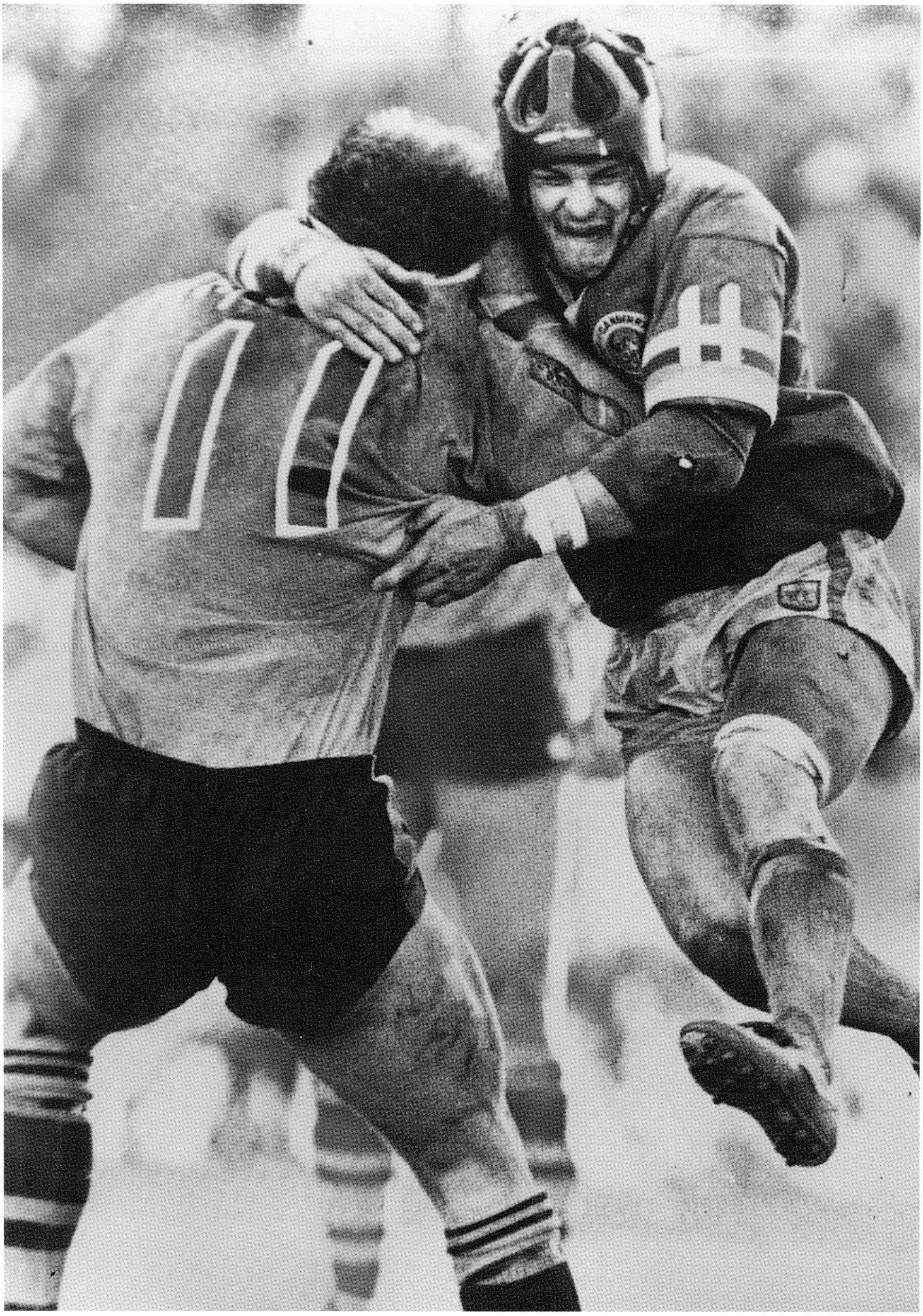

towards the goal-line. There was nothing subtle about the big man's approach — on he came, as straight as possible, as hard as possible. But as this seemingly irresistible force charged at our line he ran into an immovable object by the name of Lance. Dean Lance. Suddenly Roach was an irresistible force no more. It was the first time I had ever seen Blocker stopped stone-dead in his tracks. I'm sure his pride was hurt — and quite possibly his ribs as well — but one thing I will never forget was the way he reacted to that extraordinary tackle. He made no wild gesture, there were no ludicrous histrionics, just an unobtrusive but sincere pat on Deano's back to acknowledge what was a great moment in the history of rugby league defence.

There has been much discussion over the years about the decision by the Balmain coach Warren Ryan to replace Blocker in the second half. With 15 minutes remaining, Ryan took the big prop out of the game and replaced him with the noted defender Kevin Hardwick. Blocker couldn't believe it. Ryan's strategy was to close the game out by having his best defensive unit on the paddock, something for which he has been roundly criticised. Yet, in my opinion, he did the right thing. He put on a fresh defensive player with the intention of stopping us from scoring. We were on a march for much of that second half, and always looked likely to cross the Tigers' try-line. Ryan, shrewd coach that he is, was attempting to stem the tide. But, unluckily for him, his tactical change didn't bring the result he wanted.

Then, with about three minutes left, Ryan decided to replace Paul Sironen with another tough defender, Michael Pobjie. But while Pobjie was waiting on the sideline, Chicka Ferguson scored his magic late try to level the scores. The substitution still had to be made, as the touch judge had been notified about the switch. At full-time, Ryan made another change, taking Pobjie off and bringing on the acclaimed attacker, Englishman Shaun Edwards, who had an unhappy time that season, spending most of it in the reserves.

I'm not even sure if Pobjie touched the ball. But I am certain that Warren Ryan would have liked Paul Sironen on the field once the game was tied. As it turned out, circumstances had worked against him.

For myself, I have no doubt that no matter what Ryan did, we would still have won.

Thankfully, Chicka managed to score his try adjacent to the posts. I was the goal kicker who had to land the goal to send the match into extra time. I'm not sure I would have wanted to try and make such a pressure kick from out near the sideline.

We were never going to be beaten in extra time. Just two minutes into the first period, Garry Jack, the Tigers' impressive fullback, dropped a

Opposite: Dean Lance collars Balmain's Paul Sironen in the 1989 grand final. A similar tackle by Dean on the Tigers' Test prop, Steve Roach, the impact of which echoed around the ground, was one of the most important single moments of the game.

straightforward catch near his own goal-line. As I tried to decide which attacking move we would mount from the resulting scrum, five-eighth Chris O'Sullivan strolled over and told me he was going to kick a field goal. My first reaction was that that was a ridiculous idea. We had six tackles in their quarter, ample time to try and cross their line. Or, if we didn't, then we could think about getting Ricky Stuart (our drop goal specialist) into position to give us the lead. But Chris wanted to get in front as soon as possible, and the ultra-confident look on his face told me to let him have his way. Sometimes you have to trust your instincts. Chris's instincts said go for the point, and my instinct was to trust him.

We won the scrum, Ricky fired the ball back to Chris and he kicked the one-point as if this was a practice session in the local park.

We were ahead, by just one point on the scoreboard. Psychologically, though, we were a mile in front, and pulling further away by the minute.

The Tigers rarely threatened our line for the remainder of the match. And as the match approached its 100th and final minute, our replacement prop Steve Jackson scored the try of his life, taking a squad of Tigers over the line with him as he made an inspired 20-metre charge to the line. The final score was 19–14 to the Raiders.

The emotions displayed after the game were memorable, heartfelt and desperately cruel in their contrast to the devastation of the Balmain players. The image of Junior's exhausted face of anguish is one that will stay with me for ever. He had yearned for that precious victory just as much as I had. Across the ground, weary Tigers sat silently amid the Raiders' celebrations, scarcely believing what had happened to them. I was in tears, my football career at its absolute peak so soon after it had appeared shattered by that series of arm breaks.

The crowds of people at Canberra airport when we returned to the ACT were colossal, but nothing compared to the reception we received at our Mawson club — here, around 10,000 people waited for us and we partied into the night. Then we moved on to Queanbeyan Leagues Club, where another 5,000 to 6,000 fans helped us to celebrate some more. All up, the party continued on for about three days.

In all that time I could not buy one drink; none of the players could. The only money I spent in 72 hours was $5 for some Kentucky fried chicken. For an entire week, people around town continued to invite us to have drinks with them or to share a meal. The whole experience showed just how much the Canberra supporters relished our win, and how much they appreciated the identity the Raiders had given them. It was a flashback to my days in St Helens in 1984–85, when the team I was then a part of was able to give the citizens of that great little town some victories to savour. By 1989, the Raiders were an integral part of the ACT. The

CHAMPIONS!

The 1989 premiership-winning Raiders. Back row (left to right): Dean Lance, Craig Bellamy, Gary Belcher, Ashley Gilbert, Paul Martin, Laurie Daley. Third row: John Ferguson, Wayne Collins, Mark Lowry, Matthew Wood, Gary Coyne. Second row: Shaun McRae (trainer), Mark Bell, Bradley Clyde, Chris Houghton, Glenn Lazarus, Steve Jackson, Brent Todd, Tim Sheens (coach). Front row: Ricky Stuart, Chris O'Sullivan, Kevin Walters, Mal Meninga, Steve Walters, Phil Carey, Ivan Henjak.

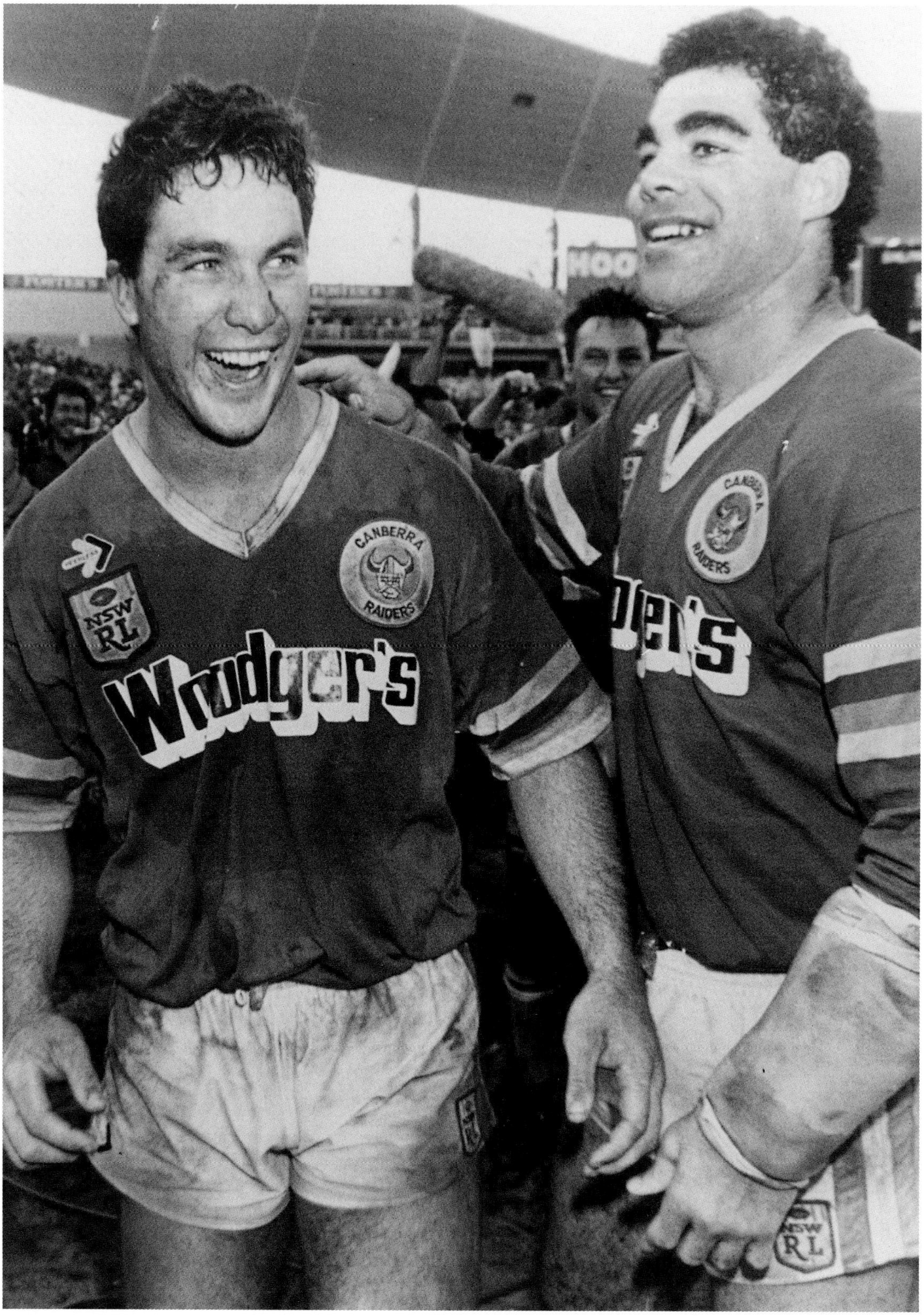
Woodger's
CANBERRA
RAIDERS
NSW
RL

Champions

Scenes following the '89 grand final.

Opposite: With a very happy Clive Churchill medal-winner, Bradley Clyde.

Above: Sharing the moment with Dean Lance, the man I replaced as first-grade captain.

Left: Some of the guys with the J.J. Giltinan Shield: (left to right) Laurie Daley, Chris O'Sullivan, John Ferguson (and his children), Glenn Lazarus, Steve Walters, Tim Sheens and Matthew Wood.

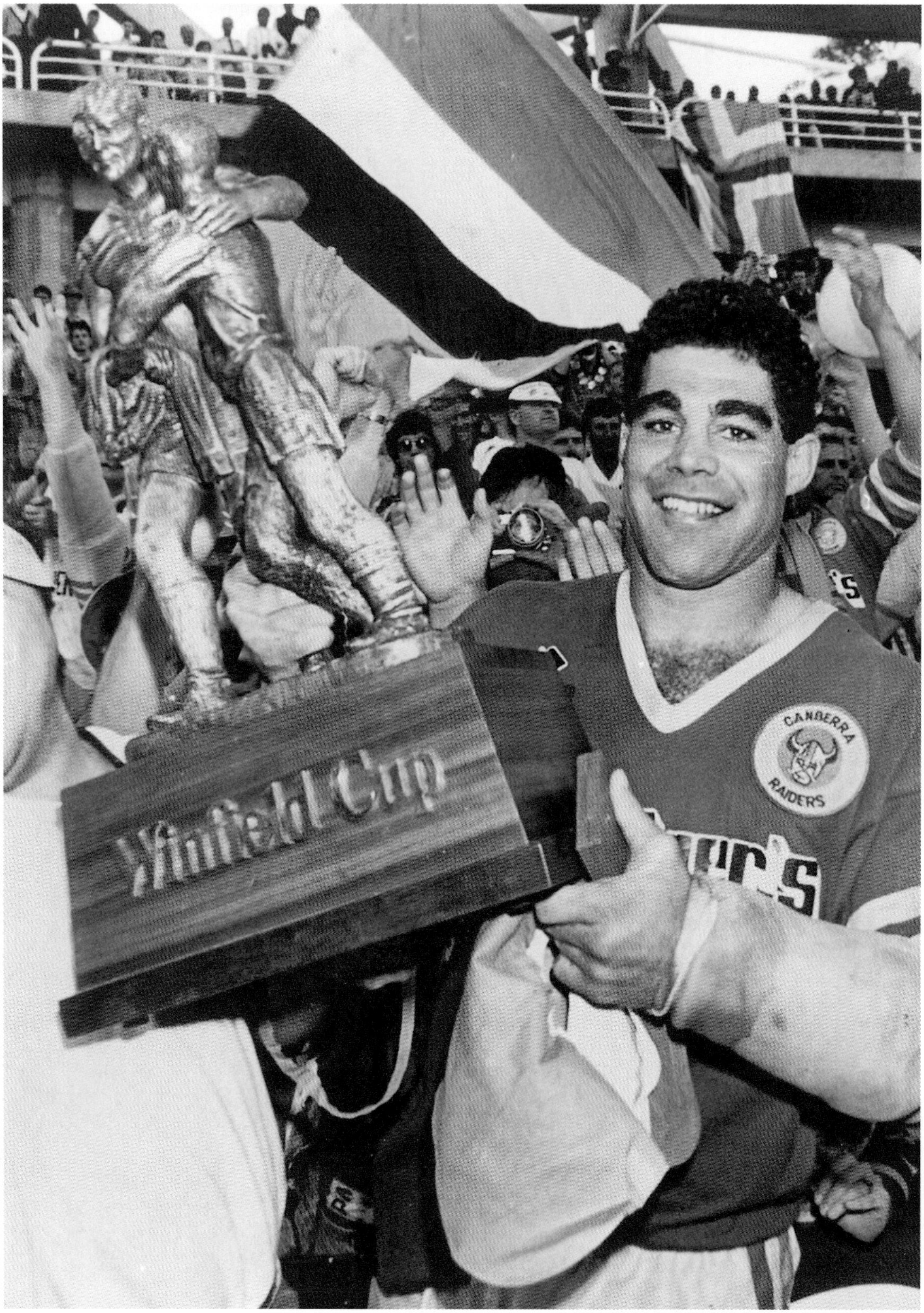
Winfield Cup
CANBERRA
RAIDERS

people were proud of their team, and we were proud of them.

Before I leave that famous time in the Raiders' history, there is one other fact I would like to underline. I have watched tapes of that match many, many times and I am always amazed at the speed of the game. It was without doubt one of the quickest games I ever played in. I can remember when State of Origin football was first deemed the state of the art. In the early and mid '80s, there was no shortage of commentators who kept insisting that State of Origin football was a step up in standard from first-grade. Origin matches, we were told, were the ultimate in speed and intensity.

Yet, if you compare the '89 grand final to one of the early Origin games, the Canberra–Balmain classic was 10 times quicker. In a very short space of time, the standard of first-grade football increased dramatically, right up to the level of Origin football. Today, there is no doubt that first-grade matches between the top-rated clubs are the equal of anything produced in inter-state clashes.

Above: Showing most of the Winfield Cup to the people of Canberra. The towel was necessary because the base of the trophy had parted company with the statue of Norm Provan and Arthur Summons during the post-match celebrations.

Opposite: Near the end of our victory lap after the grand final. The satisfied smile, though, lasted for many days.

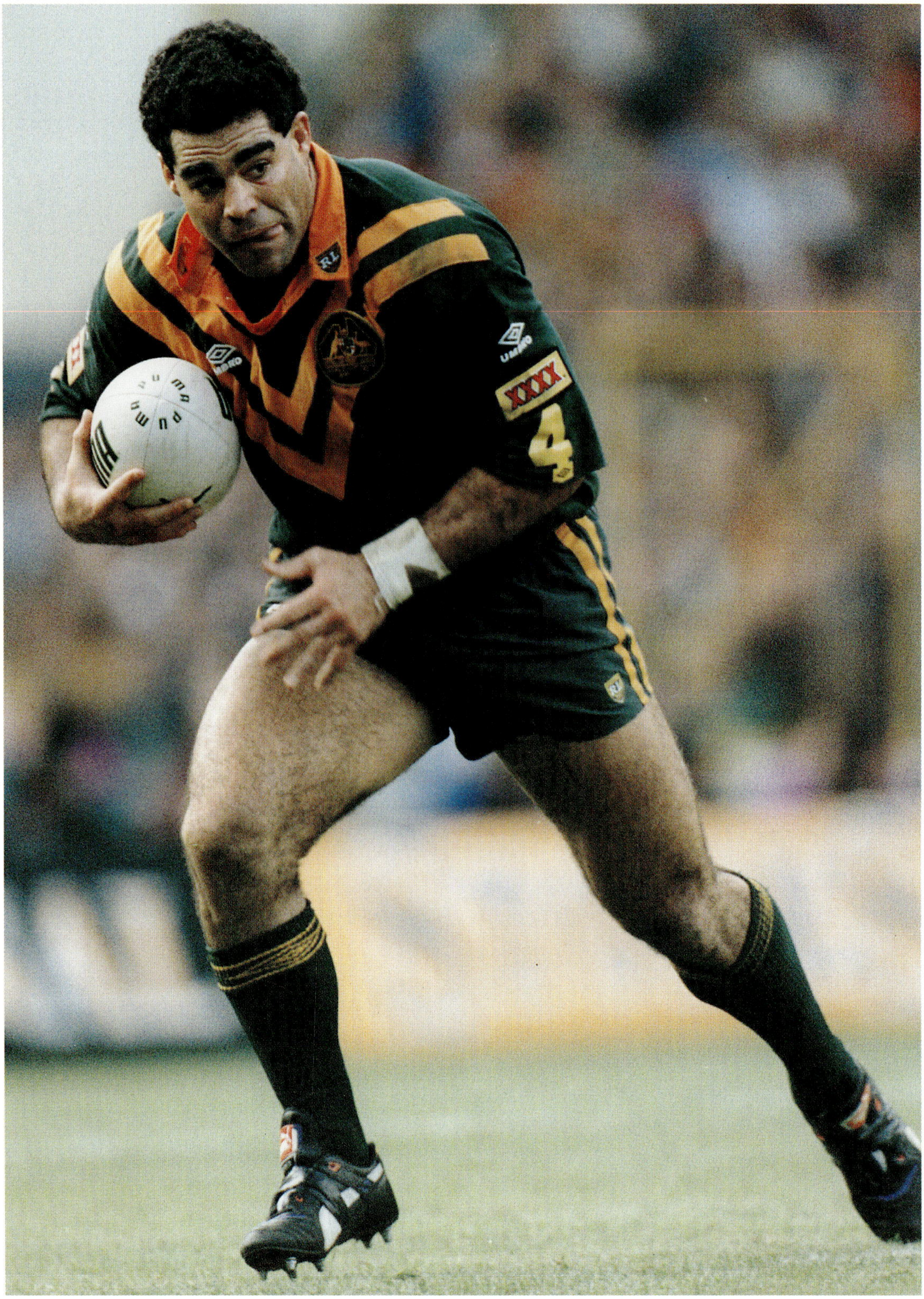
XXXX
4

8: THE WINNING EDGE

The recipe for success in life and in football depends on a number of ingredients — talent, luck and a lot of hard work. Success does not just happen in life or in football. You have to be prepared to meet the challenges and, if you have a bit of luck, you need to grab the opportunity and make the most of it.

My luck started when I was born into a family that enjoyed sport. Both my parents were very talented sports people. Dad was an outstanding rugby league player and my mother was a fine sportswoman who was very good at a variety of sports and outstanding in athletics. As a girl, she competed in school and state titles.

I believe the combination of having two parents with sporting talent, and then the good fortune to be introduced to the game at an early age, helped to foster what football talent I had.

Talent is bred into you. You can't train talent and I believe if any sports person or business person has talent, it is up to that individual to utilise and expand it. It is critical to recognise what you are good at and to work towards your goal with the particular talent you have. I was fortunate at an early age to recognise that I had the potential to be a very good rugby league player.

Obviously, there are a lot of things that can happen along the way. There can be injuries and bad luck and not getting the right breaks. If you can get through your career without too many injuries, you are one of the luckiest people in sport, particularly a sport like rugby league that has such heavy contact.

In my playing career, I suffered four breaks to my arm but it wasn't that big a deal. I knew I was going to come back and play football, I was never going to give the game away. At no stage did I even consider not playing again. My injuries were just a series of unfortunate incidents and I believe I came back a little too early on three occasions. The last time I broke my arm, I had learned my lesson and I made sure I gave myself plenty of time to recover. I then played for another six years without any worries.

Those injuries made me appreciate the game and become aware of my passion for football. I became mentally stronger, more determined, more committed and more conscious of the fact that I had to work hard

Opposite: World Cup final, 1992.

Every club I have played for has featured a number of representative players, and inevitably these are the men who attract most of the publicity. This, I have always believed, is a little unfair, as it means that the "tradesmen" in the team rarely get the attention they deserve. On this and the next two pages are photographs of just five Canberra Raiders who are perfect examples of players who rarely won the headlines afforded to stars such as Laurie Daley, Bradley Clyde and Ricky Stuart, but who all made telling contributions to the development of the club.

Chris O'Sullivan (right), played 204 first-grade games for the Canberra Raiders between 1982 (the club's inaugural season) and 1992. Sully was a genuine stalwart in those early years, playing consistently good football despite being part of a struggling side. That he battled through those difficult seasons to become an important part of our premiership success in 1989 and 1990 is testimony to his ability and his never-say-die character.

Sully often played halfback for the Raiders, and many times his five-eighth was Craig Bellamy (opposite). In all, Craig played 148 first-grade games over 10 seasons with the

to leave the game the way I wanted to leave it — as good a footballer as I could possibly be.

At the time I suffered the breaks, I was probably a good player running around and having a fair bit of success. But after those injuries I think I became a better player. I trained harder than I had ever trained in my life. I put in three hours a day and I enjoyed it.

I was lucky in my career — my father was a good coach and taught me the basics and then, when I was ready to move from junior football to first grade at Southern Suburbs, Wayne Bennett was there.

At that time there were players leaving the club and I was able to come in and take their place — I didn't have to wait on the backburner or in reserve grade to come through. I was thrown in at the deep end from the start. The next challenge was representative football. In the right place at the right time again, I was lucky enough to play first-grade when there were spots available in the Queensland team. So I represented my state in my first year.

My father was a great coach. He taught me how to pass, to tackle effectively, to kick properly and to be a good sportsman. He was firm, but not overbearing. If I came off the field crying or with a long face he would kick my butt and put me back on again. Early guidance from parents and coaches is important, but the worst thing that can happen to any youngster in any area is to have pushy people in the background.

As I've said, goal-setting has been an important ingredient in my success and under the guidance of Wayne Bennett I started setting goals

Raiders, in a variety of positions, including five-eighth, centre and lock.

It was men such as Craig and Chris, and captain Dean Lance and second-rower Ashley Gilbert (next page), who made my original transfer south to Canberra so comfortable. They were quality football professionals who realised that new acquisitions would help the club. They were also quality blokes, whose camaraderie and support made the move into a new environment a rewarding experience.

Our respect for Ashley Gilbert was such that we all took a pay cut in 1990 so that salary-cap restrictions wouldn't force him out of the club. He had been fighting for the Raiders since day one and we needed him to continue at least a little bit longer.

*The third man in the photograph with Dean (left) and Ashley (right) is second-rower Gary Coyne, a Queenslander who came down to the Raiders in 1986, the year Gary Belcher, Steve Walters and I also ventured south. His most publicised day for the Raiders came in 1991, when he scored four tries in a semi-final win over Manly. And a few weeks later, he was selected to play for Australia. This was a great and deserved reward for **(continued on next page ...)***

*(... from previous page)
a man who had toiled in the background for many years, but whose work had always been greatly appreciated by his comrades.*

Playing representative football is a great privilege, and one that I treasured. But winning a premiership with my close mates was the rugby league experience I rated highest. These were the guys who I trained with, socialised with and played football with week after week after week. To share the glory of a grand final triumph with them was as good as it can get.

when I was 16. When we were preparing for a match at the Police Academy, we used to write down our goals and this helped us to mentally prepare for our games — I don't want to make a bad pass ... I don't want to miss a tackle — simple things to help us play better. Perhaps you'd missed a couple of tackles in your last game so that would be one area to concentrate on: your target this time is not to miss ONE tackle.

Though it is easy to write that down on a piece of paper, realistically you have to be more specific and think about why and how you missed those tackles. Perhaps your leg drive is not as strong as it should be, or you are not using your shoulder or not wrapping your arms firmly enough about your opponent, or your head positioning is not good enough. You need to analyse these things and then pinpoint the problem area in your defence work.

You should also think about longer term goals. When I was in the police force, I wanted to play for the Queensland Academy against the NSW Academy. I achieved that first step up the rugby league ladder and I just kept on going, later setting my sights on making the Queensland team. My first step towards this goal was to make the Southern Suburbs first-grade team and then to be selected for the Queensland team. Despite the doubts from some of my team-mates, I made it.

The Winning Edge

151

Previous page (clockwise from top left): Joshua and me looking our best in matching "Big Mal" T-shirts; with Joshua and Tamika after the 1994 grand final; a studio shot of the Meninga family — (from left) my mother Lee, me, Bevan, Geoff and Cameron; one of the Queensland league team's greatest fans, Jim Banaghan, with Laurie Daley at the Raiders presentation night in 1991. Jim's a top bloke, and has been associated with the Queensland Origin team for as long as I can remember; with the best man at my wedding, Peter McIlwain; Debbie's family — (from left) sisters Lynette (in front) and Brenda, her mother Gloria, father Stan, and Deb.

If you set yourself realistic goals and work towards them diligently, more often than not you will achieve them and in the process you learn the value of discipline. In matches — and in life — sometimes you make your own luck, but opportunities only come your way because you have been willing to put in the hard yards. You have to dig in and really put in the effort.

In Canberra we all dug in and everyone reached their personal goals in the grand final against Canterbury in 1994 when we all played to the best of our ability. In the end, we won easily and that is the pinnacle of goal-setting.

When you play as a team, you must have team goals as well as personal goals. If you achieve both, you are virtually unstoppable.

In the 1989 grand final against Balmain, our chances of success seemed slim at half-time. Things just did not go our way in the first half, though we were playing well individually. We were trailing 12–2. However, we were confident that if we could stick to our team goal and keep on playing well individually — as we had in the first half — things would come our way. And they did. We reached our goal with a never-to-be-forgotten grand final victory.

When I was with the Raiders, we used to have open discussions on team goals. First, the coach would suggest a team goal for the week. He would explain why we needed that particular team goal and, if the players agreed, then that was the target of the round.

The team goals varied, according to who we were up against. If we were playing a team with a good forward pack who were strong up the middle, we'd work to combat that area. We might concentrate on the gang tackles that slow the ball down and provide time to readjust. Or we might work on our defence around the rucks to make sure the attacking side didn't get to the advantage line. It all depended on how we saw the opposition. We would set our goals to counter their strengths.

I can't stress too strongly how critical self-discipline is, particularly at the professional level. What may seem humdrum, like getting to training on time, having the right gear and making sure all your equipment is in top order, is all part of the mental discipline of preparing for the game.

Goal-setting applies to training as well as matches. When you are training, discipline is especially important. Try to do your best all the time and work on minimising mistakes — ask yourself why you dropped a ball during a skill session or why you finished second or third in the sprints. If you do this, you will benefit when it's crunch time on the big day.

As team captain for the Raiders, I felt it was important to set an example both on and off the field. I would get filthy on myself if I dropped a ball at training, really filthy, because I was not setting the standard. I didn't want to drop even one ball during a game. To limit that sort of mistake, you try to be as good as possible during training sessions. Of course, nobody is perfect, but you need to keep striving for the unattainable.

No matter who you are or how good you are, you should never forget to focus on the basic skills of the game. Passing skills, tackling skills, kicking skills and other vital areas have to be worked on week in and week out, season in and season out, to enable you to keep on top. These are critical for your confidence and for your game. Sometimes this may seem boring over a season or over a couple of years but, personally, I never found it boring. I knew it was an important part of my rugby league make-up. A good grounding in basic skills was what enabled me to overcome a lot of players.

I also believe it is a great help if you are your own strongest critic. Wayne Bennett and Tim Sheens had players analyse their own games and give themselves a rating out of 10. Then they would discuss how they felt the team went. In this way, you become good at assessing your own performance and I think that is very important because no-one plays a perfect game. There is always room for improvement. Every time you finish a game, look back over it and there will always be something you wish you had done better.

On the other side of the coin, it's good to be praised, to read your name in the paper and to hear people say you are a good player or had a fine match. If there is praise, appreciate it, learn to accept it, but don't get carried away by it. This is when you appreciate all the hard work you put in during the preparation for the match. Of course, there will also be criticism from time to time, but you have to learn to accept that along with the praise.

Another part of the mental discipline you need in rugby league is the ability to become single-minded. I've had traumas in my personal life, the drama of the Super League, speculation that I might be dropped from a team, or sometimes a crowd giving me a hard time. But during the 80 minutes of a game I concentrated on playing well and doing the best I possibly could — I never let the worry take over until the siren had gone. I believe this single-mindedness is one of my major strengths.

Exercise, discipline and single-mindedness — there are certainly sacrifices to be made. But there also has to be a play time, a balance between hard work and relaxation. When you are training, rest is just as important as the physical side of your preparation, whether you're a young man coming into the game or a seasoned campaigner. Without proper rest, you will never reach your peak because you will always be tired. Learning to switch off can be one of the hardest things to do, but it

Meninga

One of the unsung heroes of modern rugby league is the former Raider, now Bronco, Kevin Walters (right). I believe that without him Brisbane would not be the great side they are. He provides the team play to complement Allan Langer's attacking genius and is the perfect link between his forwards and the backs. The Broncos' superb three-quarters — Steve Renouf, Chris Johns, Michael Hancock, Wendell Sailor and Willie Carne — need a player of Kevin's vision and ability in their side.

Kevin is also extremely versatile, with the ability to play with style at hooker, halfback, five-eighth and centre. I'm sure he could handle lock as well. However, his utility value might have hurt him at the Origin level because he was always the guy who was dropped if things went wrong. In one game he even won a Man of the Match award, but was still dropped for the next game! Not all selectors appreciate skill, vision and talent.

Kevvie is also one of the funniest blokes I know. When he and Alf are together you're never short of a laugh. For two little blokes, they're not backward in bagging people.

What makes the 1995 Australian captain, Brad Fittler (left), such a magnificent footballer is the fact that he can play superbly at Test level in a variety of positions. There have surely been few utility men of his ability in the entire history of the game. And as well as being very talented, he is also extremely dedicated — a man deserving of all the success he has found in the sport.

comes with experience. Laurie Daley has said quite often that one of the things he learned from me is when to train and do the right things that help you play well and when to relax and have a few beers.

Our training routine at the Raiders varied because we could either play on a Friday, Saturday or Sunday. It was a good mix of hard physical work and relaxation. If we played on a Sunday, then Monday was designated as a rest day. You could go for a swim to ease the soreness or you might go to the gym to do some light weights. Or you might have what we call an active rest — a game of tennis or a round of golf.

We trained on Tuesday, either in the morning or the afternoon, depending on what the coach wanted. Then we'd get together and discuss the match we had played and go over our team goals, our personal goals and evaluate how the team went.

We would train for 90 minutes to two hours, mainly on skills and fitness with some time spent on ball work. On Wednesday we did weights and on Thursday there could be more weights, skills sessions and ball work in preparation for the weekend's match. Friday was an active rest day and on Saturday we had an hour of pure ball work and ball skills.

We tried to fit in at least one weight session a week, although the pre-season period is when we really developed our fitness and strength in the gym.

Leading up to the start of the season, we would do three or four sessions on weights per week to build our strength base and two or three sessions of running to build our stamina base. But when we got into the season proper, we relied on a maintenance program. In this type of program we would do one or two sessions of weights a week to maintain our physical strength during the season.

A key ingredient to success is to lead by example. It is essential in any club that the coach, the administration, the captain and the senior players behave well off the field as well as on it. This goes a long way towards a club being successful and accepted by the public.

The Raiders have excellent role models in Laurie Daley, Bradley Clyde, Ricky Stuart and Steve Walters who all set good examples off the field. That is why the youngsters coming through the Canberra juniors also have the right attitude.

To be a winner in rugby league, you also need to look to the future, beyond football. When I came to Canberra, I used my money to buy a house and the majority of my earnings from football went into that house. Now Ricky, Laurie, Bradley and Steve have done the same.

In the game's history there have been so many cases of players who earned good money but wasted it. Now the lesson has been learned and the players of today are looking for work and investment opportunities during their careers that will help them handle life after football.

There is one other area of a footballer's life that I have not mentioned. But it is vitally important — in fact, it's probably the single most important feature of your career as a footballer. This is the quality of your home life. This can have a major impact on your career. If you have a happy home environment, you take that happiness and security with you, and you are a much better player than someone who has drama and insecurity in their life off the field.

It takes some doing, but it is not impossible to manage your time so that everything runs smoothly with your training, your family commitments and your work commitments. If these can be managed without too many disruptions you are well on the way to success.

THE WINNING EDGE

Two photographs from the Australia Day awards, presented on 25 January 1995.

*(**Above**) With Prime Minister, Paul Keating, and the other award recipients.*

*(**Left**) With Debbie, Tamika and Joshua.*

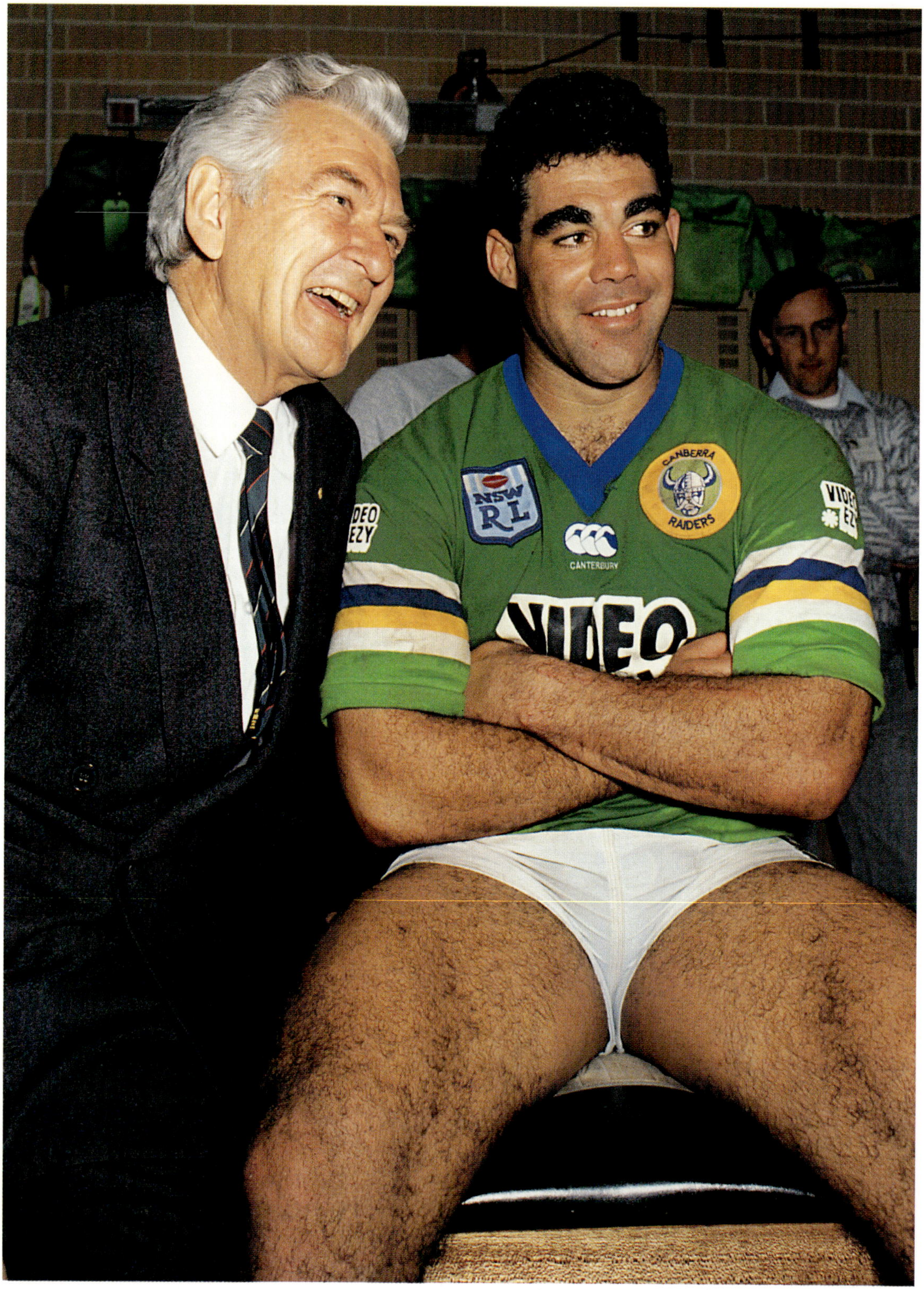
NSW
RL
CANBERRA
RAIDERS
CANTERBURY

9: ONE TOWN, ONE TEAM

In 1990, the Raiders won the club championship, the pre-season, the minor premiership, the President's Cup grand final and the first-grade grand final. In reserve grade, we made the grand final but lost to the Broncos in extra time. Rarely has a club so dominated the premiership scene.

Our win in the pre-season knock-out, the Channel Ten Cup, was at the expense of Penrith, whom we defeated 12–2 at Parramatta Stadium. First prize was $200,000, but just as satisfying was our defensive effort in both the semi-final (against Norths) and the final. In neither match did we concede a try.

Our premiership defence began with a resounding win over St George, before a big crowd of 22,257 at our new home ground, Bruce Stadium. The club had decided, reluctantly, to move our home from Seiffert to the more luxurious and therefore more lucrative facilities of Bruce, the centrepiece arena of the Australian Institute of Sport in Canberra. The crowd at that first game was a record for the ground, and our performance augured well for a successful defence of our title. However, after another comfortable victory, over the Steelers in Wollongong, we crashed to consecutive defeats at the hands of Canterbury and then Cronulla. Some critics were questioning our prowess, which annoyed us and fired us up for our round-5 clash with Eastern Suburbs.

This game developed into a famous day for the Raiders. The final score was 66–4 and my contribution was 38 points, from five tries and nine goals. This was, I was told later, the most points scored by a player in a single first-grade match since the legendary Dave Brown managed 45 in 1935. Brown's individual achievement then must have been truly awesome. Back in those days, of course, a try was only worth three points, not four as it was in 1990. However, as good as his Easts' team-mates were (they won the premiership in 1935, 1936 and 1937), I doubt they could have been as lethal as my Raider colleagues. All 66 points we managed against Easts in 1990 were scored by the backs, and most of my five tries involved little more than placing the ball down over the line.

This victory was the first of six in a row, a run that ended on June 8 when we crashed to Parramatta on our hoodoo ground, Parramatta Stadium. It was not until 1991 that the Raiders finally defeated the Eels

Opposite: With Prime Minister and Raiders fan Bob Hawke in 1991.

A pat on the back for Clive Churchill medal-winner Ricky Stuart, during our victory lap after the 1990 grand final.

on their home ground.

Round 14 was a major event for the Raiders, a clash at Lang Park with the Brisbane Broncos, who were enjoying their best season in the Winfield Cup since entering the premiership in 1988. The afternoon was also a highly significant one for me, as I was presented with the Adidas Golden Boot award for being the best player in the world in 1989. This award was judged by an international panel of league writers and correspondents and meant a great deal to me, coming as it did so soon after my two horror years out of the game. And it made for something of a dual personal celebration, for four days earlier I had captained the Australian team for the first time, in the only home Test of the season, against France in Parkes. Wally Lewis, who had been the Aussie skipper since 1984, was injured at the time.

Brisbane won in a thriller, 22–20, and a week later we lost again, to another of the premiership front-runners, Penrith, at Bruce Stadium. But that was to be our last loss of the regular season, as we went through our remaining games undefeated, to clinch the club's maiden first-grade minor premiership from Brisbane, Penrith and Manly.

ONE TOWN, ONE TEAM

Most commentators were predicting a Raiders–Broncos premiership showdown, but the Panthers stunned Wayne Bennett's team by defeating them 26–16 in the minor preliminary semi-final. Then they surprised us as well, winning a place in the grand final, courtesy of a runaway victory in extra time. We had led that game 18–16 with only five minutes remaining, but a 35-metre penalty goal by their captain Greg Alexander took the game past 80 minutes, and in the added time we were weary and our opponents unstoppable.

Our performance against Brisbane, in the preliminary final, was one of our very best, as we swept past them and into the grand final by 32 points to 4. This was one of those games in which every Raider was at, or near, his best. It was 12–0 at half-time, 16–0 soon after, and although the Broncos introduced Wally Lewis into proceedings at this point (for his first appearance since June 23) there was no way back for the men from up north. Their only try came just two minutes from the end.

The 1990 grand final lacked much of the electricity, emotion and theatre of the previous year's classic, but was still an exciting game that went all the way to the finish line. We took control early on, and by the

Celebrations after our grand-final victory over Penrith. The men visible are (left to right): Chris O'Sullivan, myself, Dean Lance, Craig Bellamy, Ricky Stuart, Phil Carey, Paul Martin, Laurie Daley (at back), Glenn Lazarus (in front), John Ferguson (behind Lazarus), Gary Coyne (behind Ferguson), Tim Sheens, Steve Walters, Mark Bell (in front of Walters), Matthew Wood, Nigel Gaffey (partly obscured), Gary Belcher, Alex Corvo, Jason Croker and Brent Todd.

midway point of the first half led 12–0 through tries by Chicka Ferguson and Laurie Daley. Six minutes before half-time, the Panthers' teenage sensation Brad Fittler scored and then seven minutes into the second half there was only two points' difference after their winger, Paul Smith, touched down wide out.

It was at this point that our experience in grand final football took over. Penrith had the momentum, but a couple of mistakes at crucial times turned the game and ensured the Winfield Cup stayed with Canberra. Five minutes from full-time, a Panthers forward spilt the ball near halfway and, five tackles later, our replacement centre Matthew Wood was racing over for the match-sealing try. A last-gasp four-pointer to Alexander was no more than a consolation — we were home, 18–14.

The celebrations after the win were not as raucous or as sustained as in 1989, but there was still plenty of spirit in the post-grand final festivities. In many ways, the predominant emotion this time was relief; the pressure of being defending premiers had created stresses that had not existed the year before. For five Raiders — Gary Belcher, Ricky Stuart, Laurie Daley, Glenn Lazarus and myself — there was a bonus: selection in the Kangaroo touring party. And with Wally Lewis having been ruled out of the team through injury, I was named captain. This was a great honour for me and for the Canberra club.

The 1991 season was one of the most turbulent of my career. For the first few months of the season we had no more to worry about than a succession of injuries that had put in jeopardy our intention of "three-peating" as premiers. But then a story with huge ramifications for rugby league and for the Raiders broke. It was revealed in mid-July that, in keeping our all-star line-up together, club management had broken the NSWRL's salary cap, which had been put in place by the League to control the amounts clubs could pay their playing staff. The Raiders' breach had come to light after the League had investigated the extent of the football club's financial difficulties. The club was seriously in debt, and public appeals had to be organised to try and keep the city's pride and joy afloat.

It was a horror period for the players, a time of indecision when we did not know exactly what was going on, whether we would be paid and what the future held for our team. None of us knew what the others were being paid, and it was hardly our job to get the calculator out to check whether the club was within the salary cap. Yet, publicly at least, we had to bear much of the resultant furore.

Media stories about the club being in financial strife had been about for weeks. In early May, the *Canberra Times* had reported that the combined debt of the Queanbeyan Leagues Club, the Raiders' licensed club at Mawson and the Rugby League football club was "in the vicinity of

$5 million". Just about every player in Canberra and Queanbeyan had heard rumours about this financial mess, and naturally we wanted to know what was going on. So did the NSW Rugby League, and not long after their investigation began club officials came to us and admitted they were in some trouble. That was when we found out the club was over the salary cap.

Earlier in the season, I had received some tentative but potentially highly profitable approaches from a number of English clubs, including St Helens and Wigan. I was under contract to the Raiders until the end of 1992, but with all the uncertainty, I wanted to clarify what was happening. When I couldn't get the answers I was looking for, I sought a release from the final year of my contract. That didn't necessarily mean I wanted to depart, but with such a release I would be a lot surer about where I stood when handling any negotiations with the English clubs.

Rumours abounded, including a strong one that the players would be forced to take pay cuts. The Raiders' chief executive, John McIntyre, resigned. A new management committee was appointed for the club, with Bernie Fraser, the Governor of the Reserve Bank, as its head. The Raiders' joint patrons, the federal member for Canberra (and Minister for Sport), Ros Kelly, and that remarkable old politician and lover of football, Fred Daly, became two of a number of prominent spearheads of the official "Save The Raiders" trust fund. Richard Farmer, a well-known local identity with close ties to the Labor Party, became the fund's chief spokesman. Within minutes of the fund's opening, money was pouring in.

The Canberra public's support at this time was a poignant reminder of the ties that had developed between the club and the fans. In a quite ironic way, the Raiders' financial plight accentuated this close relationship even more than any of our greatest wins. Donations of more than $20 to the fund were acknowledged in the *Canberra Times*. One family attached a simple note to their cheque which read: "We believe the Raiders are good for Canberra and we want them to stay."

On July 23, the *Canberra Times* ran an editorial on why it was so important for the region to retain its team. Here is just a part of what that editorial said:

> *The Raiders live, train and play right here in Canberra. We can watch them play every second week at Bruce Stadium and hear and read reports of the away games. They belong to us, they are our team and there were few ACT residents left unmoved by the magnificent last-minute victory against Balmain in the 1989 grand final and the second grand final win against Penrith a year later. The crowds that gathered at the airport and the leagues club to welcome their heroes home were*

Grand final day, 1990.

testament enough to the pride the national capital felt in these achievements ...

The [trust] fund represents an effort by the people of Canberra to hang on to something they treasure. In a sense, the Raiders have put Canberra on the map. They have shown the rest of Australia that this is not a city without a soul but one full of vibrant people who can cheer as loudly as any others when their champions win and equally loudly bemoan their losses ...

In the days of old the people had their champions in the form of knights who took up the challenge of intruders on their behalf. Mal Meninga and the Raiders are Canberra's knights, except they carry a football rather than a lance.

A meeting was arranged between Bernie Fraser and the ANZ Bank. Also in attendance was the general manager of the NSWRL, John Quayle. After that get-together, it was announced that the bank, which was already owed in the region of $5 million, had agreed to lend the club a further $700,000, provided the Raiders reduced their player payments to within the salary cap set by the NSWRL. Without that loan, the club might have died. However, when this agreement was announced, there was no indication as to how such a cut was going to be achieved. To us, it either meant a pay cut for some or all of the players, or that some people were going to get sacked. Frustratingly, the players were left largely in the dark as these developments occurred.

Allegations were flying all over the place. Statements were made that the Raiders had exceeded the cap by as much as $600,000 (this was later shown to be way over the mark). There were suggestions we should give back the premierships we had won. Some believed we should have been kicked out of the League. "Other clubs have breached the salary cap, but they have been of a minor nature only," one unnamed chief executive told *Rugby League Week*'s David Middleton. "Those breaches have been the result of miscalculations. This is far more blatant. Canberra are openly cheating the system."

A proposal was raised that the club cut player payments by a specific percentage across the board. This was something the players naturally wanted to avoid. So did the club, because legal opinion was that such a move would make us all free agents. But as more facts came to light there seemed no alternative. It was clear the club was over the cap, and just as clear that neither the bank nor the NSWRL was going to let that situation continue.

Rumours abounded that some of the players were leaving at the end of the year. "Naturally I'd like to stay," Bradley Clyde told Middleton, "but if the worst comes to the worst, I'm prepared to leave." In the *Daily Telegraph*, Ricky Stuart told journalist Mike Colman: "I want to do the right thing by the club, but I also have to look after my future."

The players were told they would have to take a 15 per cent cut in pay — there was no other way of keeping the club in the competition. At the same time, it was confirmed that all contracts would have to be renegotiated. What the future held, none of us knew, as there was no indication of how much, if any, money the club would have available in 1992 to spend on the players. The team would remain together for the remainder of the 1991 premiership season, earning 15 per cent less than expected. But as we tried to concentrate on getting the Raiders into the semi-finals, constantly in the back of our minds was the realisation that once the '91 season was completed, the side which had grown up together since 1986 could quite easily be destroyed.

What seemed most unfair about this situation was the fact that of the 13 Canberra players who had started the 1990 grand final, John Ferguson and I were the only two to have played any state or Test football before we came to Canberra. The rest had developed into representative league footballers after they arrived at the club. Of the 1990 grand final side, only Chicka (Newtown and Easts) and Dean Lance (Newtown) had come from other NSWRL premiership clubs. Brent Todd was from New Zealand. Gary Belcher, Gary Coyne, Steve Walters and I were products of the Brisbane premiership. Ricky Stuart came from Canberra rugby union. Paul Martin, Chris O'Sullivan, Laurie Daley, Glenn Lazarus and Nigel Gaffey were either locally produced or products of the nearby country leagues. Bradley Clyde, another local product, had missed the 1990 grand final because of a severe knee injury.

I maintain that clubs which produce juniors with the ability to make first-grade who then step up into representative football should be exempt, to some extent, from the hard-and-fast rules of the salary cap. I also believe that if a player stays with a club for a set period — say, five, six, eight or 10 years — then allowances should be made to reward this loyal service.

But this wasn't how things worked in 1991, and it meant that in Canberra the entire first-grade was up for sale. Inevitably, the sharks moved in. Laurie Daley fielded a lucrative bid from St George. Manly renewed the invitation to Steve Walters they had made earlier in the season. Daley and Brad Clyde received a massive package deal offer from Wigan. Glenn Lazarus had talks with the Brisbane Broncos. I had offers from two Sydney clubs and a tentative approach from Brisbane, but the most amazing potential deal came from St Helens. Their approach of earlier in the year became a firm offer of a four-year contract worth £100,000 a year. In addition, they indicated the player–coach job was mine after a year if I wanted it, and that they were keen for me to stay on as coach once my four-year playing contract was completed.

This was extremely tempting — free accommodation and meals, unlimited access to a car and my tax bill paid. All I had to do was to front up and play football. As the crisis in Canberra reached its stormy peak, I was very close to accepting.

For a while, the stresses and accusations made me a very agitated man. Everything was taking its toll. Debbie got thoroughly sick and tired of me bringing these worries home, and more than once told me she had had enough. More than once I felt the same. There was a stage where she was very keen for us to return to St Helens.

But in the end we decided to stay. To explain why is not simple, but it goes back to the bonds with team-mates that had been created over the previous five and a half seasons. Not to mention the bond with the supporters. If you talk to footballers who have been with a successful club,

ONE TOWN, ONE TEAM

How Fraser saved the Raiders

Directors faced criminal liability: lawyer

By IAN DAVIS, Finance Editor

The appointment last week of the Reserve Bank Governor, Bernie Fraser... ...and the Raiders manager... ...the ANZ Bank... ...cision to let $700,000... Raiders fr...

that without a disciplined commercial approach to running the football club, the Queanbeyan Leagues Club will be unable to cope with the demands placed on its cash flow by both the football club and the Raiders Leagues Club and will ultimately fail.

The Queanbeyan Leagues Club has been propping up the rest of the organisation by guaranteeing to pay the ...the Mawson club...

RESCUE A RAIDER — Page 2

Hawke jokes about luck as Raiders just smile at Manly

By KEVIN HEPWORTH

Bob Hawke said yesterday that he'd better begin rearranging his schedule to make certain he would be available to attend all matches in Canberra Raiders' finals campaign.

"I'd certainly hate to miss any of them," Mr Hawke joked.

The Prime Minister was speaking after watching the Raiders score a 14-13 win over Manly in a Winfield Cup match at Seiffert Oval.

...have to try and work things... with a winning wager against the former Manly official.

"It's nice to see a bit of redistribution of income," he grinned. Mr Arthurson, when asked about his afternoon with the PM, smiled and added, "We kissed and made up."

When it was suggested that Mr Hawke and his Treasurer, John Kerin, might have found room in tomorrow's Budget for a grant to the Canberra club, the Prime Minister said, "I'd win some votes in Canberra, but I'd lose them elsewhere. But I hope [the club's financial...

Meninga tipped to stay Raider

By JOHN HOGAN

AUSTRALIAN captain Mal Meninga is expected to announce today that he will remain with Canberra.

Meninga, who sought a release from the embattled club a month ago following a massive two-year offer from St Helens, reportedly rang the Lancashire club last night to advise Saints he would not be moving to England.

Canberra lobbyist and spokesman for the "Rescue a Raider" fund-raising committee, Mr Richard Farmer, said Meninga would hold a press conference in Canberra today.

"If I was a betting man I'd have a dollar on Mal staying with Canberra," Mr Farmer said last night.

"The offer made to him is not an unattractive one and his family likes it here.

"I'll be disappointed, as will all the people of Canberra, if we have been unable to come up with enough encouragement for Mal to stay. But I can fully understand his position.

"None of the players want to leave..."

...capital and Queanbeyan, such is his standing in the community.

His choice to stay will be a breath of fresh air in the territory, exactly three months after it was revealed the Raiders were labouring under a group debt of more than $5 million.

The financial crisis came to a head last Sunday when angry players and coaching staff were left no alternative but to accept a 15 per cent pay cut, saving the club about $500,000 this year.

All contracted players immediately became free agents and rival Winfield Cup clubs and rich English clubs quickly organised talks with senior players left in limbo.

Meninga knows his decision, either way, will have a domino effect.

Staying will help coach Tim Sheens and new chief executive Kevin Grace retain most of his team-mates; going would result in a mass fallout of the ranks.

This is the second time in...

...bane to join the Broncos.

At the time, Canberra officials believed Meninga, who had an escape clause in his contract, would depart with Bennett.

But he chose to stay, as Canberra had stuck by him through a miserable injury period (broken arms) and he repaid them by leading the Raiders to back-to-back premierships (1989-90).

The Canberra team was built around Meninga and it would be a shame if the entertaining Green Machine were put up on blocks and stripped.

'No players want to leave'

Although the league will reduce Canberra's salary cap from $1.5 million to about $1.3m, the fund-raising committee is confident of placing more than $200,000 in a trust fund to help retain players.

"We have raised more than $100,000 already and I have no doubt we will get over the...

...players last night how the trust fund worked and he gained a positive impression of team morale from their reactions.

"They didn't seem like a side which had lost its spirit," he said.

"Obviously we will have trouble keeping all of them but we're doing our best."

Meninga's Test team-mates Laurie Daley and Bradley Clyde have been tempted with a massive package deal offer for two years from English champion club Wigan.

Daley and Clyde will consider the offer but are uncertain about their eligibility for international selection should they opt to join John Monie's side at Central Park.

Daley is obligated to Wakefield Trinity for a guest stint immediately after Australia's brief tour of Papua New Guinea in October, but would then be free to join Wigan if conditions were suitable.

Halfback Ricky Stuart is expected to have a groin operation at the end of the season.

---

very few want to leave. Friendships have been developed, and a strong link has evolved with the loyal fans who have played such an important part in the days of glory. In my case, the Raiders followers had been especially good to me and I felt I owed them something.

Through late July and early August I was in an awkward position because St Helens were pressing me for a decision. Before I made up my mind, I wanted to know how my team-mates were thinking, and at a meeting at the Raiders Club at Mawson one morning, I realised that almost to a man they wanted to stay. No-one was happy about what had happened, and many felt that in having their pay cut they had been

Opposite: In my opinion, Steve Walters is the best hooker-forward of all time. Simple as that.

No-one had really heard of him when he first arrived in Canberra back in 1986, but they certainly know him now. It was that shrewd judge of talent, Don Furner, who recognised his potential and offered him a contract, but I'm sure even Don would not have forecast just how good a player he would turn into.

When Steve first arrived, Canberra had a capable first-grade hooker in Jay Hoffman, and in 1986 the pair battled hard for the top spot. However, from 1987 Jay had to take a back seat to Steve which, in one way, was a great shame, because Jay was one of the best club men you could ever imagine. But Steve was on his way to the top.

Steve's second half performance in the third Ashes Test of 1994 was absolutely majestic. Running up the middle of the field through the forwards is not dissimilar to hitting your head repeatedly against a brick wall, but there were times in this game when it seemed not even concrete and mortar could stop him. Every time I watch the video of that great victory, I marvel at his skill and ability to pick when is the right time to run.

scapegoated for the dreadful mistakes of management. But the great spirit among the team seemed to outweigh the bitterness against those who had created the turmoil.

Tim Sheens played a very significant role in preventing the episode destroying the club. In the three weeks between the confirmation in mid-July that the club was in severe financial trouble and the final decision to cut the players' salaries, the team had matches to play. Tim tried desperately to prevent us from being distracted completely. We all listened to him, and he did a magnificent job in keeping us together through this tempestuous time.

Tim had faith in the Canberra establishment and was the first to re-sign. He told us he had decided to stay solid to the club and although he never at any point insisted that we should do the same, his decision helped a lot of us to follow him down the same road.

A crucial episode in my decision to remain a Raider was a lunch at which Debbie and I discussed the furore with Tim and Kevin Grace, the newly appointed Raiders chief executive. We talked about where the club was going, its ability to pay the players and where the money was coming from. I became convinced that there was a viable plan in place, and at the same time it also became clear that the club needed me to agree to stay to help convince others that this was the way to go. Tim stressed this point. The fact that the coach and then the captain had signed would show others — players, fans and rival clubs — that the Raiders really had a future.

I made my decision on August 7, two days after the players had held a crisis meeting at Queanbeyan Leagues Club, at which we demanded that those who had been responsible for the fiasco be dismissed. At a press conference I told reporters of my decision: "I had always wanted to play in the Sydney competition and Canberra seemed the logical choice because I didn't want to live in Sydney. That decision really wasn't that hard. This time I have taken a big gamble, but I think it's well worthwhile.

"I am very happy and sort of relieved."

The crisis was far from over, but for me much of the stress had gone. Not long after I announced my decision, the NSWRL set our salary cap for 1992 at $1.3 million, $300,000 below the top level, and refused to allow the money raised by the Save the Raider trust fund (which eventually amounted to upwards of $250,000) to count towards the cap. That provoked outrage in Canberra, with even the Prime Minister getting involved. But before the year was out, that decision had been changed. Every cent raised by that fund went towards the retention of the Raiders team. There was never any possibility that the money would be used to help alleviate the club's debt. When the fund had been established, legal eagles had been brought in to ensure that the terms and provisions under

ONE TOWN, ONE TEAM

which the trust was executed made it impossible for the money raised to be used for any purpose other than the retention of the club's players.

Not long after, Laurie Daley signed a new deal with the club. Then it was Bradley Clyde, who agreed to stay despite a rumoured offer from the Gold Coast that amounted to not much less than a blank cheque. "I thought very seriously about that one," Brad told a reporter, "but I would have missed getting up to go to work when the temperature is minus two." It was apparent by this time that at least most of the Raiders' best players were going to remain with the club, albeit on less money than they had received in previous seasons.

One extremely positive thing that did come out of the trouble was that many of the players started to look to their own futures. Some bought a house, others invested in businesses to make sure that when their playing days were over they would have something to show for it.

Ricky Stuart, Steve Walters and Brett Mullins, an exciting young back the club had brought down from the NSW country town of Young, agreed to terms on the Monday after we thrashed St George 40–8 in a final round clash at Bruce Stadium. This victory, before another record crowd, confirmed our place in the semi-finals and left the Saints, who had been in contention for a finals place all year, to make plans for 1992. This was our fourth win in a row; in fact, we hadn't been defeated since the Broncos had won 18–8 at Bruce Stadium on the weekend after the salary cap furore really hit the headlines in late July. And that loss to Brisbane had come at a time when the two clubs' representative players (Willie Carne, Allan Langer and Chris Johns for Brisbane; Laurie Daley, Bradley Clyde, Steve Walters, Brent Todd and myself for Canberra) were absent preparing for the final Test of the series against New Zealand.

Just as we had in 1989, in 1991 we progressed from the minor preliminary semi-final all the way to the grand final. First up, we put paid to Wests 22–8. Then we saw off Manly 34–26, in a brilliant game that featured a four-try performance by our workaholic second-rower Gary Coyne. In the final, we faced North Sydney and early on fell behind 12–0. But from that point, we were outstanding, and eventually careered away to win 30–14.

Our effort in getting to the grand final was a remarkable feat, considering the distractions we faced. Whenever we travelled to Sydney, we had to put up with people making jibes about our "cheating". I was caught up in a drama of a different kind when I was labelled in some sections of the media as being in favour of the legalisation of marijuana use. This was outrageous. I had been quoted as saying that I felt that the NSWRL's stance on testing players for marijuana use was "humiliating", but I was fully behind the League's tough stance on performance-enhancing drugs. That didn't mean I wanted marijuana legalised. Far from it.

And our injury toll kept rising. Glenn Lazarus had a fractured sternum but kept on playing, while halfback Ricky Stuart, the courageous, creative schemer, was virtually playing on one leg because of a bad groin problem. When the season finally ended, he went straight into hospital for a major operation, but throughout the finals series he kept getting injections to help him on to the field. And there was also Laurie Daley, who has won so many matches for Canberra but was severely handicapped by knee and shoulder injuries.

We were the walking wounded that season, but we kept plugging away. Such were our courage and persistence, that I think our greatest achievement as a team was in making the 1991 grand final. Team spirit was unprecedented. Far from giving up, we had actually been spurred on by all the garbage that had been tipped over us. We were battling on for each other and for Canberra. And as we did so we became an extremely close-knit group.

Sadly, we stumbled at the final hurdle. Penrith, inspired by their veteran hooker Royce Simmons, who was playing his final game in the Winfield Cup, played very well, but for most of the game we held the lead. At half-time we were in front 12–6, and kept that advantage until the 70th minute, when centre Brad Izzard crossed for the Panthers. Greg Alexander's conversion levelled the scores. By this point, Ricky and Laurie were really struggling, and we knew when Alexander kicked a superb field goal six minutes from the end that our dream of a premiership trifecta was gone. Simmons' late try, his second of the grand final, iced the cake on the Panthers' greatest day. Our only consolation was the announcement that Bradley Clyde had won the Clive Churchill medal as the best player on the field. It was his second win (after 1989), and the third time in a row that a Raiders player had won the award (Ricky Stuart was the recipient in 1990).

During the 1991–92 off-season, the erosion of the club's playing strength began. First to go was Glenn Lazarus, who accepted the big deal he had been offered by the Broncos. Then winger Paul Martin signed a contract with the Gold Coast. Soon after, Brent Todd followed Martin north. Then it was three-quarter Mark Bell (to Wests) and back-rowers David Barnhill (St George) and Nigel Gaffey (Easts). In all, we lost 39 players, an obstacle that made 1992 the toughest year we had experienced at the club since 1986.

The season developed into a disaster, one of only two years we did not make the finals in my time at the club (the other was 1986). Our lack of depth meant other teams' defences could zero in on what was termed the "Big Five" (Steve Walters, Laurie Daley, Ricky Stuart, Bradley Clyde and myself) and in doing so they stifled many of our attacking options.

MENINGA

The closest thing I have seen to Wally Lewis, as far as effective running is concerned, is the Raiders' sensational five-eighth, Laurie Daley (right). He has everything you could wish for in a player: he runs the ball brilliantly, tackles extremely well, has great vision, communicates well, has a good kicking game and can be an inspirational leader, as he has shown often in State of Origin matches.

When something has to be done on the football field, Laurie is the guy who usually does it.

One Town, One Team

I believe Canberra's Bradley Clyde (left) is currently the best player in the world. A superb athlete, there is basically nothing he cannot do on the football field. His defence is immaculate, he can kick if he wants to, he can off-load, his work-rate is tremendous, making tackle after tackle, and he's always available to take the ball up when necessary. If the opposition puts a kick through, you can bet with certainty that Brad will be back there to assist the fullback or the winger. He really is an incredible player.

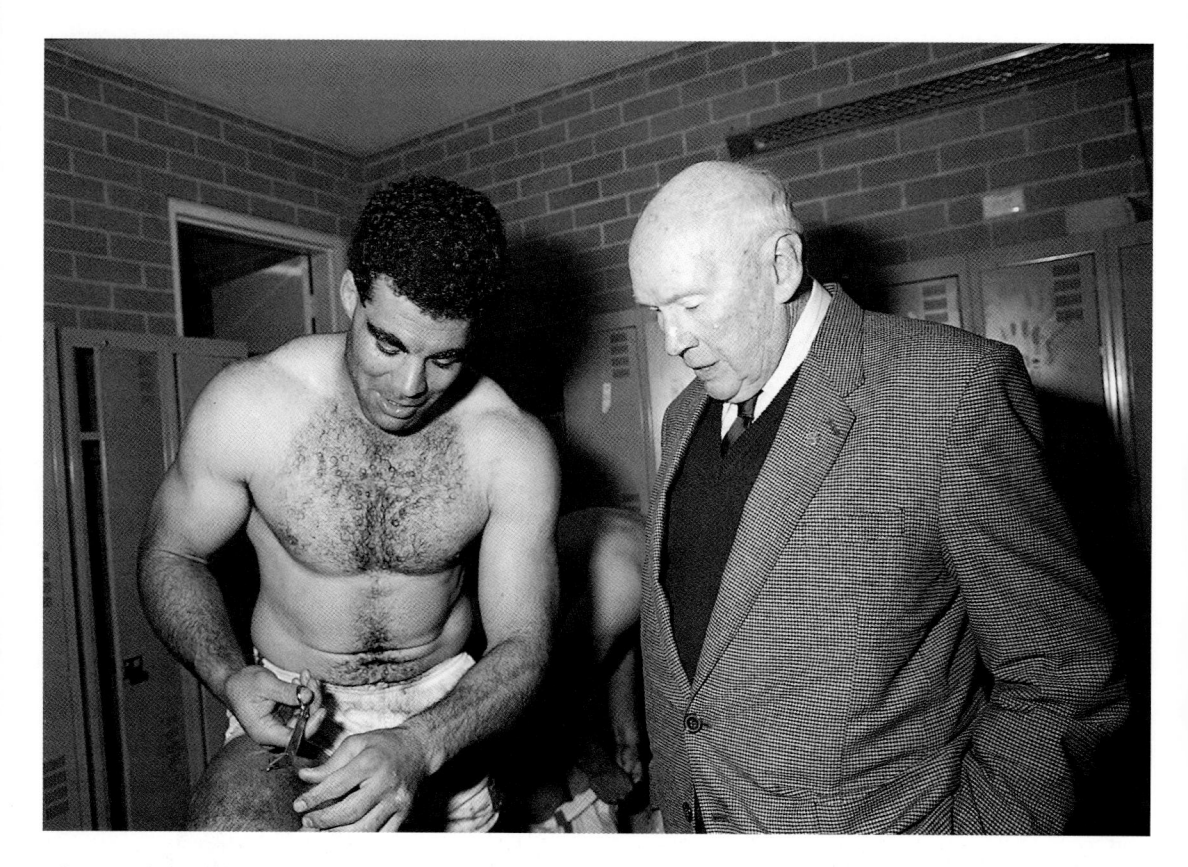

Above: With that great fan of the Raiders, the former politician and present-day patron of the club, Fred Daly.

Opposite: Moving across to try to apprehend Penrith hooker Royce Simmons during the 1991 grand final. Royce, a team-mate on the 1986 Kangaroo tour, was playing his final game of league, and the occasion developed into a fairytale for him, as he scored two tries in the Panthers' 19–12 victory.

That Big Five probably would have been a Big Six had Gary Belcher been able to play more than a single game during the year. Out because of a knee injury, Badge wasn't alone on the sidelines: Ricky Stuart missed five early matches after suffering a knee injury against Manly in round 2, Bradley Clyde played only 14 games, Laurie Daley a paltry seven. In previous years, we might have had the substitutes to cover these setbacks, but not in 1992. Eventually, we finished 12th, five competition points from the semi-finals.

One bloke I did feel desperately sorry for was prop Paul Osborne, who had signed for the club at the start of the season after playing a number of seasons at St George. From 1986 to 1991, Saints never even made the semi-finals, while the Raiders made it five years in a row from 1987. Then in '92, we missed the play-offs while Ossie's old club bravely fought their way to the grand final. All he could do on grand final day was sit in his new Canberra home and think of what might have been. Fortunately, though, for Paul, his time would eventually come.

When a club has to go through a massive rebuilding process such as the one the Raiders were obliged to do, it can take many years before the club is able to return to the top of the premiership tree. However, such was the astute nature of the scouting process instigated by Tim Sheens

ONE TOWN, ONE TEAM

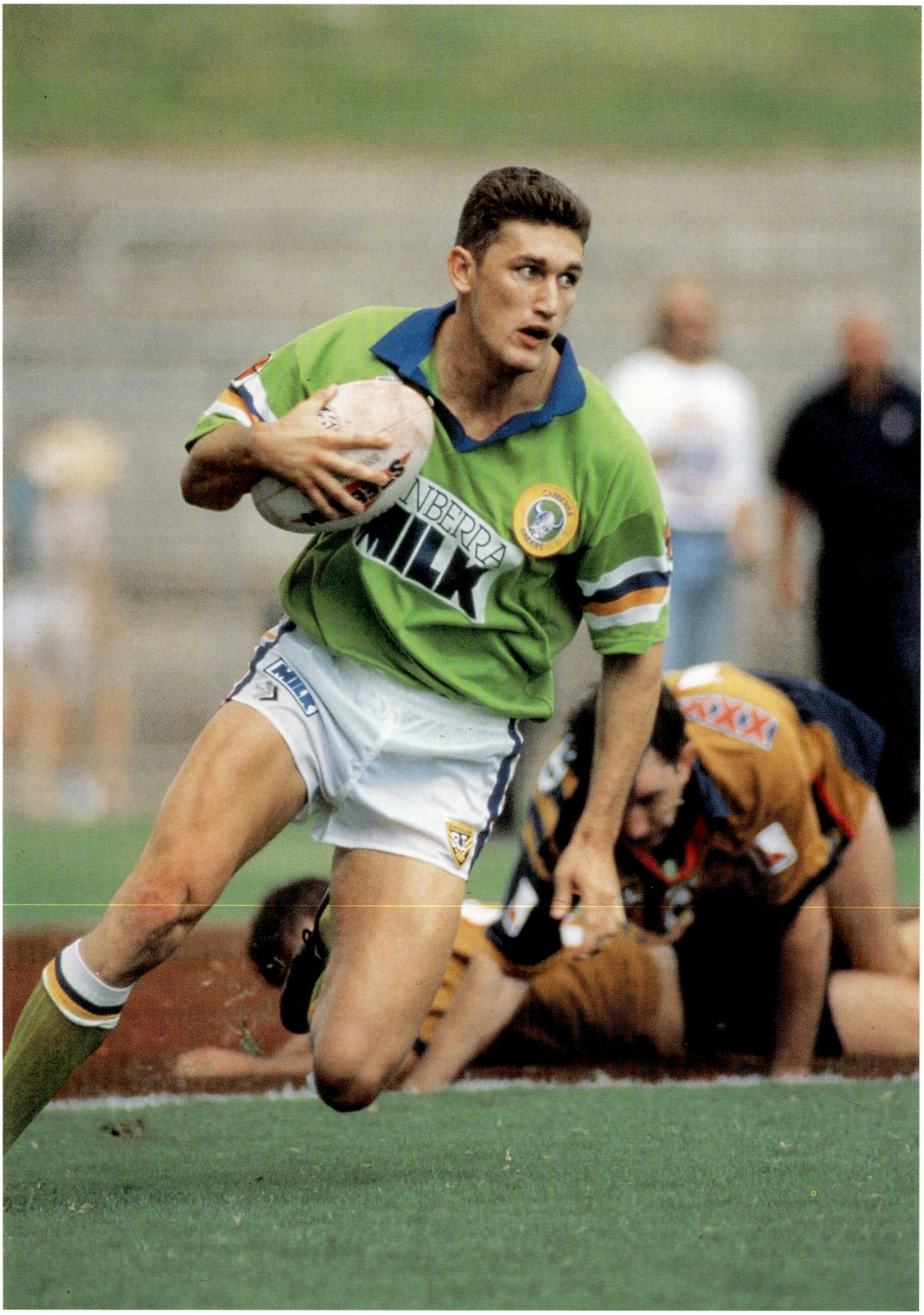
CANBERRA
MILK
MILK
XXXX

and the club's new chief executive Kevin Neil (Kevin Grace had stepped aside to concentrate on his job as the Raiders group general manager), that the Raiders became a real force in the competition again as early as 1993. Kevin had been given the job in late February 1992 and commented on his appointment: "My primary task is to help make sure the Canberra Raiders have a 1993."

This he and Tim did, signing up a range of young prospects who were earmarked as potential first-graders. In addition, they set about re-signing all the established stars who had only agreed to one-year deals in the wake of the 1991 crisis. This was a re-establishment period for us. The club had the basis of a very good side with the six or seven experienced representative players. All we needed were some talented young footballers to come through and, fortunately, that is exactly what occurred.

In 1993, outstanding young talents such Brett Mullins, Jason Croker, David Boyle, David Furner and Ken Nagas confirmed they were genuine first-graders. From New Zealand, winger Sean Hoppe arrived and by season's end was the second leading try-scorer. The only man ahead of him was another Raider in his first Winfield Cup season, the Fijian sensation Noa Nadruku, who finished the regular season with 19 tries, and then scored three more in the semi-finals.

After 20 rounds in '93, we were running second, just a point behind the premiership pace-setters, Canterbury. A point adrift of us were the previous season's grand finalists, St George and Brisbane. Despite the good form of the Saints and the Bulldogs, most bookmakers saw the season as a match-race between ourselves and the Broncos.

But then came a disaster that totally wrecked our year.

In round 21, at Bruce Stadium, we humiliated Parramatta by 68–0, scoring 12 tries. It was the biggest win in Raider history, and with Canterbury losing to St George we moved to the outright competition lead. Yet we were in sombre mood afterwards. Ricky Stuart, in the middle of a brilliant season that would see him win the Rothmans Medal, the Dally M Player of the Year trophy and the NSW Press Writers' Player of the Year award, suffered a horrific injury — a badly dislocated and fractured ankle.

From the first minute of our first game without Ricky, we played like premiership longshots, and disappeared out of the competition. In the final round, we were thrashed by Canterbury at Belmore and then in the semis we lost successive games to the Saints and Brisbane.

To some extent, I blame myself for our abrupt departure. After Ricky's injury, we rapidly developed a phobia about his absence. Rather than accepting the fact he was gone and focusing on the job at hand, we

Opposite: Brett Mullins, who took over as the Raiders' fullback following the retirement of Gary Belcher, is an extraordinary talent. Already a superb running fullback, he needs only a fraction more maturity to completely realise his potential. When that happens he could be anything he wants to be.

I put Brett and the Broncos' Steve Renouf in the same "excitement stakes" category. Both guys have the ability to get spectators on their feet. There is a real buzz in the air when the ball looks like going to them.

Playing against Manly at Brookvale Oval in 1993, a game we won 21–10.

panicked about what was going to go wrong because he wasn't there. As captain, I should have arrested this negative attitude, but before we realised what was going on, we were out of the competition.

However, when we sat down to assess our 1993 season, we acknowledged that a lot more good had come from the season than bad. Even our dismal exit had taught us lessons, and for the younger players in the squad this had been an invaluable experience. They knew now how much they had relied on the genius of Ricky to keep the team afloat. In 1994, a number of these players would become high-flyers in their own right.

Still recovering from his awful injury, Ricky did not play in 1994 pre-season. But he was back for the season opener, a shock 24–16 loss to Cronulla on a Saturday night at Caltex Field. Our team included some more new faces — Ruben Wiki, an exciting centre who ended the year with 15 tries, and the uncompromising forwards, John Lomax and Quentin Pongia. All three were from New Zealand, where Tim Sheens had headed in the off-season to bolster the club's ranks. It said a lot for Tim's methods and his judgement that he put these guys straight into the top grade. I have always admired the fact that he is not afraid to introduce young players into the first-grade team if he thinks they are good enough and talented enough to be there.

For my final game at Bruce Stadium, I was accompanied on to the field by two of my most loyal fans — Tamika and Joshua.

The team played well right through 1994, although there were a couple of losses when we expected wins, against the Gold Coast and against Penrith. However, we weren't overly worried by these setbacks, as they came at awkward times in the season. The Gold Coast match came after the City–Country game, while the loss to Penrith occurred on the weekend after a bruising State of Origin match.

I knew that because of the way we were playing we would be very hard to beat for the premiership. Towards the end of the season I thought we played some of our best football: we amassed a record 779 points from our 26 premiership matches, an average of just a fraction under 30 points per game. Our season's try tally of 146 was another record, while the number of Raiders picked in the Kangaroo team (seven — Brett Mullins, Ricky Stuart, Laurie Daley, Bradley Clyde, Steve Walters, David Furner and myself) equalled the highest representation by one club on a 'Roo tour.

The individual form of some of our team during the year was simply awesome. Brett Mullins, stepping into the fullback role that had been so grandly filled by Gary Belcher in previous seasons, had a remarkable year. His attacking displays were such that some critics were comparing him to giants of yesteryear such as Graeme Langlands and even Clive Churchill.

Steve Walters confirmed what we in Canberra had known for quite a while — that he is without peer as a modern-day hooker-forward. Ricky had another magnificent season, while Laurie and Bradley were no better than their usual brilliant selves. Winger Ken Nagas struggled a bit with injury, but in the semi-finals was devastating. Jason Croker, playing in a number of positions at different times, scored 19 tries. David Furner kicked 75 goals and played himself into the Australian team.

Such was the competitive nature of the premiership, we still needed to win our final match of the regular season, against Manly at Brookvale, to seal a place in the top three. Which we did, with a victory more comfortable than the 21–18 final scoreline suggested. Eight minutes from time, we led 21–6, a position that reflected the way we had dominated the game, especially in the first 20 minutes of the second half.

As I explained in the opening chapter, we struggled through the semi-finals, but did enough to reach the season decider.

Tim pulled off a master stroke in the grand final with his decision to use Paul Osborne. Although Ossie had begun the season in the top grade, by season's end, Quentin Pongia and John Lomax had taken over in the front row. And we had a number of promising young players — Mark Corvo, David Westley and Brett Hetherington — who could fill at prop when needed. Ossie had indicated that he was going to call it quits at the end of the season, so with reserve grade not qualifying for the semis, it appeared his career was at an end. He kept training, but with the conviction of a man who knew he was wasting his time.

But then Johnny Lomax was sent off in the final against Norths, and later suspended. Tim went through all the alternatives and decided to use Ossie because of his good skills with the ball and the fact that he was a very hard man to tackle.

The rest is history. Ossie's one big regret was that he had never played in a grand final before. Now he had that opportunity and he gave it everything he had. Tim told us Canterbury were a little vulnerable down the blind side, an area where Ossie likes to work, and that's where we attacked early on. The first two Raiders tries both came from Ossie passes, and the match developed into something of a dream for the big man.

While we celebrated after the event with Ossie, we all felt desperately sorry for John Lomax. We made sure that John was part of the day, the victory lap around the Sydney Football Stadium, the celebrations and the speeches. He missed only two matches all season yet, cruelly, one of them was the one that really mattered. As some compensation, he was later voted as the club's first-grade player of the year.

And so ended my life as a Raider. Well, at least it was the end of my playing career with the club. But I will always be a Canberra man in spirit.

What a fabulous way to end my playing days with the Canberra Raiders.

When I joined the club back in 1986 I could not have believed just how well it was all going to turn out. And I'm not talking about the trophies and the glory either. The other things — the rapport with the fans, the identification with the city and surrounding region, the links with local business and even politics — have made me feel as if I have lived in Canberra for ever. I feel as though I contributed to the community and that, through playing rugby league, I was able to make the lives of the people of Canberra that little bit more significant.

I think Richard Farmer, the spokesman for the Save the Raiders trust fund, summed it all up during an interview he gave the *Australian* on August 7, 1991. "None of the players want to leave," Farmer told reporter John Hogan, alluding to the fact that the alternative was a substantial cut in salary. "They're more than just footballers down here."

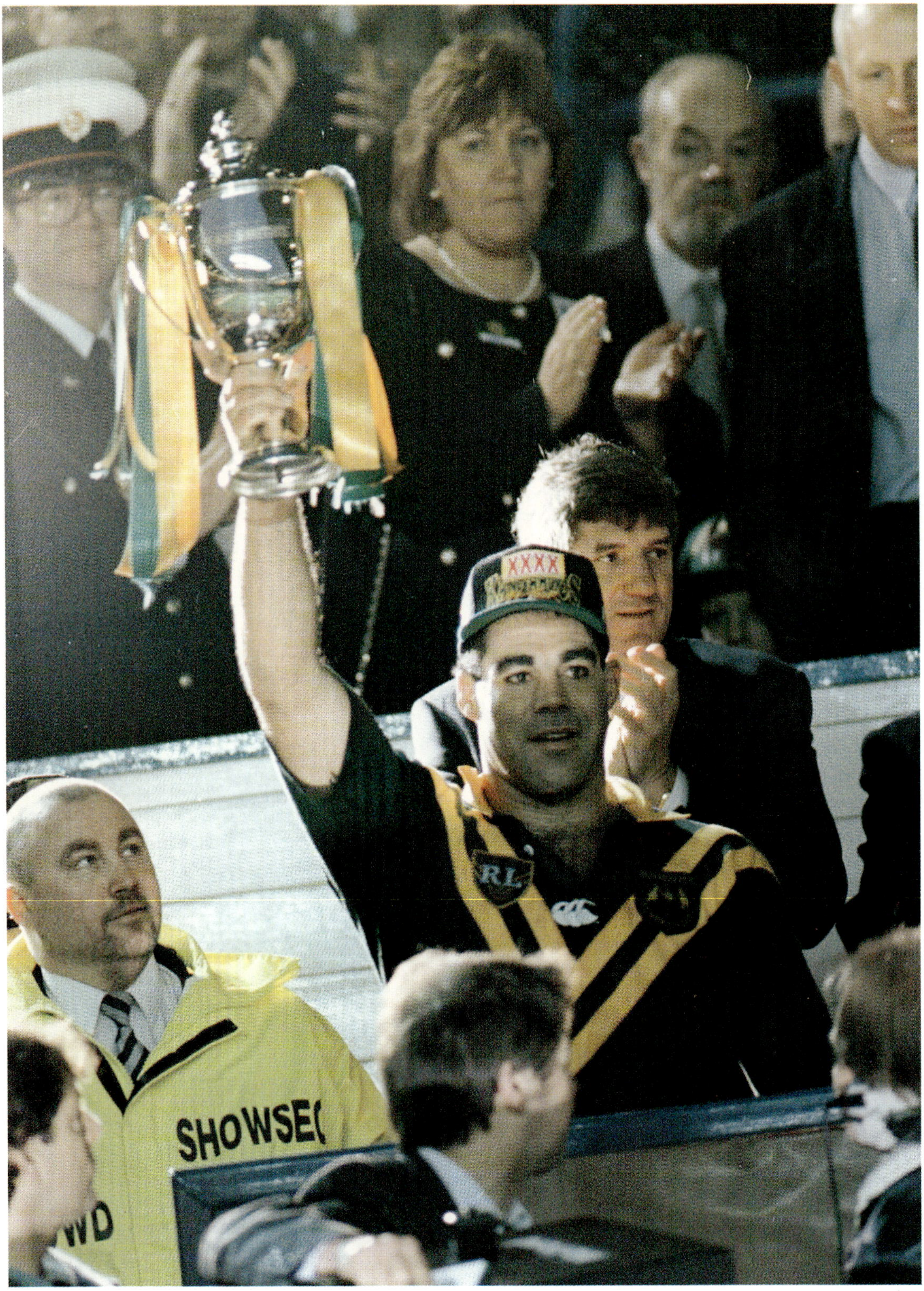
XXXX
RL
SHOWSE

10: AUSTRALIAN CAPTAIN

I was surprised by just how nervous I was when I first captained the Australian rugby league team. The game was a one-off Test against France in the New South Wales country town of Parkes, on July 27, 1990. As the most experienced captain in the team (the only other guy in the side then captaining his club side was Manly's Michael O'Connor, who was on the wing for Australia and had only begun leading the Sea Eagles at the start of 1990), I was a long way from a surprise choice. But the buzz I felt as I came to terms with my elevation was unforgettable. I was so honoured — here I was, the leader of some of the very best players in the world. I didn't want to let anyone down.

I quickly found that being captain of Australia is a lot different to leading a club team. Because I needed to earn the players' respect for my leadership skills in a hurry, the pressure to do the off-field things right was accentuated. Bob Fulton encouraged me and I made a conscious effort to talk to all the guys, from established players like Blocker Roach and Paul Sironen right though to the debutants, St George's Brad Mackay and Souths' Mark Carroll.

In Canberra, where the players are together for much of the year, I had had a number of matches to convince my Raiders team-mates that I had the ability to lead them through the tough times. But in this one-off Test, I had only the pre-game camp. Of all my team-mates, only Gary Belcher and Laurie Daley had played in a team captained by Mal Meninga.

Gaining my Test team-mates' respect proved to be a seemingly never-ending endeavour. It was also highly rewarding. In the seasons that followed, every time a fresh face came into the squad, I needed to go through the process of convincing that newcomer that I would be there when he needed me.

It was especially difficult taking over the captaincy from an icon like Wally Lewis, a person everyone respected as a player. I knew I could play the game pretty well, but I also wanted to be an influential captain.

As it turned out, I actually found the Australian job easier than club captaincy in at least one sense: the men in the Australian side were the very best footballers available and, inevitably, their approach to the game was of the highest order. These guys were strictly professional — if they hadn't been, they wouldn't have been there, for nowadays you have to

Opposite: With the spoils of another Ashes triumph at Elland Road, Leeds, 1994.

have total dedication to get to international rugby league. And they all appreciated the honour of playing for their country. One thing I didn't have to worry about was convincing the guys to put the effort in, or that the cause they were fighting for was worthwhile.

The night of my Australian captaincy debut was one of the coldest of my life, as temperatures plummeted towards zero. At one point, we asked for buckets of hot water to be brought to the sideline, because our hands were freezing up. The final score was 34–2, with two aspects of the game being of note. First was the performance of Brad Mackay, who celebrated his Australian call-up with a trifecta of tries. Second was the deplorable Australian goal-kicking. I missed two out of two, Michael O'Connor missed three out of three and Dale Shearer and Laurie Daley missed their only attempts. Finally, Gary Belcher stepped up to land one from right in front, to scenes of great jubilation from the frozen Australian bench.

Three weeks later, the Australian team travelled to Wellington to play the Kiwis in a Test staged as rugby league's contribution to New Zealand's 150th birthday celebrations. The day before, the rugby union Wallabies had defeated the All Blacks, and we managed to complete the double, with an emphatic 24–6 victory. It was an excellent performance, so good that after the game Bob Fulton told the media that, as far as he was concerned, unless injuries took a hand, all 17 members of the Australian squad were guaranteed spots in the Kangaroo team that would travel to Great Britain and France at the end of the Australian season.

The biggest league story in the weeks leading up to the announcement of the 1990 Kangaroo team was whether Wally Lewis was going to be available. Conflicting news reports suggested his arm was right, it wasn't right, it might be right, it might not be right. I was aware that if Wally were ruled out, I was a very short-priced favourite to get what is one of the most privileged jobs in football. I also knew that Wally was still a great and influential footballer and that the Australian side would lose something if he wasn't there. But really, I couldn't afford to even think about it — the Raiders were up to their necks in the premiership race, and whether Wally was fit or not had absolutely nothing to do with me.

In the end, he was ruled out after the ARL's doctors decided his arm was not quite right. Soon after, I was named as captain of the side — one of the genuine highlights of my career. The names of the tour squad had been released just as we boarded the plane to fly back to Canberra after our grand final win over Penrith and in a brief moment during the flight, away from the celebrations, I thought back to some of the absolute legends of the game who had led previous Kangaroo sides — Fulton, Langlands, Gasnier, Churchill ... The name Meninga didn't look quite right beside them, but I was determined to try and change that if I could.

Every member of the Kangaroo squad was aware of just how tough the tour was going to be. Memories remained of the way a spare-parts British side had stunned the Australians at the Sydney Football Stadium in the final Test of the 1988 Ashes series. The recent performance of quality players like Ellery Hanley, Garry Schofield, Martin Offiah, Joe Lydon and Kevin Ward in the Winfield Cup underlined the fact that the team from Great Britain was going to be a powerful one.

Then there was the pressure on us to emulate the undefeated performances of the 1982 and 1986 Kangaroo teams. But I had a great deal of faith in the ability and integrity of the team I captained, confidence that was boosted even further by our efforts in the five lead-up games to the first Test. All were won handsomely, the highlight being a 34–6 thrashing of the English champions Wigan in game 3.

However, we then travelled to Wembley Stadium in London for the first Test, and were soundly beaten. The final score was 19–12, on a day when Hanley and Schofield were superb, and we struggled to come to terms with the stop–start pace of the game. Afterwards, both Bob and I tried to be positive, and others pointed out that at least the stress of trying to remain undefeated was gone.

Why did we lose? First and foremost, our opponents were clearly the better side. Perhaps we were complacent. It did seem that some of us had forgotten on the day about the things (intensity, hard work, desire) that had made the Australian team so powerful for so long. Perhaps the huge promotional push the game received in the week leading up to the kick-off worked against us. Certainly that second point may well have been a factor in my own mediocre display. I agreed to appear on a number of early-morning TV and radio programs, which meant getting up at 6 a.m. to be on air an hour later. That is not my usual routine.

I recall that our training sessions were very, very ordinary, which might have had something to do with the hour-long journey from our London hotel to our training ground. There were a lot of dropped balls and a lack of intensity. Training took on an almost carnival-like atmosphere: subconsciously, we might have forgotten the importance of the Test match to be played.

Whatever the causes, our performance was embarrassing, but it served as a very effective kick in the butt for us.

Changes were made for the second Test in order to regroup and regain the confidence we had lost. The hardest choice for Bob Fulton was at halfback — whether to choose Allan Langer (one of the better players at Wembley) or Ricky Stuart. Ricky had played five-eighth in the first Test because Laurie was out with a broken hand (Bob wanted to use Ricky's brilliant kicking ability), but for the second he was moved to the

Meninga

Australian Captain

In the 1990s, there was an almost never-ending debate as to who was the top Australian halfback — Canberra's Ricky Stuart (opposite) or Brisbane's Allan Langer (left). I'm afraid I have no intention of buying into this argument — frankly I'm not sure what the correct answer is (and, anyway, they're both good friends of mine).

Ricky and Allan are both superb halfbacks, but they are very different types of footballers. Ricky thrives on running the show, with his extraordinary vision, passing and kicking ability. In contrast, Alfie is more of an individualist who strives to make the breaks and create chances. Both are excellent leaders, great characters and match-winners.

The great Australian halfback of the 1980s was Peter Sterling, but as grand a player as Sterlo was, I believe Ricky and Alfie are better.

MENINGA

scrumbase, which was desperately unfortunate for little Alfie. I think Bob saw Ricky as providing a slightly better link between the forwards and the backs. Laurie moved into the centres, instead of Mark McGaw (our best at Wembley), who had wrecked a shoulder. Cliff Lyons, of Manly, was the new five-eighth. Dale Shearer replaced Mick Hancock on the wing. And Glenn Lazarus, Ben Elias and Brad Mackay came into the forwards, replacing Martin Bella, Kerrod Walters and John Cartwright respectively.

In the second Test we were much, much better and should in truth have won the game quite easily. There were many occasions where we produced some magic play, but then the last pass would go astray. Then, in the second half, with just 12 minutes left and Australia ahead 10–6, Ricky threw that infamous pass that the Poms' replacement centre Paul Loughlin intercepted, to race away and score. Standing behind the goalposts after that try was a unique experience in my football career. The British winger Paul Eastwood had a relatively simple conversion attempt that, if successful, would have put his side in front 12–10. But we had been so dominant, it was almost impossible to come to terms with the fact that we were about to fall behind. Ricky was terribly upset. He commented later that he felt as if there had been a death in his family. As captain, I had to try to stay positive. I told the guys that all we had to do was to keep playing the way we had and everything would be okay. There was no need to panic, I said, even though deep in my mind I really wondered whether the rugby league gods were against us. Then Eastwood missed the kick. The score stayed at 10-all and, in terms of the series and the retention of the Ashes, we had some breathing-space. There really was no need to panic. From that point on, we just kept plugging away, plugging away and, right on full-time, the unbelievable happened.

Ricky Stuart — the same Ricky Stuart who had thrown the intercepted pass — had the ball in his hands about 15 metres from his own line. He ran right, straightened, then dummied and took off. Fortunately, I had enough legs at that point of the game to back him up. He passed me the ball about 20 metres from the line, so I didn't have too far to go.

As you can imagine, I remember this moment very vividly. And I remember the emotion I felt very clearly, too. I was relieved. Not thrilled, just relieved. Despite our excellent preparation, undoubted ability and huge effort, things could have gone horribly wrong. But they didn't, and the relief I felt, and all the squad felt, was very evident. We were so thankful we still had the opportunity to retain the Ashes.

In the fortnight between the second and third Tests, we were very, very focussed. Our preparation was spot-on and, despite the fact the series decider was played in cold, bleak, very English conditions, we produced

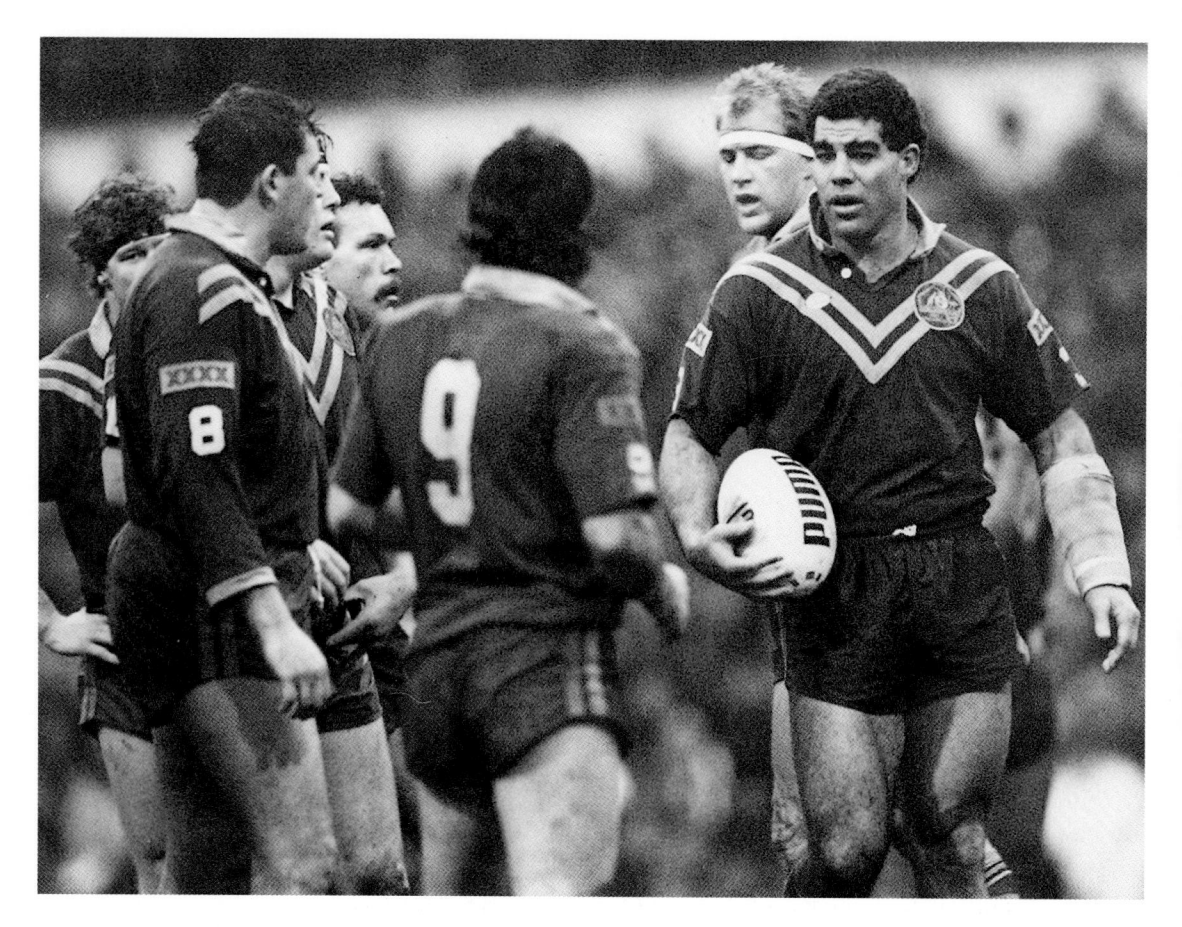

A tense moment in the second Ashes Test of 1990 at Old Trafford. The other players are (left to right): Brad Mackay, Steve Roach, Glenn Lazarus (obscured by Roach), Cliff Lyons, Ben Elias (no. 9) and Paul Sironen.

our most dominating display of the tour, to win 14–0. The entire defensive effort of the Kangaroos that day was quite exceptional, especially the role played by Paul Sironen, who blotted Ellery Hanley completely out of the game. We led only 4–0 at half-time, but we had battled biting winds in the first 40 minutes and in the sheds at the break we were one extremely confident football side.

Holding up the Ashes trophy after the game was obviously one of the best moments of my career. It was just a pity then, that I didn't get it right. On the front of the Ashes trophy is the simple insignia:

International
Rugby League Football
Australia v. England
The Ashes
Presented by City Tattersalls Club
Sydney 1928

The great tradition, after being handed the trophy following the series' conclusion, is to turn to the crowd and show them the cup. Which I did

— only I showed them the back of the thing, not the front! It was only a little thing, but Gary Belcher still reminds me of it ...

The English leg of the tour completed, we then travelled to France for a series of easy games against very ordinary teams. From a football point of view, there is little I recall of this tour. Our opponents were just not up to international standard, and though we didn't train that often (about once before each of the two Tests, if my memory is right) we still belted our opponents in each of the five games.

I found that on tour, one of the most crucial roles of the captain was to try and monitor the players' feelings, and to make sure that they were getting as much out of the training and preparations as the coaching staff intended. I made sure the guys knew that if they had a problem or even a suggestion, I was always available to listen to their thoughts. I became something of an advocate for the players, and at the same time Bob and trainer Shaun McRae would sound me out to ensure that the players were happy and comfortable with what was going on. I also saw it as my role to help make sure that things didn't become too mundane or tedious from day to day.

By the end of the Kangaroo adventure, I had settled into the role of Australian rugby league captain, so I was delighted when the selectors decided to keep me in charge for the first Test of the 1991 home series against New Zealand. The squad chosen included 11 of the successful Kangaroo touring party and six new players — five of whom were full-back Paul Hauff, lock Bradley Clyde (who had missed the tour through injury), second-rower Ian Roberts, hooker Steve Walters and replacement back Peter Jackson. The sixth was Wally Lewis, fully recovered from his broken arm and back in the side at five-eighth after leading Queensland to another State of Origin triumph.

Once the Test squad came together, I quickly had the impression Wally was disappointed I had not stepped aside so he could regain the team captaincy. But I didn't see why I should. I wanted the job, and had just captained the Kangaroos on a successful tour of England and France. But Wally didn't see things my way, and I believe his disappointment at not regaining the leadership had a disruptive effect on the team.

We crashed to a 24–8 loss. Our preparation was dreadful; there was a feeling that all we had to do was to turn up and victory would be ours. It was an embarrassing performance, made worse for me by the 10 minutes I spent in the sin-bin in the second half. This is not the right place for a Test captain to be at any time, but especially so when the team was struggling for cohesion and inspiration. I was terribly disappointed — with some members of the team for their lack of discipline and intensity, and with myself for allowing my frustration to get the better of me.

Opposite: 1991: Wally Lewis (standing, left), Bob Lindner (standing, right), coach Bob Fulton and I prepare for the first Test team photo to be taken.

After the game, I wondered whether I should remain as captain. Stepping down was a definite option and, had I decided the team would have had a better chance of focussing on the job at hand, that's exactly what I would have done. If the same negative attitude that ruined our first Test performance remained, I knew we were in grave danger of losing the series. However, I talked things over with a number of people within the team, and they all said the same thing — that giving up the captaincy was not the way to go. Instead, we vowed to turn things around in a hurry.

A number of changes were made to the side, with wingers Willie Carne and Rod Wishart, centre Laurie Daley (back from injury), five-eighth Peter Jackson, second-rowers David Gillespie and Mark Geyer and prop Craig Salvatori all coming into the starting line-up. Jacko's inclusion at five-eighth marked the end of Wally's remarkable international career. At the end of the following season, he retired from the game to concentrate on coaching his new club, the Gold Coast Seagulls, and the Queensland State of Origin team.

Just how much the embarrassment of our first Test performance had impacted on us was reflected in the way we approached the second Test. The intensity was back, the effort on the training tracks sensational and the final score — 44–0 to Australia — was a fair indication of how well we had played. This was a very disciplined display; by sticking to Bob Fulton's game plan to the letter, I believe we produced one of the best performances by an Australian team I was ever involved in.

Our good form then carried over into the deciding Test in Brisbane, which we won 40–12. After the game, Bob Fulton suggested this effort might have been even better than the second Test win. I wasn't so sure, but I was still very impressed with the way the guys had put in. Our entire forward pack — Bradley Clyde, Mark Geyer, David Gillespie, Martin Bella, Steve Walters and Craig Salvatori — were at their intimidating best, while for me the game was a statistically important one, as my 16 points (from a try and six goals) took me past Michael Cronin as Australia's highest points-scorer in Test rugby league.

At season's end, the Australian team travelled north for a very humid but extremely interesting five-match tour of Papua New Guinea. Whatever our expectations were before we arrived, they were nothing compared to what we actually experienced. The PNG players we faced were unbelievably enthusiastic, while the fans' reaction to our visit was simply incredible.

This was as close as I will ever get to feeling like a movie star. I remember when we first arrived in Goroka for the first Test, our public relations officer asked us to duck out on to the balcony for a minute, because there were some league followers outside the hotel. So out we

Australian Captain

Meninga

Above and right: Two snapshots from the Australian team's tour of Papua New Guinea in 1991, when we met many devoted followers of the game.

went, like the Royal Family at Buckingham Palace, to wave to a crowd of a few thousand people. It was extraordinary. This was all they wanted — to be acknowledged. Soon afterwards, we returned inside, and the throng headed off, happy to have been this close to the Australian rugby league touring team.

One morning, we decided to play golf. The course appeared to be deserted. Until about the third hole. By then, there was a gallery of around 1,000 league fans following us around, making us feel as if we were involved in the final day of the US Masters at Augusta! Every time a good shot was struck, an "oooh!" or an "aaah …" would go up from the crowd, and there was genuine disappointment if anyone hit a bad shot.

Although Laurie Daley and Ricky Stuart were both unavailable because of injury, there were still six Canberra Raiders in the touring party, including Gary Coyne, who was making his first international tour (the others were Bradley Clyde, Glenn Lazarus, Steve Walters, Gary Belcher and myself). Gary won his first Test cap in the first Test, at Goroka, which we won by 58–2.

Three days later, we played a match against a Highlands Zone XIII at

A month before the 1992 World Cup final, the Brisbane Broncos won the first first-grade premiership. In the after-match celebrations, the entire Broncos squad ventured out to get identical short-back-and-sides haircuts, which featured each player's number razored into the back of his head. The three Broncos here are Alfie Langer (left), Kevvie Walters (centre) and Willie Carne.

Mount Hagen. Unfortunately, this was marred by a near riot among the fans. Tear gas, semi-automatic machine-gun fire and a thunderstorm combined to make this one of the more unusual days in my career.

The trouble resulted from a decision to make the game an all-ticket affair, a concept foreign to many of the league fans who had journeyed for up to four days to see the encounter. Usually, getting in was as simple as turning up at the ground. So, when people began arriving without tickets and found they wouldn't be able to get in, a very ugly situation developed and climaxed when the football started with thousands left outside the ground. We were never in any danger, but it was still a very unpleasant experience to have to try and concentrate on a game of football while the screaming sounds of a riot were emanating from beyond the sidelines. At one point, the game had to be stopped because tear gas was wafting its way across the ground. Towels were rushed out to us, and we were obliged to crouch low to the ground until the fumes dispersed.

We eventually won that game 28–3, and four days later we won the second and final Test by 40–6, to clinch a place in the 1992 World Cup final. We would not know whether our opponents would be Great Britain or New Zealand in that game until the final qualifying matches were played in 1992.

Our main Test rivals in 1992 were Great Britain, who came to Australia for a three-match Ashes series. This was a contest I was eagerly looking forward to. After the tight 1990 series, international rugby league competition between Great Britain and Australia was back to its glorious best, and for me there was the chance to play against the Poms at home for the first time since 1984.

Again, we won a series by two Tests to one, with our defeat this time coming in the second match, at Melbourne's Princes Park. This was a loss that reminded me of the defeat at Wembley nearly two years earlier, when we again got caught up in much of the pre-match promotion. And again, Great Britain were brilliant, with fullback Graham Steadman in superb touch and forwards Denis Betts and Phil Clarke magnificent as well.

The third Test, which we won 16–10 to retain the Ashes trophy, was one of the most memorable nights of my career. It was my 37th Test, which edged me past Reg Gasnier's previous record for the number of Test match appearances by an Australian. And the 12 points I scored in the game, from a try and four goals, made me the highest points-scorer in Anglo-Australian Test rugby league. But, most importantly, I was captain of a side that on a night when it really mattered, produced an awesome team effort. In the end, the six-point margin between the two sides was in no way a reflection of the decisive way we controlled the game.

Our next assignment of the 1992 international season was a Test against Papua New Guinea in Townsville, which we won 36–14. Then, following the end of the Australian season, we travelled to Wembley for the World Cup final against Great Britain. This was a match that developed into a gruelling defensive battle, and was won by the only try of the game, a real Broncos' effort between our super substitute Kevvie Walters and his club-mate from Brisbane, centre Steve Renouf. The final score was 10–6, a win which broke the "Wembley hoodoo", a so-called jinx that the media had been hyping up ever since our Test defeat at the famous stadium in 1990.

In 1993, I missed the first Test of a three-match series against New Zealand when I was suspended for illegally using a forearm on Manly's British import John Devereux in a club match at Brookvale Oval. It was the first Test I had missed since the 1988 Test against PNG in Parkes, ruining a run of 20 straight appearances.

There was a lot of pressure on the NSW Rugby League to give me a suspension over the Devereux incident, which happened when the Sea Eagles three-quarter moved in to tackle me and I got my fend a little wrong.

Unfortunately, a few people in the game believed I had already escaped censure for a clash with the then Manly captain Michael O'Connor in a State of Origin match in 1991. That had been a hard tackle, and O'Connor came out of it with a broken nose, but I do not believe there was anything illegal in it. I think some of the people who pushed for me to be cited over the Devereux affair saw my subsequent two-match suspension as a "get-square" for the incident two years before.

My fend on Devereux had been awkward and careless, but I knew there had been no malice in it. However, I also realised there was little chance of getting off the charge, given the pressure that had been applied through the media. As I stood before the judiciary on that particular night, I knew I was going to be suspended. However, I was prepared for it and accepted it philosophically — you have to take the good with the bad in this game.

One good thing that did come from the episode was the reaction of Bob Fulton, who earlier in the year had taken over the coaching job at Manly, to go with his position as the Australian coach. Bob insisted I travel over with the team, as something of an assistant coach, which was a gesture I appreciated enormously.

What was not so enjoyable was watching the first Test, in Auckland, from the coaches' bench. The match ended in a 14–all draw, after stand-in captain Laurie Daley dropped a field goal in the dying minutes to level the scores.

From Auckland, we travelled down to Palmerston North for the second Test, which developed into a bizarre night. The game was played

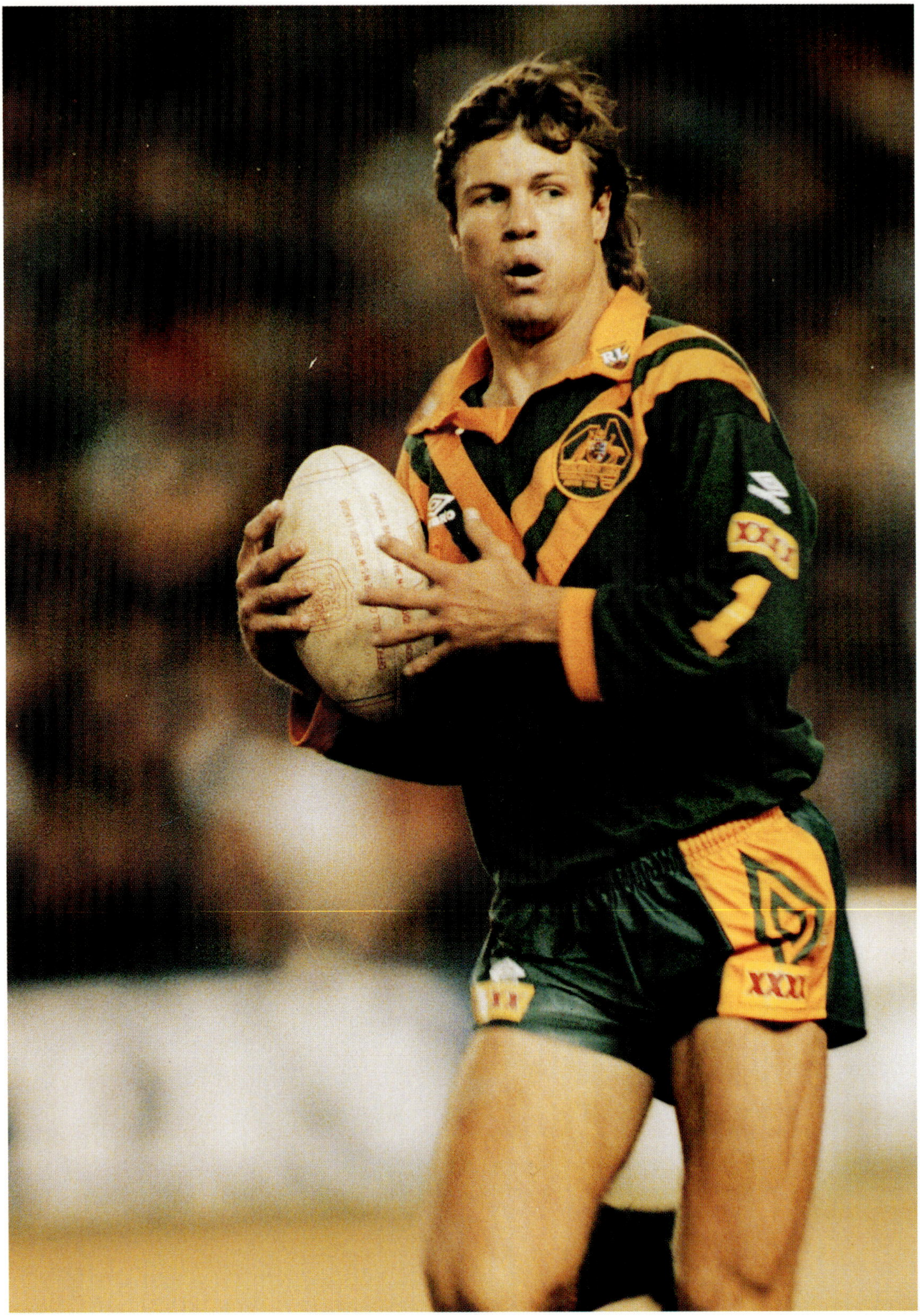

before a full house, and the start was held up while the ground staff tried to convince the crowd to get back behind the ground perimeter. When play finally began, we set about producing one of our finest ever wet-weather displays, while the crowd amused themselves by getting right into the game, and refusing to return the ball if it was kicked to them. They were no more than a little over-exuberant, but in the game's final minutes things became a little farcical when the one ball that hadn't been pinched to that point was, and officials had a devil of a time finding a pumped-up piece of leather so we could finish the game! It was cold and wet, and then some mug threw a bottle on to the field which nearly collected Laurie. The Kiwis' captain, Gary Freeman, wanted to end the game there and then, but I thought, seeing as we were 16–8 in front, we might as well wait until the final whistle.

Five days later, we sealed another series win with a 16–4 victory at Lang Park. This was a pretty emotional night for me. I knew, having seen the Test schedule for 1994, which involved just a single home Test against France, that there was little chance of me playing another international at Lang Park. So I was very pleased to score a try late in proceedings, and to acknowledge the Queensland crowd after the game. However, I was quite happy to take a back seat to the emotional tribute paid to Bob Lindner, who had just played the final Test of his exceptional international career. And I liked Bobby's comment to the media after the game. He was off at the end of the season to play for Oldham in England which, one reporter pointed out, created the very possible scenario of him playing against the Kangaroos on their 1994 tour. But Bob was having none of it. "There's no way," he remarked, "I would ever play against Australia."

My own farewell to Test football in Australia came 12 months later at the Parramatta Stadium, where we thrashed the French by 58–0. I would have preferred a more competitive fixture for this farewell, but the fans did turn out in force, and I appreciated the manner in which they acknowledged it was my last home Test.

●●●

It was an absolute thrill to captain my country from 1990 to 1994. This opportunity was, without doubt, the pinnacle of my rugby league career.

I'm not being cynical when I say that I didn't feel any more proud when I was captain of Australia than when I was playing under Wally Lewis or Max Krilich. I was already as proud as I could be just being a member of the side. It's a special feeling being able to pull on the green and gold jersey, whether you're the fullback, in the front row, or the captain. I didn't consider myself any better than any of my team-mates, just because I had the 'c' beside my name. Far from it. However, I was

Opposite: Because Andrew Ettingshausen is good-looking, some critics tend to think he's a little soft. However, that assessment is a long way from the truth. Defensively, "ET" is very strong, his timing is perfect both in attack and defence, and he can perform brilliantly as a centre, winger and fullback. And he's a very intelligent player, as was shown by the try he scored in the second Test of the 1994 Kangaroo tour, when he slid into the corner. Had he stayed on his feet, there was every chance he would have been knocked into touch.

Meninga

Above: The last Test-match try I scored in Australia, against France at Parramatta Stadium in 1994.

Opposite: Surrounded by students from Auckland Grammar, following the completion of a training session conducted on the school ovals during the lead-up to the first Test of the 1993 tour.

always aware that being the captain was a great privilege, and a very prestigious position.

Once I had the captaincy, there was never one moment when I didn't want the job. I relished the opportunity to be in charge and was aware of the responsibility the job entailed. From my first day in charge, I wanted to make sure I did the job properly. First and foremost, I realised that I couldn't allow the pressures of the captaincy to have a negative impact on my football (and I don't think that ever happened). And I also wanted to be as close to the perfect ambassador for my team, my sport and my country as I could possibly be.

Apart from playing to the best of my ability, I always considered that this ambassadorial role was the most important part of being the Australian rugby league captain.

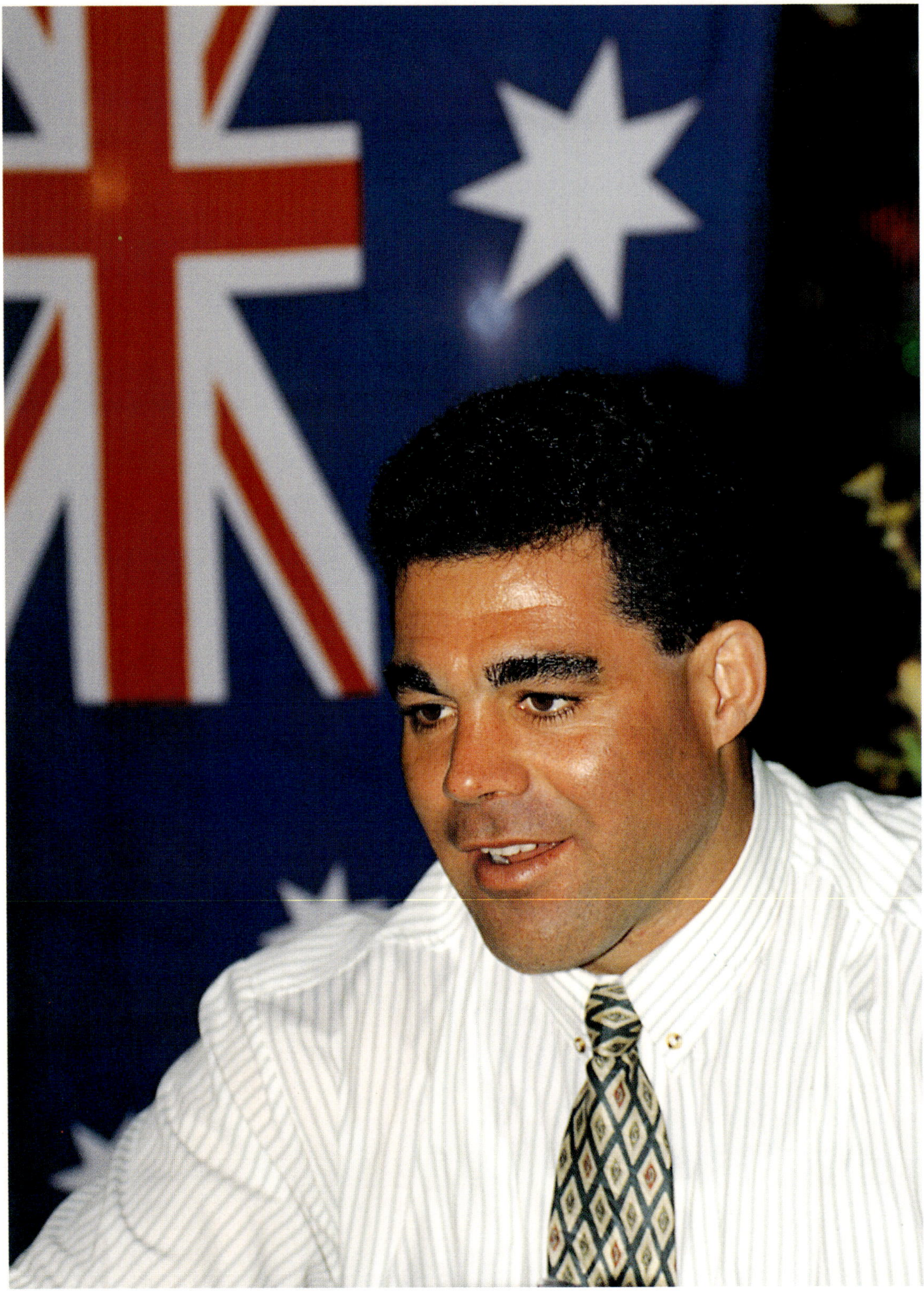

11. SUPER LEAGUE

Rugby league had been both my sport and work for nearly a decade when I decided that 1994 would be my last season. It was not a decision I came to easily. I still loved the game but, despite apprehension about what I would do with the rest of my life, I knew it was best to retire when still playing at the highest level.

Throughout the year I did my best not to think too much about what the future would hold. I wanted to concentrate on doing my best one last time for the Raiders, Queensland and Australia and I knew that worrying about the next job would interfere with the task of playing football.

Yet naturally there were moments when Debbie and I wondered what 1995 could bring. We wanted to stay in Canberra where the kids were settled, so I had a few chats with Tim Sheens about a career in coaching and making a start under him with one of the junior sides. The club spoke to me about entering Raiders management in the promotions department. John Ribot of the Broncos suggested a final fling as a player in their London team combined with some work as a television commentator.

There were obviously opportunities to remain involved in the game, but I was aware that I was not really trained to take on any of them. Whatever I did would mean buckling down and learning new skills and the middle of a football season was not the time to do that. My future was put into the too-hard basket until the end of the Kangaroo tour when there would be time enough to contemplate the options.

A summer break without the grind of pre-season training was a luxury, though I knew that decisions finally had to be made. By the end of January when the holiday had come to an end, the rumour mill was working overtime about a plan by News Limited to reshape the Winfield Cup from a 20-team competition into one with only 12 or 14 teams.

At this stage I had heard the scuttlebutt but had no direct knowledge of what the Super League concept was all about. I could understand the talk about the need to reduce the number of Sydney clubs if the competition was not going to become uneven, but I was firm in the belief that the Australian Rugby League was the body to sort that problem out. When in early February 1995 the ARL rejected the News Limited proposal, I thought that that was what was going to happen.

My personal relations with the administrators of the game has always been friendly and as captain of the Australian side I had enjoyed the support of Ken Arthurson and John Quayle. Both of them had kindly spoken to me, in fact, about a future career in ARL administration. One suggestion was that I work as a liaison officer between them and the senior players. To me, this seemed a sensible idea that augured well for the future of the game because players were regularly the forgotten people when major decisions were made. When I travelled to Sydney to join in the black-tie opening of the season I mentioned to John that my interest in such a position continued.

I had also been approached by Ken Cowley, chief executive of News Limited in Australia, who spoke of employment and training opportunities with companies in the News Limited group. The offer of management training was appealing. I wanted to get a real job for myself rather than becoming just another ex-football glad-hander trotted out for business functions. Ken was talking about this with Ansett, his newspaper business and the Foxtel pay television organisation. In our discussions Super League was not on the agenda. Officially at least, that News Limited proposal was dead.

Yet obviously the future of rugby league was in my mind too, and I took the counsel of friends as I struggled with my decision. Richard Farmer, a Canberra journalist I got to know during the salary cap crisis at the Raiders back in 1991, introduced me to Sydney company adviser David Block as someone to talk through the issues with. David, a man chosen by the Hawke Labor government to restructure the public service, certainly helped clarify my thoughts. I spoke again with John Quayle but was disappointed at what I took to be a lack of enthusiasm about having me at the ARL. There would be none of the management training that News Limited offered and the financial remuneration was very modest by comparison. In the end, I had to do what was best for the future of myself and my family.

At this point, I was still unaware of the plans to push ahead with Super League and my support for that concept was not a condition of the contract offered to me when I met David Smith of News Limited in Canberra. My lawyer, Terry Chamberlain, my accountant, Peter Wesley, and Richard Farmer all sat in on this meeting with Debbie and me as we went through the details. Only when agreement had been reached on what I was to do for Ansett and News Limited did I raise the question about the future of rugby league. David Smith very decently said that he did not want me to get involved because he understood the long and close association I had with the ARL, but he did outline the concept.

I left that meeting relieved about having settled my own future. While apprehensive about the upheaval that would occur in rugby league,

I was confident that News Limited would merely be the catalyst for necessary change and that the ARL would continue to run the sport.

I was, in fact, quite excited about what I had heard and wished I was starting in the game instead of finishing! A reduction in the number of teams to 12, when combined with increased payments for television rights, meant that there would be a $4 million (rather than a $1.8 million) salary cap to be shared among players. So there would be higher payments to go with the honour and glory of playing in State of Origin and Test matches. And for the first time players would get proper financial protection when injured, with half the contract amount being paid even if they were forced out of the game. Under this new arrangement there would also be the top level of medical benefits coverage for players and their families and a form of superannuation to make the transition to another career easier. The elite players of the game would be offered the chance of training for a career in the News Limited Group.

I could see that taking the game to the world on the News Limited television networks was a way of assuring its future. Rugby league might have developed well on television in Australia under Messrs Arthurson and Quayle, but it was in trouble in England and virtually dead in France. To grow, it need an international dimension and David Smith had talked about giving it one. For the top players, the increased exposure, when combined with a direct share in marketing revenue, would do wonders for their income.

Somewhere down the track I knew there would be a role for me in helping to bring about this new era for rugby league, but for the moment I thought it would be back to school to learn the new skills I would need in my new career. I had certainly not imagined being thrust into the hurly-burly of a fight between the Nine Network and News Limited because I thought that players, when they themselves became aware of the advantages of Super League, would welcome it and that the ARL would reach a sensible accommodation with the new competition.

However, I reckoned without the passions of some of rugby league's founding Sydney clubs and their ability to spread disinformation. When players were virtually blackmailed into signing loyalty agreements with the ARL, under the threat that this was the only way to play representative football, I chose to enter the fray. I believed Super League was in the best interest of the game and I did not want its potential sabotaged before it had even begun.

I was soon to learn that good intentions about the future of the code and its players were not enough to play in this contest. Spreading the Super League message required the skills of a politician — not a footballer — and I was certainly no slick orator. I proved that when I addressed a meeting at the Cronulla Leagues Club and my words did not exactly come out as I had intended. That all-time great player John Raper jumped on the impression I had inadvertently given, that I was ungrateful about what football had done for me. I had actually been trying to get across the serious point that professional sports people are often left ill-equipped for their next career when they have finished with football.

That is something which, if I had said it properly, John Raper would surely have understood. That I failed to get the point across does not make it any less valid. There are few sadder sights than old footballers with nothing to live on but their past glories, and I am delighted that others in the future will be given the same opportunities that News Limited has given me to learn new skills. It should come as no surprise to anyone, incidentally, to learn that one of the first training courses Ansett has since given me was in the art of preparing and giving public addresses!

Not that I want to give speeches for a living, but a continuing involvement in Super League is on the agenda. The game can only be the better for the efforts News Limited has put in to save the English and New Zealand Leagues. And its involvement in developing the game in Papua New Guinea and the Pacific Islands — something close to my heart — means that the game will also get a boost in those regions. Rugby league is now on the way to becoming a major international sport and it has an increasingly exciting profile within Australia. The scars will take time to heal, but heal they will in a way that I am sure will leave the greatest game even stronger.

Opposite: Steve Renouf, the excitement machine from the Brisbane Broncos, is one of the best centres I have ever seen. He has pace, blistering acceleration and the ability to score a try from nothing. Early in his career, there was a question mark over his defensive ability, but not any more. Perhaps more than any other player in the 1990s, Steve advertises how skilful and exhilarating modern rugby league can be.

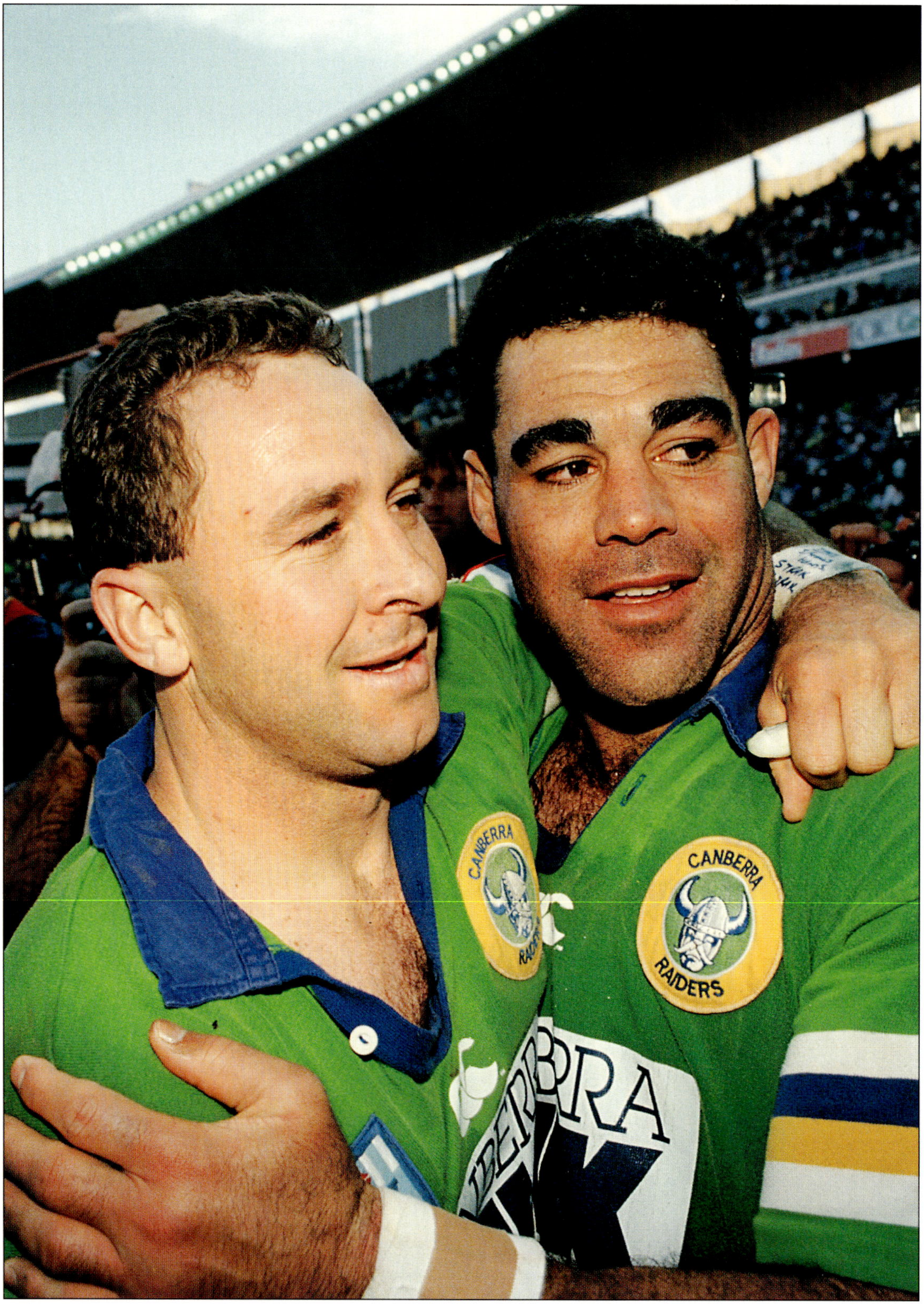
CANBERRA
RAIDERS
CANBERRA
RAIDERS

EPILOGUE: A VERY LUCKY MAN

I am the first to admit I have had a lot of luck in my rugby league career. My good fortune started very early on. I was lucky to be the son of athletic, sports-minded and caring parents. And I was lucky to be coached in my junior days by my father, a man so adept at the game and at passing his knowledge on to others. My father gave me the grounding that allowed me to play rugby league successfully. He taught me the football basics, took me to all his training sessions and gave me the chance to play against the bigger guys. Dad instilled in me a great passion for the game, while off the field both he and my mother taught me a lot of important characteristics that helped me in football and in life — things such as patience and self-control.

My good fortune continued when I ventured into the world of senior rugby league. I was lucky to have a smooth transition from the junior ranks of rugby league to the senior grades — it is not so comfortable a ride for others. I am grateful for my choice of senior clubs — first, Souths in Brisbane, and then the Canberra Raiders. St Helens, too. There is always a little luck in choosing the right club. And at the time when my professional career was under its greatest stress, in 1987–88, I was fortunate the four breaks to my arm were able to be repaired.

However, if I had to pinpoint the greatest luck I have had during my senior football career, it would be my involvement with three of the most professional coaches anyone could wish for: Wayne Bennett, Tim Sheens and Bob Fulton.

There would have been something very wrong with me if I had not learned or achieved anything from teachers like Wayne, Tim and Bob. They were the best in their field in my time. It has been a sheer pleasure playing rugby league for them.

•••

When I first came into contact with Wayne Bennett, back in my early days at the Queensland Police Academy, I was a very impressionable 15-year-old

Opposite: With Ricky Stuart, grand final day, 1994.

boy. Wayne set me on the right track, and gave me confidence both in my ability as a footballer and in my standing in life. I started believing I could go a bit further in the game and I wanted to achieve things.

In 1979, when I returned to the Police Academy and joined Souths (where Wayne was first-grade coach), Wayne became something of a father figure to me. Just as I had three years earlier, I looked up to him then, and admired his moral approach — whatever he did was based around what he thought was the right thing to do.

As a coach, Wayne emphasises the significance of a measured mental attitude to the game, the importance of fitness and the value of skills and goals. Goal-setting is one of the cornerstones of his way of life, and a technique he insists his players adopt. And he is fully aware of the physical requirements and demands involved in succeeding in the stressful domain of top-level rugby league.

He is brilliant when talking to players, in geeing them up and getting them to think the right way. And he is really outstanding in the way he teaches football skills.

I think that to be a successful coach you have to be a bit of a clairvoyant and you have to be able to read players' minds. Wayne has an uncanny ability, scary at times, to know when a player is troubled by something. And better than that, when someone has worries, Wayne can get him to open up, to get his problems off his chest. The end result is his players play better football and, perhaps more importantly, they are able to face the stresses that are sabotaging their life.

Since the Brisbane Broncos' debut premiership in 1988, that club has had only one coach — Wayne Bennett. Like the Canberra Raiders, who have been coached since 1988 by Tim Sheens, they have had absolutely no reason to change. Yet it has never been an easy ride. In three of their first four seasons, the Broncos failed to reach the semi-finals. The owners of this ambitious club didn't like such a situation at all. But Wayne never lost faith in his methods, or his approach to life. And the Broncos shrewdly stuck by him. His (and the club's) reward came in 1992 and 1993, when the Broncos were clearly the best team in football.

When tough decisions were needed, he made them. In 1994, he showed a lot of courage when he dropped the game's best front-rower, Glenn Lazarus, because he felt the big bloke was not playing well enough. At the time Glenn referred to the sacking as a "wake up call", but elite sportsmen don't appreciate being treated in this way. It was a massive kick in the guts for a man who had played in the previous five grand finals, and in the previous year had starred in the team that won the premiership, the State of Origin series and the Test series. But Wayne knew his man. Like a champion, Lazzo fought back. Through the 1994 Kangaroo tour and into

Epilogue

1995, I believe he was a better footballer than he was before his sacking.

There are times when a coach has to make a difficult, controversial and often unpopular change because he feels it will help his team win. The mistake, surely, would be to leave things the way they are. That is Wayne Bennett's philosophy. Perhaps there has been no tougher decision for Wayne to make than the one he instigated in the 1989–90 off-season, when he took the Broncos' captaincy off the legend, Wally Lewis, and gave it to Gene Miles. It was an extremely brave move, considering Wally's god-like status throughout Brisbane.

But it was one that the coach was convinced the Broncos needed at that time.

And so it was done, for Wayne Bennett is a man of convictions. His place in the history of the game, alongside other terrific coaches such as Jack Gibson, Harry Bath and the like is assured. However, for his players and for all those who have come into contact with him — and for the life and football career of one Mal Meninga — he is simply a very great man.

I have the highest admiration for Tim Sheens both personally and as a coach. One simple example illustrates this. It was Tim Sheens' decision in 1991 to stay with the Raiders, despite the financial minefield around the club. Tim's show of faith brought stability in troubled times because

The 1985 Southern Suburbs team which won the Brisbane A-Grade premiership.
Back row (left to right): R. Emonuel (masseur), G. Prior (masseur), P. Jennings (doctor), K. Rach (masseur), J. Elder (manager), W. Gardiner (trainer). **Standing:** E. Muller, M. Meskell, C. Phelan, S. Tronc, K. Gittins, H. Abbott, G. Grienke, A. Lumby. **Sitting:** G. Belcher, M. Meninga, W. Bennett (coach), N. Carr (captain), J. Elias, P. Jackson, G. Thompson. **In front:** G. French, D. Bourke, P. Wallace, W. Cullen.

> ## WAYNE BENNETT ON MAL MENINGA
>
> by Alan Clarkson
>
> Wayne Bennett has said the same thing about Mal Meninga so many times over the years that he feels he is like a record stuck in one groove. But he never tires of it. He remembers first meeting Meninga, then an eager young cadet, at the Queensland Police Academy in 1977.
>
> "He was only 15 at the time, but there was a great presence and a special quality about him," Bennett recalled. "One of the officers at the Academy said some of the young cadets were playing touch football and one of them looked to have a bit of class about him. I went down, watched them for a while and there was no doubt Mal Meninga was a player of the future.
>
> "He had extraordinary skills. In passing the ball, he generally took the right options and he was a remarkable athlete. He could joke with the best of them but when it came time to be serious, he was a dedicated professional.
>
> "Mal was, and remains, an exceptional young man, both on and off the field. And I think it says a lot for him that some of his closest mates now are the young fellows he first met during those Police Academy days.
>
> "I think the greatest accolade he could receive is that he is a winner. Every club he went to won. When Mal signed with Southern Suburbs they were well down the premiership ladder but in his time there they became one of the top teams in the competition. It was the same story when he went to the Raiders — they won three premierships.
>
> "I doubt if the career records he has established will ever be bettered."

we all had faith in Tim. Had he decided to leave, I believe the majority of the players would have gone as well.

Tim came to the club in 1988 and was in many ways in an unenviable position. The previous year, the club had made the grand final. There was only one way to improve, and that was to win the premiership. Despite being under a lot of pressure in his first year, he came through as you would expect from a man with such strength of character. In the seasons since, he has been a major figure in the success story of the Raiders.

EPILOGUE

With coach Tim Sheens after the 1994 grand final. This triumph vindicated Tim's brave decision to stick with the club during the financial crisis of 1991. Had he decided to go, I have no idea what the future might have held, but I'm pretty certain it wouldn't have included a Raiders' premiership victory within three years.

When Tim came to the Raiders we did not know much about him. As is the case when a new coach arrives at a club, unless he is already known as a great achiever, he really does have to earn the respect of the players. In Tim's case, that happened quickly, a key factor in his success. It is imperative that the players respect the coach, not only for his coaching ability, but for his personal qualities, too.

In 1987, Wayne Bennett and his fitness co-ordinator, Kelvin Giles, introduced weight training to the club, and we gradually developed in size and strength. And when Tim arrived, he increased the emphasis on weights in our training regime, which led to snide insinuations from some quarters outside the club that we were on steroids.

There is no doubt that from one season to the next we bulked up quite dramatically, but this had nothing to do with drugs. It was simply the result of the new, state-of-the-art training methods which Tim had introduced. We became a bigger, stronger and a more powerful side, who were, because of our added power, able to add intimidation to our ever-expanding armoury.

Tim is a very thorough coach. His preparation is extraordinary, probably the best I have experienced. It goes down to the most minute detail, describing the goals we should be setting, what the team we are playing will be doing and what we are going to do.

He insisted we kept notebooks to document our play. I would not call Tim a great motivator, but because his preparation was so thorough (and because we all had such faith in his methods) he did not need to motivate us with rousing speeches or dramatic videos.

Tim is very strong on discipline and club loyalty and adamant that players' families be kept involved in the club scene. I don't think there has ever been a footballer at the Raiders who has not appreciated that last point. And, like all the great coaches I have played under, Tim is a man of conviction. He lays down the rules and sticks by them. If a player is going to get on the grog or misses training, that player will suffer the consequences. In Tim's view, there are many young kids in reserve grade

---

TIM SHEENS ON MAL MENINGA

by Alan Clarkson

When Tim Sheens came to the Raiders in 1988, to succeed the successful coaching partnership of Don Furner and Wayne Bennett he was, to many critics, a surprise choice. Sheens had played 258 grade games with Penrith between 1971 and 1982, and then, as coach (1984–87) had steered that club to their first semi-final appearance in 1985.

Sheens' record with the Raiders has been quite superb, although his career was not always without its controversies. One of the toughest decisions Sheens had to make was in 1989, when he took the captaincy away from club stalwart Dean Lance and gave it to Mal Meninga. When I spoke to him in 1995, the first question I asked him was about Mal's leadership qualities.

"I like to think that the added responsibility helped him to develop into such a great player," Sheens said. "There was always a sort of magnetic aura about Mal and there was obvious leadership quality there too.

"Before being given the captaincy, Mal really did not push himself. He was great with his team-mates, but at functions he was sometimes a little shy. The captaincy helped to bring him out of his shell. His football improved and he led by example."

Sheens remembers one highly significant confrontation between Raiders players at half-time in a match against Canterbury.

"We were trailing at the time and Mal took to the forwards.

EPILOGUE

just itching for a chance to have a crack at the big time. So he has little time for the senior men who lose their ambition, even for a moment.

All the top coaches in the game have great back-up staff, inevitably hand-picked. Tim brought to the club Shaun McRae and Bryan Hider, who sorted out the training schedules and put Tim's plans and strategies into operation. The contribution of these guys to the Raiders has been enormous. With them around, the players have not had to worry about anything other than simply playing rugby league as well as they can.

Australia has played some great Test matches under Bob Fulton's wing since he took over as the Australian coach in 1989, and, fortunately, I was involved in all but one of them in the seasons between 1989 and 1994.

They reacted to his criticism by stating that he was the biggest player in the team and he wasn't doing very much.

"Mal led his team by example in the second half and we won the match. I believe the captaincy got him out of a 'traffic cop' syndrome and he became a more dominant figure in matches. He did a fine job for the Raiders."

Sheens has no doubts as to Mal's place in the game's history. "I have not seen a finer centre," he contends. "Generally, you get a player who either has good hands or he is a good runner with the ball, but Mal had both. You will never get the perfect player, but Mal does come close.

"When you look at his record — four Kangaroo tours, twice the captain of the Kangaroo touring team and so many points-scoring records — he is, on figures alone, the greatest ever. There will be arguments about who is the greatest but, in my time, Mal is the best to play the game."

Sheens also praises Mal's humble approach to the game. "One of the many things I admired about Mal was he was continually trying to learn, to improve some area of his play," he said. "Even in his last couple of years he was always prepared to listen and try to add something to his game.

"I remember after the 1990 Kangaroo tour he came to my office, sat down and we had a long talk. He wondered where he could go in football. At this time he had had his third Kangaroo tour, he had played in successive premiership-winning teams and had had success at State of Origin level. We talked about a fourth Kangaroo tour and the records it would create.

"As history now shows, he responded magnificently to that goal."

Opposite: Chaired from the field after Australia had retained the Ashes by winning the third Test of the 1992 series, at Lang Park. The Australian players are (left to right): Andrew Ettingshausen, David Gillespie, Laurie Daley, Bradley Clyde and Allan Langer.

Bob had a big advantage when he first took up the Australian coaching job. Unlike most new coaches, he did not need to generate respect among the players — he had earned that on the football field through his many brilliant performances which, deservedly, saw him named in 1981 as one of rugby league's immortals. And, as a coach, he was a premiership winner with Manly in 1987, after some successful seasons in the early '80s with Eastern Suburbs.

My first impression of Bob as a coach was that he was very good. Not in the Bennett class, but still very good. However, the more I got to know him, the more I appreciated just how thorough and effective he was. He really is in the very top bracket. I have always said that Wayne Bennett and Tim Sheens were the most influential coaches in my career, but Bob comes in a very close third.

Bob (or "Bozo", as he is better known) would spend hours going over videos of past games to assess the other side's strengths and weaknesses. His players were always aware of the opposition's pet moves. And he also used the video to help his own players. I remember on the 1990 Kangaroo tour, Bob spent time going through a video one day to pick out a couple of incidents involving Mark Carroll and Mark Geyer. They were both going for the big shoulder charge in defence which is always great when it comes off. But Bob used the video to show the pair the gaps created in the defence when they missed.

This helping of individuals makes him a very special coach. And this trait sits well alongside another of his major strengths — his ability to mix well with the players.

In fact, Bob Fulton does everything well. His skill sessions are good because he knows how important this aspect of the game is. Bozo is a strong advocate of both ball and skill sessions, and he also places importance on weight training. He is an advocate of giving players time to recover from the stress of matches. He also enjoys varying training sessions — something that is very important with touring sides. It is highly probable on Kangaroo tours that, after a long domestic season, the daily training routine will become boring.

On the 1994 tour, Bozo made sure the training was interesting. We still did the work, but we did it in a variety of ways. Unlike the Frank Stanton approach in 1982, there wasn't that grind of training twice a day and doing the same sort of thing time and time again. Frank's style worked in 1982, but I don't think the players would have accepted it as comfortably in 1994. By '94, the pressure and demands on players in the Winfield Cup was such that elite players would not have responded well to the older style of training, even though it proved so effective 12 years before. Bob was smart enough to realise this. I'm sure Frank Stanton would have been as well.

Epilogue

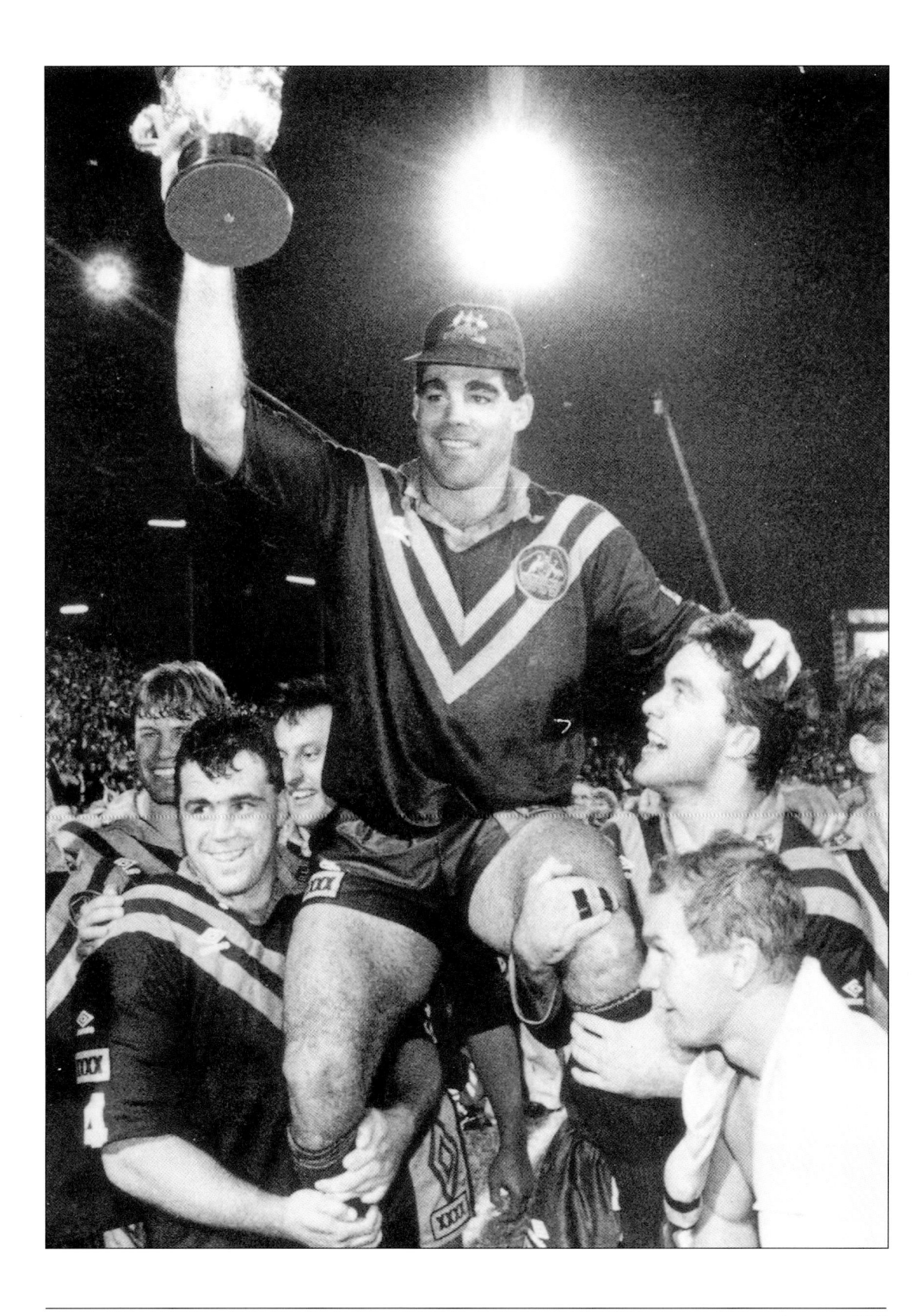

BOB FULTON ON MAL MENINGA

by Alan Clarkson

Bob Fulton was one of rugby league's all-time great footballers and in the years since his playing career ended in 1979 has forged a reputation as one of the game's best coaches.

In 1980, he steered his Eastern Suburbs side to the grand final, and did likewise at Manly in 1983 and 1987, the year of the Sea Eagles' fifth premiership success. In 1989, he was appointed to the Australian job, which is when he first had the chance to coach a side that included Mal Meninga. A year later, Mal became Australian captain and the pair remained at the helm of the national side until the end of the '94 Kangaroo tour.

In 1995, I asked Bob Fulton to identify Mal's strengths as a captain. "He had that great ability to produce when it mattered," he told me. "When we needed a big effort from him on the field, to spearhead the team, he invariably came up with it.

"I found Mal fantastic to work with. He had remarkable leadership qualities both on and off the field. The coach and the captain can both be 'boys' for some of the time the Australian team is together, but a line has to be drawn when it's time for business. Mal knew when to draw that line and be business-like at the appropriate moment."

The Fulton–Meninga team lost only four of 23 Tests between 1990 and 1994, a tribute to the special quality of their alliance. However, there were still many occasions when the pressure was well and truly on. In such situations, it is essential that the relationship between the captain, coach and team management is as positive and harmonious as it was in the Australian team during this five-year period. Fulton acknowledges Mal's role in this, and also the contribution of the managers.

"Mal and I were fortunate to have managers such as Keith Barnes (1990) and Geoff Carr (1994) on the Kangaroo tours," Bob said. "Geoff has been the longest serving Australian manager and he, Mal and I became a very good team."

I asked Bob to sum up his former captain. I thought he would say something about Mal's great football ability, or the calibre of his leadership. Instead, he said simply …

"I think the best way I can sum up Mal Meninga is to say that he's a good bloke."

Epilogue

Celebrations after the 1992 World Cup final.
Standing (left to right): Chris Johns, Shaun McRae (trainer), Allan Langer, Bob Fulton (coach), Brian Hollis (trainer), Tim Brasher, Michael Hancock, Steve Renouf, Willie Carne, David Gillespie, Paul Sironen, John Cartwright, myself, Brad Fittler.
In front: Steve Walters, Bob Lindner, Kevin Walters, Mark Sargent, Glenn Lazarus.

There would be a weight session in the morning and we might run in the afternoon. We did a bit of swimming, there was indoor tennis and soccer. The variety made the training enjoyable and I always found that when you enjoy your training sessions, you put more into them.

During the 1990 and 1994 Kangaroo tours, I felt Bob and I formed a great captain–coach partnership, even though we always seemed to do it the hard way by winning the last Test to win the series. It was in pressured situations that his coaching skill and thorough preparation always came to the fore. When it came to the crunch games, we always won them well.

There are, of course, many other outstanding league men who helped my career, and I'd like to pay a brief tribute to some of them.

Bob McCarthy coached me at Southern Suburbs in Brisbane from 1980 to 1983, a period during which we reached three grand finals and won the premiership in 1981. He was a very different coach to anybody I had previously come into contact with. Bob was one of the greatest running forwards of all time, the man who, as part of the famous South Sydney side of the late 1960s, introduced the concept of the big, fast forward running out wide with the backs. He was also one of the fittest men to play the game. So it was no surprise that he built his coaching style around fitness and pace. As far as Bob McCarthy was concerned, there was just one hard and fast rule — you had to be as fit as possible.

One of his greatest attributes was his personal familiarity — he mixed well with the players and always treated them as adults. Everyone at Souths respected him for what he had done as a player, and in a very short space of time he gained our respect as a coach as well. Once he had our respect, he drove us hard. And we responded.

"Macca" placed great importance on our mental preparation for games, organising relaxation sessions and instructions from a psychologist. I can remember Dr Ian Lynagh, the father of Australian rugby union's champion fly-half Michael Lynagh, coming in to talk about goal-setting and how best to prepare mentally for important matches.

While Bob McCarthy was leading Souths to the Brisbane grand final in 1982, Frank Stanton was the Australian coach for the series in Australia

---

BOB McCARTHY ON MAL MENINGA

by Alan Clarkson

Bob McCarthy was one of the best second-rowers in league history, a giant in the Souths side that dominated the premiership between 1967 and 1971. In 1976 and 1977 he played successfully with Canterbury, before returning to Souths for one last season.

In September 1979, McCarthy, by then retired from league, was in Brisbane in his role as a company sales representative. It was the day after the Brisbane grand final, and he had time to call into a hotel to visit a friend he hadn't seen in quite a while. Among the patrons in that bar was a collection of players and officials from the Southern Suburbs club, all of them shattered after being crushed 26–0 by Valleys in the big game the previous afternoon.

Souths president Tony Testa recognised the league great and strode over. Testa was aware his first-grade coach, Wayne Bennett, had accepted an offer from the rival Brothers club for the 1980 season. When he reached McCarthy, he shot out his hand, but rather than saying, "G'day," he said simply, "Can you coach?"

A stunned McCarthy's reply was equally forthright. "I don't do coaching deals in pubs," he told the Souths president. "If you want to talk to me, give me a call tomorrow." And he handed Testa his business card.

against New Zealand and for that season's Kangaroo tour. I enjoyed playing under Frank's guidance. He was very strong on discipline. On tour, we had to get up every morning at 7.30 a.m., just to go for a walk! Then we'd train twice a day. This went on for almost the entire trip, and there were times when it seemed like a real grind. But we were highly successful, even if the opposition were below international standard.

Frank Stanton reinforced in me the maxim that you don't achieve anything without hard work. Despite the lack of quality in our opponents, there was never any relaxation as far as Frank was concerned. Even if we won a match by 40 points, the routine never changed … just more of the same hard slog. But we all knew why we were putting in the effort. Like our coach, we wanted to be the best.

Frank did not play favourites. He selected players on form and not on reputation. That year, Steve Mortimer and Wally Lewis arrived in England as

---

The next day, Tony Testa rang and, soon after, a three-year deal was signed. Souths had wanted to keep the agreement to just 24 months, but McCarthy was insistent.

"I told Tony that it was no use me shifting my family out of Sydney to Brisbane for just a two-year guarantee," McCarthy remembers. "And before I signed I wanted to know what players they were going after and who of their current players had signed up. I really wanted to know if Mal Meninga would still be there. I had seen him play before and he impressed me as a player of enormous potential.

"I knew he was a shy kid, but he had what it takes."

McCarthy remembers being in a hurry to turn the young Mal into a champion.

"There were times when I thought he could have done a little more, but then I realised he was only a kid, still learning the game. He was a laid-back type. He did not have that hunger early in his career. I remember, not long into my time coaching at Souths, that I spoke to Ernie Hammerton, the chairman of the Australian selectors, about Mal. I told Ernie how much potential Mal had. Ernie explained that he knew all about him already. Soon after, they picked him in the Test team against New Zealand, but he only lasted a short time before he had to come off with a dislocated elbow.

"To reach his full football maturity, I felt Mal had to get out of Brisbane. Of course, he went to the Raiders and the rest is history.

"The only thing I regret is that he did not end up at Redfern Oval playing for South Sydney."

the Australian halfback pairing, but Frank thought the Parramatta pair, Peter Sterling and Brett Kenny, were going better. So he trusted his judgement, selected them in the early games, and stuck by his decision when Peter and Brett played well. Given the way the Test team went, winning all three matches by handsome margins, it was very hard to say that he was wrong.

Frank Stanton coached NSW in State of Origin football in 1982 and 1984. His rival coach for both of those series was one of the true giants of the code, the great Arthur Beetson, who had starred in the first State of Origin match in 1980 and then coached the Maroons to Origin success in 1981 through to 1984 and then to further glory in 1989.

I have tremendous admiration for Arthur personally, as well as for his qualities as a coach. He is an extraordinary character who is extremely proud of his Aboriginal heritage. That pride he displayed was important to me, for it underlined what I had always been taught by my parents.

Arthur's greatest strength as a coach was simple ... everyone loved him and wanted to do the best for him. Every single person in football respected Arthur for the gentleman he is, for what he has done in and for the game, and for what a superb player he was. It was never difficult to play well for such a man.

One of my greatest football memories is Arthur coaching the Queensland side in the early State of Origin matches. When it came to preparation for a match, he wasn't totally disciplined but, almost despite this, we trained well and hard. And we played well.

However, in the hours before a game he was very business-like. He would bring in reams of paper with information about the strengths and weaknesses of the opposition players. Then Arthur would explain what our individual roles were and he would go through the overall game plan. He was very strong on game plans, on the precise things we needed to do. He might stress one area — say, the need to work harder at marker defence. That done, as the kick-off approached, Arthur would become one very nervous puppy. He was afraid he had missed something that might have helped our cause. We appreciated that he cared so much.

All these men I have referred to in this chapter had very different methods of coaching a top-grade rugby league team. Yet, despite these contrasts, all were highly successful. My Raiders and Kangaroo coach in 1986, Don Furner, was different again.

Don's philosophy was that though he might not be coaching the best football team in the world, he would certainly be in charge of the fittest group of players in the competition. His reasoning was that the extra stamina and strength might just allow his team of triers to sneak up and win late in the day. This was certainly how he was thinking in 1986, my first season in Canberra.

EPILOGUE

> ## FRANK STANTON ON MAL MENINGA
>
> by Alan Clarkson
>
> The Mal Meninga who Frank Stanton remembers from the 1982 Kangaroo tour was a very different individual from the man who retired as a football legend in 1994. Stanton, who had coached Manly to premierships in 1976 and 1978 and was coach of the Australian Test side between 1978 and 1982, recalls a quiet but impressive individual, who preferred to let his deeds on the football field do the talking for him.
>
> "Back in '82, Mal was young and relatively inexperienced," Stanton recalls, "but the signs were there that he would make it. His sheer ability was apparent and he had no shortcomings in his football make-up. He had size, mobility and remarkable skill levels. He could run, tackle, and had great dexterity in passing the ball. And he could kick goals. Before that tour he had had to play the understudy role to Steve Rogers and Mick Cronin. But then Mick pulled out and the chance was there for Mal."
>
> Stanton admits that back in 1982 he didn't see Mal as a future Australian skipper. "I wouldn't have thought of him as a captain. If anything, on that first tour he was a little bit shy. But with greater experience, he gained in confidence and he went to become an exceptional leader."

Before our first trial game, Don conducted what everyone who had survived it before referred to as the "mad month". We trained right through January, 31 days in succession, for at least one hour each day. We did not touch a ball at all during that time, we were just fitness crazy. The way we laboured that month is something I will never forget!

One of Don's great assets was his ability to recognise potential in a young player. He was forever trying to lure young players with skill to the club. Long before I arrived in Canberra, he had been building for the future. The club had joined the premiership in 1982, and Don's vision was that the Raiders would have a very strong team within five years. And his dream became a reality.

Canberra and its surrounding country districts had always had a remarkable crop of local products, and Don was not going to let any of the best of them slip away. Shrewdly, he also recognised that what was needed to complement this precocious talent was a number of

Opposite: At Australian training with Bradley Clyde, who represents a perfect example of the style of footballer who will take the game into the 21st century.

experienced footballers. With such hardened performers in town, he knew Canberra could become one of the top teams in the premiership.

Every decision he made in Canberra was done with the aim of improving the club. Never once did Don's personal interests get in the way. I believe it shows the calibre of the man that he brought a coach like Wayne Bennett into the club in 1987. Don had been the first-grade coach from the Raiders' first premiership game and could have been selfish about the coaching role. But he wasn't. He saw Wayne's input as being another crucial step in the club's climb to the top, and he also realised Wayne would be helpful in introducing more quality footballers into the team.

ARTHUR BEETSON ON MAL MENINGA

by Alan Clarkson

Arthur Beetson, the man considered by some commentators to be the greatest forward ever produced by Australian rugby league, has no doubts as to Mal Meninga's place in league history. Beetson considers him to be one of the genuine legends of the game.

"For what Mal has done over the years, I have no doubt he deserves to be in that class." Beetson told me. "I consider myself lucky to have been associated with a Queensland team which included such a champion player as Mal, and also Wally Lewis, Gene Miles, Chris Close and so on."

Beetson revealed to me a not-so-well-known fact about Mal's move to the NSWRL premiership in 1986. Beetson at that time was the coach of Eastern Suburbs, the club he led to grand final victories in 1974 and 1975.

"One of the great tragedies of rugby league is that we did not get him to Eastern Suburbs. When the Queensland chairman Ron McAuliffe released the brakes and allowed some Queensland players to sign with Sydney premiership clubs, I said I would die happy if we could get Mal to Easts.

"But the Easts committee at that time was not interested. One member even said that Mal couldn't play!

"While the Easts board were dithering around and showing no interest in this superb player, Canberra went out of their way to impress him. If the 1995 Easts board had been operating then, I believe Mal Meninga would have been a Rooster and not a Raider.

"What a great footballer he became and what a great ambassador for himself and the game."

Epilogue

Opposite: The 1987 Raiders watch as Manly's Cliff Lyons steps forward to accept the Clive Churchill medal as the best player of the 1987 grand final.

The Canberra players and officials are (left to right): Gary Coyne, Kevin Walters, Jay Hoffman, Matthew Corkery, Chris O'Sullivan, Ivan Henjak (sitting, at back), Ashley Gilbert (sitting), Gary Belcher, me, Glenn Lazarus, Dean Lance (sitting, behind Lazarus), Les Morrissey, Rowan Brennan, Sam Backo (obscured), John McIntyre (secretary), Don Furner (co-coach), Phil Carey and Laurie Daley. Our other co-coach, Wayne Bennett, is behind the group, being interviewed by John Gibbs of Sydney radio station 2UE.

Although disappointed at losing, we gained great strength from our march to the grand final. From 1987 on, the Canberra Raiders were quite definitely a major premiership force.

Don had his great days as a coach. He did an exceptional job with the Kangaroos on the 1986 tour of England and France when, just as we had in 1982, we went through undefeated. But I think his greatest contribution was all he (in association with Raiders chairman Les McIntyre) did to help establish the Raiders as a premiership force. It was his vision that laid the foundation for all the success the Raiders have had in recent years, an era of glory for the club that I was so fortunate to be a part of.

DON FURNER ON MAL MENINGA

by Alan Clarkson

Don Furner, the original coach of the Canberra Raiders, had already established his premiership coaching credentials with Eastern Suburbs in the early '70s before the Raiders came into the competition in 1982. A forward good enough to tour with the Kangaroos in 1956–57, Furner has always maintained that the turning point for the Canberra Raiders was when Mal Meninga signed with the club.

"I knew Mal's signing would encourage other players to come to the club," Furner explained. "I had adopted the same principle at Easts and attracted a number of players who were keen to play in the same team as Arthur Beetson."

This strategy worked brilliantly, with players such as John Ferguson, Gary Belcher, Steve Walters, Peter Jackson, Kevin Walters, Gary Coyne and Brent Todd arriving in the national capital in Mal's first two seasons.

"You don't get too many Arthur Beetsons and you don't get too many Mal Meningas during a coaching career," Furner said. "When we signed Mal, it turned the whole club around. He was a great competitor, he had a lot of pride and he liked to win."

As the man who brought Mal to Canberra, Don Furner had watched his career with a great deal of pride. "Anyone who has played 10 years in the Winfield Cup, as Mal did, has nothing to prove," Furner commented. "He has gone to the top of his profession and he can be proud of that for the rest of his life.

"And the players around him respected him. That is one of the things you strive for in football — to get respect from your team-mates."

Epilogue

I am a very lucky man to have chosen the game of rugby league as my sport. It has been so good to me, and given me opportunities I could not have dreamed of when I first picked up a football back in Queensland in the early 1960s. I am grateful for the friendships I have made, from the guys at the Police Academy back in the '70s, at Souths in Brisbane between 1979 to 1985, at the Raiders from 1986 and in the Queensland and Australian teams between 1979 and 1994. I am proud to have met many of the great and famous people I have been introduced to through rugby league. And I have appreciated being in a position to help many people, within and outside the game, who have been far less fortunate in life than me.

Rugby league truly is the greatest game of all. No other game offers as much to its players and fans. I have enjoyed being a part of it as a player, and I hope I will still be a part of it, in some shape or form, for many, many years to come. If that does happen, I will continue to be a very lucky man.

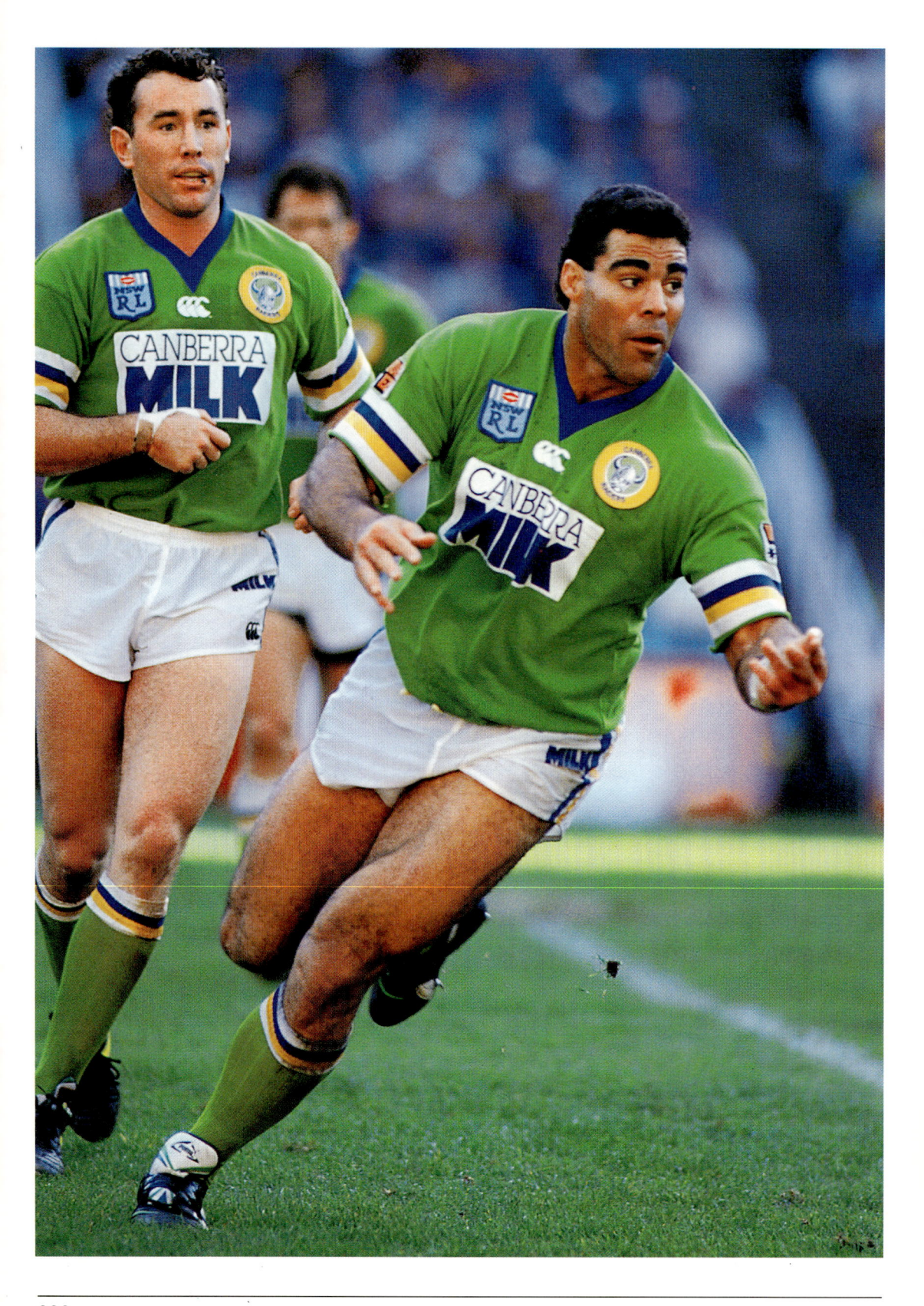

Meninga

CAREER RECORD

BY DAVID MIDDLETON

MALCOLM NORMAN MENINGA

Born: Bundaberg, July 8, 1960

CAREER OVERVIEW

	GAMES	TRS	GLS	F/G	PTS
CLUB CAREER 1979–94					
Southern Suburbs (Brisbane) 1979–85	109	77	313	–	889
St Helens 1984–85	31	28	8	–	128
Canberra 1986–94	166	74	283	2	864
TOTAL	306	179	604	2	1,881
REPRESENTATIVE CAREER 1979–94					
QUEENSLAND 1979–94					
State of Origin 1980–94	32	6	69	–	161
v. New South Wales 1979–81	6	3	9	–	27
v. touring sides 1982–84	2	1	10	–	23
Tour matches 1983	2	3	8	–	28
TOTAL	42	13	96	–	239
AUSTRALIA 1982–94					
Tests 1982–94	45	21	95	–	270
World Cup 1992	1	–	3	–	6
Tour matches 1982–84	37	29	79	–	267
v. Rest of the World 1988	1	–	3	–	6
TOTAL	84	50	180	–	549
OCEANIA 1984					
v. Europe	1	–	1	–	2
GRAND TOTAL					
All senior matches	433	242	881	2	2,671

CLUB CAREER 1979–94

SEASON	GAMES	TRS	GLS	F/G	PTS
Southern Suburbs (Brisbane)					
1979	20	9	76	–	179
1980	21	16	95	–	238
1981	20	14	47	–	136
1982	11	6	26	–	70
1983	10	8	28	–	88
1984	18	18	41	–	154
1985	9	6	–	–	24
TOTAL	109	77	313	–	889
St Helens					
1984–85	31	28	8	–	128
Canberra					
1986	20	3	65	1	143
1987	12	6	3	4	1
1988	5	3	7	–	26
1989	16	2	19	–	46
1990	24	17	72	–	212
1991	22	13	57	–	166
1992	21	6	17	–	58
1993	20	11	4	–	52
1994	26	13	8	–	68
TOTAL	166	74	283	2	864
GRAND TOTAL	306	179	604	2	1,881

Premierships: 1981, 1985, 1989, 1990, 1994

Grand Finals: 1979, 1980, 1981, 1982, 1984, 1985, 1987, 1989, 1990, 1991, 1994

Semi-finals: 1979, 1980, 1981, 1982, 1983, 1984, 1985, 1987, 1988, 1989, 1990, 1991, 1993, 1994

Club coaches: Wayne Bennett 1979, 1984–85, 1987, Bob McCarthy 1980–83, Bill Benyon 1984–85 (St Helens), Don Furner 1986–87, Tim Sheens 1988–94

First Grade debut: March 25, 1979 Souths v. Wynnum–Manly

Most points in a season: 238 in 1980 (Souths)

Most tries in a season: 18 in 1984 (Souths)

Most goals in a season: 95 in 1980 (Souths)

Most points in a match: 38 (5 tries, 9 goals), April 16, 1990 Canberra v. Easts

CAREER RECORD

JUNIOR REPRESENTATIVE CAREER 1978

DATE	WINNER	SCORE	VENUE	TRS	GLS	F/G	PTS
Queensland Under-18s v. NSW Under-18s							
July 15	NSW	21–16	Brisbane	–	–	–	–
July 22	NSW	28–25	Sydney	–	–	–	–
		2 matches, 0 points					

SENIOR REPRESENTATIVE CAREER 1979–94

DATE	WINNER	SCORE	VENUE	TRS	GLS	F/G	PTS
QUEENSLAND 1979–94							
1979–81 Queensland v. New South Wales (traditional inter-state matches)							
May 22, 1979	NSW	30–5	Brisbane	1	1	–	5
May 29, 1979	NSW	31–7	Brisbane	–	2	–	4
May 20, 1980	NSW	35–3	Brisbane	1	–	–	3
May 27, 1980	NSW	17–7	Sydney	–	2	–	4
June 2, 1981	NSW	10–2	Brisbane	–	1	–	2
June 16, 1981	NSW	22–9	Sydney	1	3	–	9
		6 matches, 3 tries, 9 goals, 27 points					
1982–84 Queensland v. touring sides							
1982 v. New Zealand							
June 27	QLD	31–16	Brisbane	1	5	–	13
1984 v. New Zealand							
June 5	QLD	18–14	Brisbane	–	5	–	10
		2 matches, 1 try, 10 goals, 23 points					
1983 tour matches							
Papua New Guinea tour							
June 15	QLD	34–16	Mt Hagen	1	1	–	6
June 18	QLD	106–3	Port Moresby	2	7	–	22
		2 matches, 3 tries, 8 goals, 28 points					
1980–1994 Queensland v. New South Wales (State of Origin)							
July 8, 1980	QLD	20–10	Brisbane	–	7	–	14
July 28, 1981	QLD	22–15	Brisbane	1	5	–	13
June 1, 1982	NSW	20–16	Brisbane	–	5	–	10
June 22, 1982	QLD	10–5	Sydney	–	2	–	4
June 7, 1983	QLD	24–12	Brisbane	–	6	–	12
June 21, 1983	NSW	10–6	Sydney	1	1	–	6

Continued

Meninga

DATE	WINNER	SCORE	VENUE	TRS	GLS	F/G	PTS
June 28, 1983	QLD	43–22	Brisbane	–	6	–	12
May 29, 1984	QLD	29–12	Brisbane	–	2	–	4
June 19, 1984	QLD	14–2	Sydney	–	3	–	6
July 17, 1984	NSW	22–12	Brisbane	–	2	–	4
May 28, 1985	NSW	18–2	Brisbane	–	1	–	2
June 11, 1985	NSW	21–14	Sydney	–	3	–	6
July 23, 1985	QLD	20–6	Brisbane	–	2	–	4
May 27, 1986	NSW	22–16	Brisbane	–	4	–	8
June 10, 1986	NSW	24–20	Sydney	–	2	–	4
July 1, 1986	NSW	18–16	Brisbane	–	–	–	–
May 23, 1989	QLD	36–6	Brisbane	2	4	–	16
June 14, 1989	QLD	16–12	Sydney	–	1	–	2
May 9, 1990	NSW	8–0	Sydney	–	–	–	–
May 30, 1990	NSW	12–6	Melbourne	–	1	–	2
May 8, 1991	QLD	6–4	Brisbane	1	1	–	6
May 29, 1991	NSW	14–12	Sydney	–	2	–	4
June 12, 1991	QLD	14–12	Brisbane	–	1	–	2
May 6, 1992	NSW	14–6	Sydney	–	1	–	2
May 20, 1992	QLD	5–4	Brisbane	–	–	–	–
June 3, 1992	NSW	16–4	Sydney	–	2	–	4
May 3, 1993	NSW	14–10	Brisbane	–	1	–	2
May 17, 1993	NSW	16–12	Sydney	1	–	–	4
May 31, 1993	QLD	24–12	Brisbane	–	2	–	4
May 23, 1994	QLD	16–12	Sydney	–	2	–	4
June 8, 1994	NSW	14–0	Melbourne	–	–	–	–
June 20, 1994	NSW	27–12	Brisbane	–	–	–	–

32 matches, 6 tries, 69 goals, 161 points
Total for Queensland: 42 matches, 13 tries, 96 goals, 239 points

Meninga's Queensland coaches: John McDonald 1979–80, Arthur Beetson 1981–84, 1989–90, Des Morris 1985, Wayne Bennett 1986, Graham Lowe 1991–92, Wally Lewis 1993–94

Meninga captained Queensland in 9 matches 1992–94

Meninga has scored the most points by any player in the history of State of Origin football and the most points for Queensland in the history of the game.

He has played more times for Queensland than any other player.

Debut for Queensland: May 22, 1979 v. New South Wales

Most points in a match for Queensland: 22 (2 tries, 7 goals) v. Papua New Guinea, June 18, 1983

State of Origin series wins: 1982, 1983, 1984, 1989, 1991

Winning Queensland teams: 19

AUSTRALIA 1982–94

DATE	WINNER	SCORE	VENUE	TRS	GLS	F/G	PTS
TESTS							
1982 v. New Zealand							
July 17 (2nd Test)	AUST	20–2	Sydney	–	–	–	–
1982 v. Papua New Guinea							
October 2	AUST	38–2	Port Moresby	1	4	–	11
1982 v. Great Britain							
October 30 (1st Test)	AUST	40–4	Hull	1	8	–	19
November 20 (2nd Test)	AUST	27–6	Wigan	1	6	–	15
November 28 (3rd Test)	AUST	32–8	Leeds	–	7	–	14
1982 v. France							
December 5 (1st Test)	AUST	15–6	Avignon	–	3	–	6
Deember 18 (2nd Test)	AUST	23–9	Narbonne	1	4	–	11
1983 v. New Zealand							
June 11 (1st Test)	AUST	16–4	Auckland	–	4	–	8
July 9 (2nd Test)	NZ	19–12	Brisbane	–	2	–	4
1984 v. Great Britain							
June 26 (2nd Test)	AUST	18–6	Brisbane	1	3	–	10
July 7 (3rd Test)	AUST	20–7	Sydney	–	4	–	8
1985 v. New Zealand							
June 18 (1st Test)	AUST	26–20	Brisbane	–	2	–	4
June 30 (2nd Test)	AUST	10–6	Auckland	–	1	–	2
July 7 (3rd Test)	NZ	18–0	Auckland	–	–	–	–
1986 v. Papua New Guinea							
October 4	AUST	62–12	Port Moresby	–	–	–	–
1986 v. Great Britain							
October 26 (1st Test)	AUST	38–16	Manchester	–	–	–	–
November 8 (2nd Test)	AUST	34–4	Leeds	–	–	–	–
November 22 (3rd Test)	AUST	24–15	Wigan	–	–	–	–
1988 v. Papua New Guinea							
July 20, 1988	AUST	70–8	Wagga	2	–	–	8
1989 v. New Zealand							
July 9 (1st Test)	AUST	26–6	Christchurch	–	5	–	10
July 16 (2nd Test)	AUST	8–0	Rotorua	–	2	–	4
July 23 (3rd Test)	AUST	22–14	Auckland	1	1	–	6
1990 v. France							
June 27	AUST	34–2	Parkes	1	–	–	4
1990 v. New Zealand							
August 19	AUST	24–6	Wellington	–	4	–	8

Continued

MENINGA

DATE	WINNER	SCORE	VENUE	TRS	GLS	F/G	PTS
1990 v. Great Britain							
October 27 (1st Test)	GB	19–12	London	1	2	–	8
November 10 (2nd Test)	AUST	14–10	Manchester	1	1	–	6
November 24 (3rd Test)	AUST	14–0	Leeds	1	1	–	6
1990 v. France							
December 2 (1st Test)	AUST	60–4	Avignon	–	1	–	2
December 9 (2nd Test)	AUST	34–10	Perpignan	1	–	–	4
1991 v. New Zealand							
July 3 (1st Test)	NZ	24–8	Melbourne	–	2	–	4
July 24 (2nd Test)	AUST	44–0	Sydney	–	6	–	12
July 31 (3rd Test)	AUST	40–12	Brisbane	1	6	–	16
1991 v. Papua New Guinea							
October 6 (1st Test)	AUST	58–2	Goroka	–	–	–	–
October 13 (2nd Test)	AUST	40–6	Port Moresby	1	2	–	8
1992 v. Great Britain							
June 12 (1st Test)	AUST	22–6	Sydney	2	–	–	8
June 26 (2nd Test)	GB	33–10	Melbourne	–	1	–	2
July 3 (3rd Test)	AUST	16–10	Brisbane	1	4	–	12
1992 v. Papua New Guinea							
July 15	AUST	36–14	Townsville	–	4	–	8
1993 v. New Zealand							
June 25 (2nd Test)	AUST	16–8	Palmerston Nth	–	–	–	–
June 30 (3rd Test)	AUST	16–4	Brisbane	1	–	–	4
1994 v. France							
July 6	AUST	58–0	Parramatta	1	5	–	14
1994 v. Great Britain							
October 22 (1st Test)	GB	8–4	London	–	–	–	–
November 5 (2nd Test)	AUST	38–8	Manchester	–	–	–	–
November 20 (3rd Test)	AUST	23–4	Leeds	–	–	–	–
1994 v. France							
December 4	AUST	74–0	Béziers	1	–	–	4

45 Tests, 1982–94, 21 tries, 95 goals, 270 points

TESTS NATION BY NATION

	GAMES	TRS	GLS	F/G	PTS
v. France	7	5	13	–	45
v. Great Britain	17	9	37	–	108
v. New Zealand	15	3	35	–	82
v. Papua New Guinea	6	4	10	–	35
TOTAL	45	21	95	–	270

Meninga has scored most points in Tests between Australia and Great Britain; Australia and New Zealand; and Australia and Papua New Guinea.

Winning Test matches: 39 out of 45

Most points in one Test: 19 (1 try, 8 goals) v. Great Britain, October 30, 1982

Most points in a Test series: 48 (2 tries, 21 goals) v. Great Britain, 1982 (Australian record)

Captaincy: Meninga captained Australia in his last 23 Tests (1990–94). His total is equal with Wally Lewis and one fewer than Australian record-holder Clive Churchill.

Meninga played in 45 Tests, 9 more than previous record-holder, Reg Gasnier.

Meninga's Australian coaches: Frank Stanton (1982, 1984), Arthur Beetson (1983), Terry Fearnley (1985), Don Furner (1986, 1988), Bob Fulton (1989–94)

TOURS 1982–94

	GAMES	TRS	GLS	F/G	PTS
1982 Kangaroo tour					
Tour matches	9	7	40	–	101
Tests	5	3	28	–	65
TOTAL	14	10	68	–	166
1985 New Zealand tour					
Tour matches	3	3	8	–	28
Tests	2	–	1	–	2
TOTAL	5	3	9	–	30
1986 Kangaroo tour					
Tour matches	10	9	7	–	50
Tests	3	–	–	–	–
TOTAL	13	9	7	–	50
1989 New Zealand tour					
Tour matches	–	–	–	–	–
Tests	3	1	8	–	20
Total	3	1	8	–	20

Continued ☛

MENINGA

	GAMES	TRS	GLS	F/G	PTS
1990 Kangaroo tour					
Tour matches	6	4	11	–	38
Tests	5	4	5	–	26
Total	11	8	16	–	64
1991 Papua New Guinea tour					
Tour matches	1	1	4	–	12
Tests	2	1	2	–	8
Total	3	2	6	–	20
1992 World Cup tour					
Tour matches	2	2	5	–	18
World Cup Final	1	–	3	–	6
Total	3	2	8	–	24
1994 Kangaroo tour					
Tour matches	6	3	4	–	20
Tests	4	1	–	–	4
Total	10	4	4	–	24
Tour matches 1982–94	37	29	79	–	267
Tour totals (including Tests)	62	39	126	–	398

Meninga toured with the Kangaroos four times (1982, 1986, 1990, 1994). This is a record for an Australian player.

He is the only Australian captain to lead two Kangaroo teams.

OTHER MAJOR MATCHES

	SCORE	VENUE	TRS	GLS	F/G	PTS
1992 World Cup Final						
October 24	AUST 10 GB 6	London	–	3	–	6
1988 v. Rest of the World						
July 27	AUST 22 REST 10	Sydney	–	3	–	6
1984 Oceania v. Europe						
April 14	OCEANIA 54 EUROPE 4	Paris	–	1	–	2
1989 World Club Challenge						
October 4	WIDNES 30 CANBERRA 18	Manchester	1	–	–	4

INDEX

Abbott, Hubie 82, *211*
Adidas Golden Boot award 1989 160
Alexander, Greg *130,* 161, 171
Anderson, Chris 79
Ansett 204
Argeros, Billy *60,* 71
Arthurson, Ken 204
Astill, Bruce *60,* 64, *68-69,* 72
Australia Day awards (1995) *157*
Australian team
 MM's ambition to join 106-109
 1982 Tests *120,* 121-124
 1983 Tests 124
 1984 Tests 124-125
 1986 Tests *125,* 126-127, *130*
 1989 Tests 127-131
 1990 Tests 8, 9, 184-191
 1990, MM's initial captaincy 183-184
 1991 Tests 191-196, *193, 194*
 1992 Tests 196-197, *217*
 1993 Tests 197-199
 1994 Tests 16, 24-26, *28,* 29-33, *45,* 49, *169,* 179, *182,* 199, *201*

Backo, Sam 106, 118, 119, *132, 227*
Baldwin, Brenda *151*
Baldwin, Gloria *151*
Baldwin, Lynette *151*
Baldwin, Stan *151*
Balmain
 1988 premiership 117, 118
 1989 premiership 16-19, 137-140, *138,* 145, 152
Banaghan, Jim *151*
Barnes, Keith 218
Barnhill, David 171
Bath, Harry 63
Beetson, Arthur 13, 70, 85-86, *87,* 113, 222, 224, 226

Belcher, Gary 13, 77, 89, 92, *93,* 95, *102,* 106-109, *112,* 127, 133-134, *134,* 136, 137, *141, 161,* 162, 166, 174, 179, 183, 184, 195, *211,* 226, *227*
Bell, Mark *141, 161,* 171
Bella, Martin 189, 192
Bellamy, Craig *141, 149, 161*
Bennett, Wayne 13, 57, 59-61, *60,* 63-65, 75, 82-83, 105, 109-113, 126, 148-149, 153, 209-211, *211,* 212, 213, 224
Bertram, Graham *53*
Betts, Denis 45, 196
Block, David 204
Bourke, David *211*
Boustead, Kerry 34, 85, 86
Boyd, Les 88-89
Boyle, David *14-15,* 177
Bracken, Allan *60,* 64, 67
Brasher, Tim *219*
Brennan, Rowan *227*
Brickland, Bret *53*
Brisbane Broncos
 1988 premiership 114-117
 1990 premiership 160, 161
 1991 premiership 170
 1992 premiership *195*
Britten, Toby *53*
Brohman, Daryl 88-89
Brothers (1985) 82-83
Brown, Dave *60,* 64, 67, 95
Brown, Dave 159
Bruce Stadium 159
Butler, Terry *80-81*

Canberra Raiders *148-150*
 1985 MM transfers to 103-106, *104*
 1985 premiership 106
 1987 premiership 109-110, *111, 112*
 1988 premiership *17,* 111-119, 133
 1989 premiership *107,* 133-145, *135, 138, 141, 142-144,* 152

1990 premiership 159-162, *160-161*
1991 financial difficulties 23-24, 162-170
1991 premiership *149,* 170-171, *175*
1991-92 erosion of players 171
1992 premiership 171-177
1993 premiership 177-178, *178*
1994 premiership *14-15, 36,* 37-44, *38-39,* 178-181, *179, 181*
1994 State of Origin 37-40, *42*
 goal-setting 152-156
 State of Origin, Raiders members play in 89-90
Cannon, Mark 78-79
Canterbury
 1988 premiership 117, 118
 1994 premiership 42
Carey, Phil *141, 161, 227*
Carne, Willie 34, *154,* 170, 192, *195, 219*
Carr, Geoff 218
Carr, Norm *80-81, 211*
Carroll, Mark 216
Cartwright, John 189, *219*
Chamberlain, Terry 204
Channel Ten Cup 159
Churchill, Clive 131, 179
Clarke, Phil *28,* 45, 196
Cleal, Noel 90, 126
Clive Churchill medal
 1987 *227*
 1989 *142*
 1990 *160*
 1991 171
Close, Chris 34, 90, 92, 95
Clyde, Bradley *14-15,* 45, 89, 119, 131, 133, 134, *141, 142,* 156, 164, 166, 170, 171, *173,* 174, 179, 180, 191, 192, 195, *217, 225*
Collins, Wayne *141*

Conescu, Greg 34, 70, 90, 114
Conlon, Ross 124
Connell, Mal *60*
Connolly, Gary 45
Corkery, Matthew *227*
Corvo, Alex *161*
Corvo, Mark 180
Costa, Carlo *68-69*
Cowley, Ken 204
Coyne, Gary 77, 106, *112,* 133, *141, 149, 161,* 166, 170, 195, 226, *227*
Coyne, Mark 34, *99*
Croker, Jason *14-15, 42,* 89, *161,* 177, 180
Cronin, Michael 70, 87, 121, 123
Cronulla 136
Cullen, Wayne *211*
Currie, Tony 79
Currier, Andy 137

Daley, Laurie 11, *14-15, 35, 47,* 89-90, 94, 95, 97, 118-119, 133, *141, 143, 151,* 155, 156, *161,* 162, 166, 170, 171, *172,* 174, 179, 180, 183, 184, 189, 192, 195, *217, 227*
Daly, Fred 163, *174*
Davico, Luke *14-15*
Davidson, Les 126
Davies, Jonathon 45
Death, Jason *14-15*
Deed, Sel *68-69*
Devereux, John 197
Dewyer, Joe *53*
Dimond, Craig 133
Dini, Dave 58
Dowling, Greg 34, 71, *74,* 77, 90, 95, 114
Durkin, Tony 105

Eastern Suburbs (Sydney)
 1987 premiership 20, 110-113
 1990 premiership 159
Eastwood, Paul 189

237

Edwards, Shaun 45, 139
Elder, Jim 60, 68-69, *211*
Elias, Benny *91*, 92, 137, 189
Elias, John *211*
Ella, Steve 92, 123
Ellis, Grant *132*
Emonuel, Ric *211*
English Premiership Trophy (1984-85) *62*
Ettingshausen, Andrew 47, *198*, *217*
Everinham, John *53*

Farmer, Richard 163, 181, 204
Fearnley, Terry 90, 92, 125
Fenech, Mario 136
Ferguson, John 18, 79, 89, 106, *107*, 133, 139, *141*, *143*, *161*, 162, 165-166, 226
Fittler, Brad *84*, *155*, 162, *219*
Folkes, Steve *130*
France
  1982 Tests 124
  1986 Tests 127
  1990 Tests 183-184, 191
  1994 Tests 10, *48*, 49, 199, *201*
Fraser, Bernie 163, 164
Freeman, Gary 199
French, Brett 72, 77
French, Gary *211*
French, Ian 77
Fulivai, Albert *14-15*
Fullerton Smith, Wally 79, 95, 103
Fulton, Bob 30, *30*, 44, 49, 74, 128, 131, 183, 184, 185, 192, *193*, 197, 209, 215-219, *219*
Furner, David *14-15*, 43, 177, 179, 180
Furner, Don 13, 105, 106, 109, 126, *169*, 222-226, *227*

Gaffey, Nigel *161*, 166, 171
Geyer, Mark 192, 216
Gibson, Tony 60
Gilbert, Ashley *141*, 149-150, *227*
Giles, Kelvin 213
Gillespie, David 192, *217*, *219*
Gittins, Ken *211*
Glynn, Steve 60, *68-69*
Golden, Don *53*
Gould, David 60
Gould, Phil 96
Goulding, Bobby 46
Grace, Kevin *24*, 168, 177

Graham, John *53*
Graham, Mark 70
Gramm, Mick 60
Grant, James 137
Great Britain
  1982 Tests 124
  1984 Tests 124
  1986 Tests 126
  1990 Tests 9, 188-190
  1992 Tests *21*, 196-197, *217*
  1992 World Cup 197
  1994 Tests *28*, 29-32, 44-49
Green, David *80-81*
Grienke, G. *211*
Grothe, Eric 59, 79

Hagan, Michael 79
Halligan, Daryl 42
Hammerton, Ernie 221
Hamson, Paul 79
Hancock, Michael 34, 94, 114, *154*, 189, *219*
Hancock, Rohan 121
Hanley, Ellery 118, 134, 185, 190
Hardwick, Kevin 139
Harry, Bruce 68-69
Hartman, Merv *53*
Harvey, Gary *58*
Hasler, Des 92, *130*, 131
Hauff, Paul 191
Hawke, Bob *158*
Heads, Ian 105
Hegarty, Allen *53*
Henjak, Ivan 106, 109, *112*, 117, 118, *141*, *227*
Hetherington, Brett *14-15*, *42*, 180
Hider, Bryan 215
Higgs, Darryl *68-69*
Hoffman, Jay 106, *169*, *227*
Hollis, Brian *219*
Holloway, Henry 65
Hoppe, Sean 177
Houghton, Chris 133, *141*
Hull Kingston Rovers (UK) 79
Hunt, Neil 79

Illawarra Steelers
  1988 premiership 117
  1989 premiership 133
Iro, Kevin 127
Izzard, Brad 171

Jack, Garry 139-140
Jackson, Lee 9
Jackson, Peter 13, 77, 82, 95, 109, 110, *115*, 117, 118, 119, 191, 192, *211*, 226
Jackson, Steve 18, 140, *141*
Jennings, Peter *68-69*, *211*
J.J. Giltinan Shield *14-15*, *143*
Johns, Chris 114, *154*, 170, *219*
Johnstone, Billy 67, *68-69*, 72

Keating, Paul *157*
Kellaway, Bob 60, 64, 79
Kelly, Ros 163
Kenny, Brett 79, 106, 123, 124, 127, *128*, *129*, 130
Kenward, Warren 60
Kerr, Graham 68-69
Kilroy, Joe 70, 114
Kovae, Dairi 118
Kurtz, Charlie *53*

Lamb, Terry *116*, 118, *130*
Lance, Dean 106, *112*, 119, *132*, 133-134, *138*, 139, *141*, *142*, *161*, 166, *227*
Lang, Johnny 86
Langer, Allan *26*, 34, 94, 95, 97, 114, *154*, 170, 185, *187*, 195, *217*, *219*
Langlands, Graeme 179
Langmack, Paul 79, *130*
Lazarus, Glenn 89, *132*, 133, 136, *141*, *143*, *161*, 162, 166, 171, 189, 195, 210, *219*, *227*
Lewis, Wally 34, 57, *66*, 67, 72, 74, 77, *80-81*, 95, 97, 114, 121, 124, 127, *130*, 131, 160, 161, 162, 184, 191, *193*, 221
Lindner, Bob 77, 94, 95, 97, *98*, *193*, 199, *219*
Logan, Jim *53*
Lomax, John *14-15*, *36*, 178, 180
Loughlin, Paul 9, 189
Lowe, Graham 67
Lowry, Mark *141*
Lumby, Ash *58*, 60, *68-69*, *211*
Lydiat, John 79
Lydon, Joe 185
Lyons, Cliff 189, *227*

McAuliffe, Ron 103, 224
McCarthy, Bob 23, 44, 67, *68-69*, 71, 72, 74, 75, *115*, 121, 126, 219-220
McClelland, Jim *68-69*
McCoulogh, Bill *53*
McGaw, Mark 189
McIlwain, Peter *151*
McIntyre, John 163, *227*

McIntyre, Les 110, 226
Mackay, Brad 184, 189
McRae, Shaun *141*, 191, 215, *219*
Manly
  1987 premiership 19, 109, 113
  1991 premiership 170
  1993 premiership *178*
  1994 premiership 180
Manson, David *80-81*
Maroochy Black Swans *58*
Martin, Paul *141*, *161*, 166, 171
Mawson Club 23
Meninga, Ada 55
Meninga, Beryl 55
Meninga, Bevan *151*
Meninga, Cameron *151*
Meninga, Debbie *58*, 75, *76-77*, 78, *130*, *157*, 203, 204
Meninga, Edward 55
Meninga, Florence 55
Meninga, Geoff 55, *58*, *151*
Meninga, Joshua *127*, *151*, *157*, 179
Meninga, Lauretta 55
Meninga, Lee 20, 22-23, 51, 55, 147, *151*
Meninga, Norman 20-22, 55, 51-54, *53*, 147, 149
Meninga, Tamika *127*, *130*, *151*, *157*, 179
Meskell, Mark *211*
Miles, Gene 34, 71, 72, *73*, 77, 90, 106, 114, 123, 124, *128*, *130*
Miller, Gavin 79
Monaghan, Bill Dr *113*
Moore, Peter *113*
Moroko, George 67
Morretti, Francis *53*
Morris, Des 71
Morris, Rod 71, 85, 86, 121
Morrissey, Les *227*
Mortimer, Steve *91*, 123, 221
Moss, Michael 109
Muggleton, John 59, 79, 121
Muller, Eddie 77, *80-81*, *211*
Mullins, Brett *14-15*, 89, *93*, 170, *176*, 177, 179
Murray, Mark 34, 67, 92, 95

Nadruku, Noa *14-15*, 177
Nagas, Ken *14-15*, *42*, 89, 177, 180
Naylor, Geoff *68-69*
Neil, Kevin 177

INDEX

Neil, Mick 16
New Zealand
  1982 Tests 71
  1983 Tests 124
  1989 Tests 127-131
  1990 Tests 184
  1991 Tests *26*, 191-192
  1993 Tests 197-199
Newcastle Knights
  1988 premiership 117
  1989 premiership 133
News Limited 203-207
Niebling, Bryan 34, 59, 126, *130*
Nine Network 205
North Sydney
  1991 premiership 170
  1994 premiership 43-44
Northern Suburbs (Brisbane)
  1979 premiership 67-70

O'Connor, Michael 183, 184, 197
Offiah, Martin 45, 185
Oliphant, Greg 86
Osborne, Paul *14-15, 36*, 43, 174, 180
O'Sullivan, Chris 18, 106, 118, 136, 140, *141, 143, 148, 161*, 166, *227*

Papua New Guinea
  1982 Tests 123
  1986 Tests 125-126
  1988 Tests 117, 125-126
  1991 Tests 192-196, *194*
  1992 Tests 197
Parramatta
  1990 premiership 159
  1993 premiership 177
Paterson, Trevor 79
Pay, Dean *36*
Pearce, Wayne 16, 137, 140
Penrith
  1987 premiership 19, 109
  1989 premiership 133, 136
  1990 premiership 159, 160-162
  1991 premiership 171
Phelan, Chris 67, *68-69*, 83, *211*
Pobjie, Michael 139
Police Academy 56-59, 150
Pongia, Quentin *14-15, 42*, 178, 180
Power, Alan *68-69*
Price, Ray 131
Prior, G. *211*

Quayle, John 164, 204
Queensland
  State of Origin beginnings 85
  1979 MM first selected 149
  1979 State of Origin 60-61, 65
  1980 State of Origin 57, 85-87
  1981 State of Origin 70, 87
  1982 State of Origin 87-88
  1983 tour of England 74-75
  1983 State of Origin 88-89
  1984 State of Origin 90
  1985 State of Origin 90-92
  1989 State of Origin 92-95, *93*
  1991 State of Origin 95
  1992 MM named captain 95-96
  1994 State of Origin 32-40, *35, 98-99*
  1995 State of Origin 97

Rach, Ken *60, 68-69, 211*
Raper, John 206-207
Reardon, Mick *68-69*, 70
Redcliffe
  1981 70-71
  1982 71
Reddy, Rod 85, 86
Renouf, Steve 34, 95, *154, 176*, 197, *206, 219*
Rest of the World (1988) *113*, 117-118
Ribot, John 95, 203
Richards, Alf *122*
Roach, Steve 137-139, *138*
Roberts, Ian 191
Rogers, Steve 70, 87, 121, *123*, 124
Rugby League Week 104, 105
Ryan, Peter *60*
Ryan, Warren 139

Sailor, Wendell *45, 154*
Salter, John *60*
Salvatori, Craig 192
Sargent, Mark *219*
Schofield, Garry 185
Scott, Colin 77, 92
Shearer, Dale 95, 184, 189
Sheens, Tim 19, 24, 43, 114, 119, 137, *141, 143*, 153, *161*, 168, 174-176, 178, 180, 203, 209, 211-215, *213*
Sigsworth, Ron *75*, 79
Simmons, Royce *130*, 171, *175*

Sironen, Paul *84*, 126, 131, *138*, 139, 190, *219*
Smith, Allan 86
Smith, Darren 34
Smith, David 204-205
Smith, Len 44
Smith, Paul 162
South Sydney
  1988 premiership 110-111, 117
  1989 premiership 136
Southern Suburbs
  1979 MM joins 148
  1979 premiership *60*, 63-70
  1980 premiership 57
  1981 premiership *68-69*, 70-71
  1982 premiership 71-74, 123
  1983 premiership 75-77
  1985 premiership *77*, 81, 82-83, *211*
  1989 premiership *135*
St George
  attempts to sign MM 63
  1988 premiership 117
  1990 premiership 159
  1991 premiership 170
St Helens (UK) 22, 24, *62*, 77-82, 105, 166-167
Stanton, Frank 123, 216, 220-222, 223
State of Origin
  beginnings 85
  1980 57, 85-87
  1981 70, 87
  1982 87-88
  1983 88-89
  1984 90
  1985 90-92
  1989 92-95, 133
  1990 95
  1991 95
  1992 95-96
  1993 98
  1994 *11*, 32-40, *35, 42, 84*
  1995 96-99
Steadman, Graham 196
Sterling, Peter 79, *125, 130*, 222
Stone, Steve *14-15*
Strudwick, Ross 67
Stuart, Ricky 9-10, *14-15, 17*, 40, *42, 88*, 89, 117, 136, 140, *141*, 156, *160, 161*, 162, 164, 166, 170, 171, 174, 177-178, 179, 185-189, *186*, 195, 208
Sully, Brad *68-69*

Super League 26-27, 98-99, 203-207

Taylor, Paul 79
Tessmann, Brad 59
Testa, Tony *68-69*, 220
Thompson, Duncan 75-76
Thompson, Gary *68-69, 211*
Todd, Brent 109, 134, *141, 161*, 166, 170, 171, 226
Tronc, Scott *211*
Tuigamala, Va'aiga *45*
Tunks, Peter 92
Turner, Bill *58*
Turner, Dick *98*

Valleys
  1979 65-67
  1982 71-72
Vautin, Paul 34, 37, 94, 95, 96-97
Veivers, Greg 64, 67
Veivers, Phil 78-79

Wacker, John *58*
Wallace, Peter *77, 211*
Walsh, Garth *53*
Walters, Kerrod 189
Walters, Kevin 13, 95, 109, 113, *141, 154, 195*, 197, *219*, 226, *227*
Walters, Steve 13, *14-15, 26*, 40, 47, 95, 106, *141, 143*, 156, *161*, 166, *169*, 170, 171, 179, 180, 191, 192, 195, *219*, 226
Ward, Kevin 185
Weir, Brian *60*
Wesley, Peter 204
Western Suburbs (Sydney)
  1989 premiership 134
  1994 premiership *38-39*
Westley, David *14-15*, 180
Widnes (UK) 79
Wigan (UK) 78
Wiki, Ruben *14-15*, 178
Williams, Darrell 109
Wishart, Rod 192
Wood, Matthew *141, 143, 161*, 162
World Cup (1992) *21, 146*, 196, 197, *219*
Wynnum-Manly
  1979 premiership 63
  1982 premiership 71-72
  1984 premiership *74*, 77
  1985 premiership *80-81*, 82-83

PHOTO CREDITS

Front cover: Richard Sellars (Sportsphoto Agency)

Back cover (both photographs): Clifford White

Title page: Clifford White

Phil Brown, page: 28

Canberra Times, pages: 38–39

Chris Cole (Australian Picture Library/All Sport), page: 33

Courier–Mail, pages: 35, 56, 64, 87, 101, 217

News Limited, pages: 17, 18, 26, 30, 114, 122, 123, 134, 135, 138, 142, 143, 144, 145, 160, 175, 179, 193, 200

Eric Piris, pages: 40–41

Rugby League Week, pages: 12, 14–15, 42, 66, 73, 74, 75, 88, 91, 93, 98, 99, 102, 104, 107, 111, 112, 115, 116, 125, 128, 129, 132, 141, 148, 149, 150, 151 (top right), 154, 155, 158, 161, 169, 172, 173, 174, 176, 181, 186, 187, 198, 206, 208, 225, 227, 228

Southern Suburbs RLFC, pages: 60, 68–69, 81, 211

Sportsphoto Agency (UK), pages: 22, 25, 146

Varley Picture Agency (UK), pages: 8, 10, 11, 21, 44, 46, 48, 62, 84, 120, 182, 190, 195, 219

Clifford White, pages: 36, 178, 201, 202, 213

ACKNOWLEDGEMENTS

Meninga: My Life in Football was written with the valued assistance of Alan Clarkson, who for many years was the rugby league correspondent for the *Sydney Morning Herald* and the *Sun–Herald*, and remains today a respected writer on the game. His support is much appreciated.

Special thanks to Wayne Goss for taking the time to provide the foreword, and to rugby league's leading historian, David Middleton, for providing the statistics at the end of the book and for checking the final manuscript.

Thanks also to the photographers and photo libraries who provided their support, and to Janette Doolan, Kevin Grace, Alan Graubard, Matt Horan, Murray Lembit, Ern McQuillan, Ken McTrusty, Tony Testa and John Wilkinson, all of whom helped make this book a reality.